The
Development of Intelligence
In Children

by

Alfred Binet *and* Theodore Simon

with marginal notes by
Lewis M. Terman

LIMITED EDITION

Copy number: *1313* /3000

Printed in the United States of America
by
Williams Printing Company
Nashville, Tennessee
1980

Photograph of Lewis Madison Terman
1877–1956

Sent from Department of Psychology
Stanford University

Preface

One day, in 1953, shortly after joining the Peabody College faculty, I found this volume in the open stacks of the Vanderbilt-Peabody-Scarritt *Joint University Library*. Of course I inquired as to how it had gotten there. The library director, A. F. Kuhlman, informed me that he had written a number of noted scholars across the country asking them to donate their books to the library. Terman responded about the time of his retirement by donating this and other volumes. After spending a stimulating evening reading what Binet and Simon had to say, and Terman's reactions in the form of handwritten marginal notes, I had this volume placed in the rare book collection where it remains. Only this year, did I make arrangements for a limited reprinting of it, though to do so has been a long-term goal of mine. (Permission to reproduce this volume was obtained from Terman's only surviving progeny, Frederick E. Terman who has now retired after a distinguished career in engineering at Stanford University.) In preparation for writing this preface, I read many accounts of the contributions of Binet and Terman to psychometric testing. The more recent they are, the more sketchy they tend to be. So let's examine briefly the work of these two great men.

Alfred Binet was born in Nice, France, in 1857, and died 54 years later, in 1911, the year the third version of his scale was released. After first studying law, he followed his father into medicine, but soon turned to abnormal psychology, and then to the field of mental retardation. By that time, he was on the faculty of the Sorbonne where he was first adjunct director and later director of the Laboratory of Physiological Psychology. In 1895, at 37 years of age, he founded the journal, *L'Année Psychologique*, in which he published most of his subsequent work—volumes of it. At about the same time, he embarked upon his search for how best to measure human intelligence. Before arriving at the Binet-Simon scales, he pursued several different lines of inquiry. First he investigated reaction time, dot counting and the like. Next he turned to head measurements. Soon he was exploring palmistry, handwriting, and then speech fluency. Often he found some relationship to intelligence, but nothing substantial.

In 1904, the French Minister of Public Instruction appointed a Commission to study strategies for educating mildly retarded children in the public schools of Paris. This Commission soon agreed to segregate the retarded into special classes. To do this, however, effective procedures were needed to differentiate between normal students who would remain in the ordinary school, and children who were special education candidates. The Commission turned for assistance to Binet, the psychologist, in collaboration with Theodore Simon, the physician, to devise a test to accomplish this. What then occurred is covered, in detail, in this volume.

As I read this book, what impressed me was that Binet had gone through his trial-and-error stage at an opportune time. Two events seem to have put him on a propitious course. One was the recognition that he should turn away from narrow, discrete measures, and shift toward the concept of general intelligence which had been formulated by Galton in England and which included the feature of a global mental ability score. This gave him a rationale for being eclectic, and for including a variety of types of items in his scales. The second event was learning of a set of test items that fit this model. These had been developed by a fellow Parisian and physician, Dr. Blin, and his student, Dr. Damaye (see pages 27-36), the *unsung heroes* in the case. For both his ideas and his items, Binet drew heavily from the work of these men and others—and gave due credit. Nevertheless, unless it can be shown that Blin and Damaye lifted their scale from some earlier source, I believe the field should refer to the Blin-type items, rather than Binet-type items. In no way is this intended to disparage the extensive work done by Binet and Simon in refining the Blin items, sorting out those that contributed most to a global measure of intelligence, finding and devising others, and arranging the array in order of difficulty. As you read this volume, I feel certain you will be as impressed as I was with the use Binet and Simon made of empirical evidence. (By the way, you will discover this is not a book in the sense that Binet and Simon put it together as such. Rather it is a translation and reprint of five major articles selected by H. H. Goddard from among those in *L'Année Psychologique*. Too, it was Goddard who chose as the title for this set of readings essentially the one used in the original 1908 article (Chapter IV).)

The second thrust of this preface is to bring some perspective to the marginal notes by Terman. Some of my library research into the early work of Terman was to ascertain what use he may have made of this volume and his notes. Here is a synopsis of that search.

Lewis Madison Terman lived from 1877 to 1956, reaching the

age of 79. He attended Normal School at 15 years of age and then taught in a one-roomed rural school. Later, after earning bachelor's and master's degrees at the University of Indiana, he enrolled in the doctoral program at Clark University where he studied under G. Stanley Hall. His dissertation, published in 1906, was entitled "Genius and stupidity: A study of some of the intellectual processes of seven bright and seven stupid boys." (Terminology has softened in the last 75 years.) In it he mentioned both Binet and Simon, but he was referring to their earlier work. I have no reason to believe he had read the Binet-Simon 1905 breakthrough article, reprinted as the first chapter of this book. Terman did not administer any of the Blin-Binet test items, though he gave dozens of other ones to his 14 subjects. Upon graduation, Terman became an instructor for four years (1906-1910) at Los Angeles Normal School. He then joined the faculty of Stanford University where he remained until his retirement.

In 1910-1911, he and H. G. Childs tested 396 children with a revision and extension of the 1908 Binet scale. I have to believe Terman read and used the original *L'Année Psychologique* article (see Chapter IV) because Goddard, in his introduction to this book, states he did not publish his first translation of this 1908 scale until January, 1910. (It would be nice to know for sure where Terman did get his lead.) Even as Terman and Childs published their tentative scale in 1912, the need for a more thorough revision, based on more extensive data, was immediately recognized by Terman. So, by 1913, the project was underway. It resulted in the now famous 1916 Stanford Revision of the 1911 Binet-Simon Intelligence Scale. The original 1911 Binet-Simon scale consisted of 54 test items while the 1916 Stanford-Binet was made up of 90 items. Of the 36 new items, some were devised by other psychologists, while others were developed by Terman and his many associates. (One thing is clear—wholesale borrowing appears to have been the order of the day. Blin has been given some credit for his items in a few textbooks on psychometric testing, but I did not find him mentioned once by Terman. The recognition went to Binet.)

Even though Goddard appears to have been the first American psychologist to translate, use and disseminate the Binet-Simon scales in this country, Terman was the person who did the careful revision and standardization. Thus, it was his versions that superseded a number of other concurrent efforts. Obviously Terman and Goddard knew of each other's work, which explains why the latter sent the former this copy of Kite's translation in June, 1916. (In reviewing the literature, I was impressed with how quickly French, Belgian, Italian, German, British and American scholars in the field learned of each other's efforts at the turn of the century. Perhaps they were more accomplished readers of foreign journals than we are today.)

I have searched through a number of Terman's books and articles related to the Stanford-Binet, some of them rather obscure, carefully studying the references which tended to be sparse. Not once did I find this Kite translation cited, but I did find some of the original Binet-Simon articles listed. It remains for someone to delve into the literature more thoroughly if we are to connect the marginal notes herein directly to Terman's test construction.

Finally, I have concluded that Binet and Terman had similar styles. Both appeared to have been practitioners rather than armchair theoreticians. Both of them were very hard working, extremely productive and remarkably prolific in their writings. Perhaps both of them would agree with the old adage that genius is 90 per cent perspiration and 10 per cent inspiration, with a little timely good fortune added as a bonus. It is my guess that neither would list test development as his major contribution to society. Probably Binet would cite his textbook *Les idées modernes sur les enfants*, wherein he outlines his procedures for training the intellect. And I believe Terman would name as his landmark accomplishment, the longitudinal study, *Genetic studies of genius*, in which he followed the achievement, adjustment, and other characteristics of intellectually gifted boys and girls as they grew up into men and women.

As this preface is written, 75 years have passed since Binet and Simon published their first scale, and 74 years since Terman completed his dissertation which launched him into psychometric measurement and the study of individual variability. An appropriate challenge for the field, it seems to me, is to refine and extend psychometrics more in the next three quarters of a century than has occurred since Blin, Binet, Terman and their associates released their pioneering works. Perhaps a major new insight will come to you as you study this classic. In any event, read and enjoy.

Lloyd M. Dunn, Ph.D.
Affiliate Professor of Educational
    Psychology and Special Education
University of Hawaii at Manoa
Fall, 1980

Lewis M. Terman

With the compliments of
The Vineland Laboratory
Henry H. Goddard

6.10.16

(1857–1911)

PUBLICATIONS OF THE TRAINING SCHOOL AT VINELAND
NEW JERSEY

DEPARTMENT OF RESEARCH

THE
DEVELOPMENT OF INTELLIGENCE
IN CHILDREN

(THE BINET-SIMON SCALE)

BY

ALFRED BINET, Sc.D and TH. SIMON, M.D.

TRANSLATED BY

ELIZABETH S. KITE

Diplome d'Instruction Primaire Superieure
Paris le 23 juillet, 1905
Member of the Staff of the Vineland
Research Laboratory

DEVOTED
TO THE
INTERESTS OF
THOSE WHOSE
MINDS HAVE NOT
DEVELOPED
NORMALLY

NO. 11, MAY, 1916

1916
WILLIAMS & WILKINS COMPANY
BALTIMORE

CONTENTS

INTRODUCTION

The first contribution of Drs. Binet and Simon to the problem of measuring intelligence appeared in L'Année Psychologique for 1905. This volume reached America early in 1906. The Vineland Research Laboratory for the psychological study of feeblemindedness was opened in September of the same year. My first work as director of this Laboratory was to search the literature for anything that bore upon the problem. The above article had attracted so little attention from the American psychologists that in spite of dilligent search in bibliographies, reviews, original sources and by appeals to personal friends, Binet's work in this line was never brought to my attention. It was not until the Spring of 1908 when I made a visit to Europe in the interests of the work that I learned of the tests. On that trip a visit was made to Dr. Decroly in Brussels. Dr. Decroly and Mlle. Degand had just completed a try-out of tests by Drs. Binet and Simon of Paris. Upon my return home I began at once to use the tests on the children of the Training School, employing Decroly's article as the source of information. Later I obtained Binet's article. These were the "1905" tests, not the scale. In December 1908 I published a six-page account of these tests.

In 1909 appeared L'Année Psychologique giving the "Scale," with the grading by years. Probably no critic of the scale during the past six years has reacted against it more positively than did I at that first reading. It seemed impossible to grade intelligence in that way. It was too easy, too simple. The article was laid aside for some weeks. One day while using the old tests, whose inadequacy was great, the new Scale came to mind and I decided to give it a fair trial. In January 1910 we published the first abstract of the scale—being a brief summary of the 1908 Binet-Simon article.

Our use of the scale was a surprise and a gratification. It met our needs. A classification of our children based on the Scale agreed with the Institution experience. Soon others began to use the scale. Then came the critics. Their criticisms showed such a thorough misunderstanding of the plan, purpose and spirit of the authors of the Scale that we realized what an injustice had been done by publishing our condensed outline— 16 pages out of 90. We at once resolved to publish a complete translation. Permission was obtained from Dr. Simon and the work was begun. It had to be crowded in with other work of the Laboratory, and, hence, there have been many delays. At last, however, the book is presented to the public. We regret the delay, but perhaps the present is the best time for presentation. Certainly it was never more needed than now.

It will seem an exaggeration to some to say that the world is talking of the Binet-Simon Scale; but consider that the Vineland Laboratory alone, has without effort or advertisement distributed to date 22,000 copies of the pamphlet describing the tests, and 88,000 record blanks.* This in spite of the fact that the same matter has been freely published in numerous other places. The Scale is used in Canada, England, Australia, New Zealand, South Africa, Germany, Switzerland, Italy, Russia, China, and has recently been translated into Japanese and Turkish.

The literature on the Scale has increased enormously; in 1914 there was already a bibliography of 254 titles; yet in all this time no complete translation of Binet's work on the Scale has appeared. A number of criticisms have appeared, many of which could not have been written if Binet's complete discussion of his Scale had been available to the critics.

It is little less than marvelous that the tests have had such a remarkable acceptance even in the mutilated form of our condensed abstract. That the Scale was so eminently useful in this abbreviated form shows the masterly work of the authors.

By many persons the Measuring Scale of Intelligence is supposed to be a mere incidental chapter in Binet's work. Scarcely anyone in America realizes to what an extent it was his *magnum opus.* That his writings on this subject fill a book of this size will be a great surprise. And yet this is only the half. Another volume the size of this (already translated and which we hope soon to publish) is devoted to the application of the Scale. Moreover, many other writings of Binet show how large a place it occupied in his thinking.

* (*Note:* This pamphlet is a 16-page condensation of Chapter IV of this book, with such revisions as our experience with the tests on American children seemed to justify.)

This book as a whole constitutes a complete history and exposition of the Measuring Scale as Binet left it.

In Chapter I the authors show the origin of the Scale and their first methods of attacking the problem.

Chapter II describes the first results—a series of test questions arranged in order of difficulty but not yet assigned to definite years. An immense amount of work had been done on this series, and the authors may have been justly proud of what they had accomplished, though it was soon to be largely discarded for a much more useful plan. This was the so called "1905 *Tests*."

Chapter III shows the laborious and painstaking methods of standardization. Nowhere does Binet more clearly show his genius. It is here that he has taught us the method which must be used in all extensions or revisions of the Scale, that lay any claim to scientific value.

In Chapter IV he gives us the Measuring Scale for Intelligence—the so called 1908 Scale. It is the most complete statement of the Scale.

Chapter V gives some of his later 1911 corrections and revisions—his last word on the subject.[1] In making up this book we have attempted to include everything Binet and Simon wrote explanatory of the Scale. The reader will find many repetitions and some contradictions, and the date of each article should be taken into account in deciding which is the authoritative statement. It has been thought best to include all of these repetitions and contradictions, in order to show the development of Binet's own thought in regard to his Scale. Only in this way does the marvelous work that he did on this subject become fully appreciated.

The translation has given rise to the usual translator's difficulties. Binet at times uses not only highly technical terms but also terms of his own invention. The usual "untranslatable expressions" are found. Moreover, it is clear that typographical errors occasionally crept in. Where this was certain and it was clear what the correct form should have been, we have taken the liberty of making the correction. Where we have been unable

[1] In this year he also prepared a final statement of the Scale for the "Bulletin de la Société libre pour l'Étude psychologique de l'Enfant." This has been translated by Dr. Clara Harrison Town, Lincoln, Illinois, 1913.

to correct, we have kept the error, leaving the reader of this book the same problem that faces the reader of the original. Cases of this sort will be discovered in some of the tables that do not "total" as they should.

In the question of free or literal translation, we have held more closely to the literal, especially with the test questions. This literalness seemed necessary in order to show as exactly as possible Binet's plan. But naturally it renders the questions, in many cases, inapplicable to American children.

In regard to the translation, the editor feels that the skill and ability of Miss Kite have given a most readable book. Miss Kite is eminently fitted for the task. She holds a "Diplome d'Instruction Primaire Supérieure, Paris le 23 juillet 1905." But more than that she is skilled in the use of the tests and is a close student of the writings of Binet and Simon.

Many persons from this Laboratory have taken part in this work, in the way of reading and suggesting revisions; notably, Miss Eleanor A. Gray, and Miss Flora Otis, Librarian, also Mr. E. A. Doll, Assistant Psychologist, and Miss Florence Mateer. We are also indebted to Rev. Ernest Monge of Faribault, Minn., for the original translation of a part of the fourth chapter.

HENRY H. GODDARD,
Editor.

Vineland, N. J., 1916.

Int. tests dev. from study of F. M.
Binet's interest and earlier work
Previous systems of tests (by faculties)

UPON THE NECESSITY OF ESTABLISHING A SCIENTIFIC DIAGNOSIS OF INFERIOR STATES OF INTELLIGENCE

L'Année Psychologique 1905 pp. 163–191

We here present the first rough sketch of a work which was directly inspired by the desire to serve the interesting cause of the education of subnormals.

In October, 1904, the Minister of Public Instruction named a commission which was charged with the study of measures to be taken for insuring the benefits of instruction to defective children. After a number of sittings, this commission regulated all that pertained to the type of establishment to be created, the conditions of admission into the school, the teaching force, and the pedagogical methods to be employed. They decided that no child suspected of retardation should be eliminated from the ordinary school and admitted into a special class, without first being subjected to a pedagogical and medical examination from which it could be certified that because of the state of his intelligence, he was unable to profit, in an average measure, from the instruction given in the ordinary schools.

But how the examination of each child should be made, what methods should be followed, what observations taken, what questions asked, what tests devised, how the child should be compared with normal children, the commission felt under no obligation to decide. It was formed to do a work of administration, not a work of science.

It has seemed to us extremely useful to furnish a guide for future Commissions' examination. Such Commissions should understand from the beginning how to get their bearings. It must be made impossible for those who belong to the Commission to fall into the habit of making haphazard decisions according to impressions which are subjective, and consequently uncontrolled. Such impressions are sometimes good, sometimes bad, and have at all times too much the nature of the arbitrary, of caprice, of indifference. Such a condition is quite unfortunate because the

9

Idiot — imbecile — débile (lack of definiteness)

interests of the child demand a more careful method. To be a member of a special class can never be a mark of distinction, and such as do not merit it, must be spared the record. Some errors are excusable in the beginning, but if they become too frequent, they may ruin the reputation of these new institutions. Furthermore, in principle, we are convinced, and we shall not cease to repeat, that the precision and exactness of science should be introduced into our practice whenever possible, and in the great majority of cases it is possible.

The problem which we have to solve presents many difficulties both theoretical and practical. It is a hackneyed remark that the definitions, thus far proposed, for the different states of subnormal intelligence, lack precision. These inferior states are indefinite in number, being composed of a series of degrees which mount from the lowest depths of idiocy, to a condition easily confounded with normal intelligence. Alienists have frequently come to an agreement concerning the terminology to be employed for designating the difference of these degrees; at least, in spite of certain individual divergence of ideas to be found in all questions, there has been an agreement to accept *idiot* as applied to the lowest state, *imbecile* to the intermediate, and *moron* (débile)* to the state nearest normality. Still among the numerous alienists, under this common and apparently precise terminology, different ideas are concealed, variable and at the same time confused. The distinction between idiot, imbecile, and moron is not understood in the same way by all practitioners. We have abundant proof of this in the strikingly divergent medical diagnoses made only a few days apart by different alienists upon the same patient.

Dr. Blin, physician of the Vaucluse Asylum, recently drew the attention of his fellow physicians to these regrettable contradictions. He states that the children who are sent to the

---

* The French word *débile* (weak) is used by Binet to designate the highest grade of mental defectives, called in England feeble-minded. In America the term feeble-minded has been used in the same sense, but unfortunately it is also applied generically to the entire group of mental defectives. To obviate this ambiguity, we coined the word MORON (Greek Moros, foolish) to designate the highest grade of mental defect. We have accordingly translated *débile* by moron, except in a few instances where the context requires a different term.—EDITOR.

Change of "labels"!

colony come provided with several dissimilar certificates. "One child, called imbecile in the first certificate, is marked idiot in the second, feeble-minded (débile) in the third, and degenerate in the fourth."[1] M. Damaye, former house surgeon of Dr. Blin, adds this observation: "One would have only to look through several folders of records belonging to children of the colony, in order to collect almost the same number of different diagnoses."[2] Perhaps this last affirmation is a little exaggerated, but a statistical study would show the exact truth on this point.

We cannot sufficiently deplore the consequence of this state of uncertainty recognized today by all alienists. The simple fact, that specialists do not agree in the use of the technical terms of their science, throws suspicion upon their diagnoses, and prevents all work of comparison. We ourselves have made similar observations. In synthesizing the diagnoses made by M. Bourneville upon patients leaving the Bicêtre, we found that in the space of four years only two feeble-minded individuals have left his institution although during that time the Bureau of Admission has sent him more than thirty. Nothing could show more clearly than this change of label, the confusion of our nomenclature.

What importance can be attached to public statistics of different countries concerning the percentage of backward children if the definition for backward children is not the same in all countries? How will it be possible to keep a record of the intelligence of pupils who are treated and instructed in a school, if the terms applied to them, feeble-minded, retarded, imbecile, idiot, vary in meaning according to the doctor who examines them? The absence of a common measure prevents comparison of statistics, and makes one lose all interest in investigations which may have been very laborious. But a still more serious fact is that, because of lack of methods, it is impossible to solve those essential questions concerning the afflicted, whose solution presents the greatest interest; for example, the real results gained by the treatment of inferior states of intelligence by doctor and educator; the educative value of one pedagogical method compared with another; the degree of curability of incomplete idiocy, etc.

[1] Blin, Les débilités mentales, *Revue de psychiatrie.* Aôut, 1902.

[2] Damaye. *Essai de diagnostic entre les états de débilité mentale.* Thèse de Paris, Steinheil, 1903.

It is not by means of *a priori* reasonings, of vague considerations, of oratorical displays, that these questions can be solved; but by minute investigation, entering into the details of fact, and considering the effects of the treatment for each particular child.   There is but one means of knowing if a child, who has passed six years in a hospital or in a special class, has profited from that stay, and to what degree he has profited; and that is to compare his certificate of entrance with his certificate of dismissal, and by that means ascertain if he shows a special amelioration of his condition beyond that which might be credited simply to the considerations of growth.   But experience has shown how imprudent it would be to place confidence in this comparison, when the two certificates come from different doctors, who do not judge in exactly the same way, or who use different words to characterize the mental status of patients.

It might happen that a child, who had really improved in school, had received in the beginning the diagnosis of moron (débile), and on leaving, the prejudicial diagnosis of imbecile, simply because the second doctor spoke a different language from the first.   If one took these certificates literally, this case would be considered a failure.   On the contrary, the appearance of amelioration would be produced if the physician who delivered the certificate of dismissal had the habit of using higher terms than the one who furnished the certificate of entrance. One can even go further.   The errors which we note, do not necessarily emanate from the disagreement of different physicians. It would suffice for the same physician to deliver the two certificates, if he did not employ for each one the same criterion; and it would certainly be possible for him to vary unconsciously after an interval of several years if he had nothing to guide him but his own subjective impressions.   Might not the same thing also happen if his good faith as a physician happened to be in conflict with the interests of the institution which he directed? Might he not unconsciously as it were, have a tendency to lower the mental status of patients on entering and to raise it on dismissal, in order to emphasize the advantages of the methods which he had applied?   We are not incriminating anyone, but simply calling attention to methods actually in use which, by their lack of precision, favor the involuntary illusions of physicians and relatives, in a word, of all those who, having an interest in the amelioration of the condition of the defective child, would have a tendency to confound their desires with the reality.

Perhaps someone will raise an objection and say this uncertainty, has no special application to diagnosis of the degrees of mental debility; it is also to be found in mental pathology and, in a general way, in the diagnosis of all maladies; it is the result of the empirical nature which is characteristic of clinical studies. It might be added, that, if anyone took the trouble to make a statistical study of the divergence in the diagnosis of different physicians upon the same patient, it would probably be found that the percentage of disagreement is very great in all branches of medicine.

We believe it worth while to examine their objection because it permits us to enter more deeply into the analysis of the question. The disagreements of practitioners might come from three very different classes of causes:

1. Ignorance, that is, the lack of aptitude of certain physicians. This is an individual failure, for which abstract science is not responsible. It is certain that, even when the symptoms of a disease are absolutely clear, such a physician might fail to recognize them through incapacity. There are many accountants who make mistakes in calculation, but these errors do not discredit mathematics. A physician might not be able to recognize a "p. g." if he is himself a "p. g."

2. The variable meaning of terms. Since the same expression has a different sense according to the person who uses it, it is possible that the disagreement of diagnosis may be simply a disagreement of words, due to the use of different nomenclature.

3. Lack of precision in the description of the symptoms which reveal or which constitute a certain particular malady; different physicians do not examine the same patient in the same manner and do not give the symptoms the same importance; or, it may be they make no effort to find out the precise symptoms, and no effort to analyze carefully in order to distinguish and interpret them.

Of these three kinds of error, which is the one that actually appears in the diagnosis of inferior states of intelligence? Let us set aside the first. There remain the faults of nomenclature, and the insufficiency of methods of examination.

The general belief seems to be that the confusion arises wholly

Confus. due to subjective meth. not merely to terminology

from an absence of a uniform nomenclature. There is some truth in this opinion. It can be proved by a comparison of terms used by authors belonging to the different countries. Even in France the terms differ somewhat according to the physician, the order of the admitted subdivisions not being rigorously followed. The classification of Magnan is not that of Voisin, and his, in turn, differs from that of Bourneville. Undoubtedly it would be a good work to bring about a unification of this nomenclature as has been done for the standard of measurements and for electric units. But this reform in itself is not sufficient and we are very sure that they deceive themselves who think that at bottom this is only a question of terminology. It is very much more serious. We find physicians who, though using the same terminology, constantly disagree in their diagnosis of the same child. The examples cited from M. Blin prove this. There the doctors had recourse to the terminology of Morel, who classifies those of inferior intelligence as idiots, imbeciles and *"débiles."* Notwithstanding this use of the same terms, they do not agree in the manner of applying them. Each one according to his own fancy, fixes the boundary line separating these states. It is in regard to the facts that the doctors disagree.

In looking closely one can see that the confusion comes principally from a fault in the method of examination. When an alienist finds himself in the presence of a child of inferior intelligence, he does not examine him by bringing out each one of the symptoms which the child manifests and by interpreting all symptoms and classifying them; he contents himself with taking a subjective impression, an impression as a whole, of his subject, and of making his diagnosis by instinct. We do not think that we are going too far in saying that at the present time very few physicians would be able to cite with absolute precision the objective and invariable sign, or signs, by which they distinguish the degrees of inferior mentality.

A study of the historical side of the question shows us very clearly that what is lacking is a *precise basis for differential diagnosis.*

A Few Historical Notes

PINEL, ESQUIROL, SEGUIN, MOREL, BOURNEVILLE, SOLLIER, BLIN

It is perfectly useless to enumerate all the authors who have attempted to classify idiocy. In medicine as in other sciences there are a number of writers of secondary rank who repeat the work of those who have gone before, making but insignificant alterations. We shall note only those who have brought new ideas and changed the direction of study.

Pinel devoted a chapter of his medico-philosophical treatise on *Mental Derangement,* to "Idiocy, or the Obliteration of the Intellectual and Affective Faculties." But he confounds the states of stupor and dementia with actual idiocy, "that which is so from the beginning," regarding which he makes one observation; one paragraph is reserved for the "Cretins of Switzerland."

Esquirol was the first to differentiate idiocy; he develops this fact in great detail and certainly understood its importance. Ordinarily when anyone cites the names of Esquirol in a history of idiocy it is to bring out the fact that we owe to him a classification of idiocy founded upon the power of speech. It is true that Esquirol has made this classification. We give the passage in its entirety.

> Speech, that essential attribute of man, which has been given him that he may express his thought, speech, being the sign most constantly associated in idiots with the intellectual capacity, gives the character to the principle varieties of idiocy. In the first degree of imbecility, speech is free and easy. In the second degree it is less easy, the vocabulary more limited. In the first degree of idiocy proper, the idiot uses only words, with short sentences. Idiots of the second degree articulate only monosyllables or some cries. Finally idiots of the third degree have neither speech, phrase, word, nor monosyllables.[3]

That is all. Esquirol relates a number of interesting observations regarding imbeciles and idiots, which form perhaps the most suggestive part of his study; but nowhere does he undertake to introduce his classification by speech; but, on the contrary, by a total of the symptoms. Moreover, if he had attempted an application, he would have seen that the condition of speech

[3]*Des Maladies mentales,* II, p. 340.

Esquirol disting. idiocy from insanity
Expl. what his distinct is:—
Insane: rich, become poor, etc

16   DEVELOPMENT OF INTELLIGENCE

is not always sufficient to characterize the degree of mental inferiority.   We are therefore disposed to see in the so-called classification only one of those accessory ideas which germinate in
the mind of an author and to which he attaches only relative
importance.   The talent of Esquirol did not develop in this line.
His real work consists in having definitely separated idiocy from
other conditions which seem to resemble it, by a lack or by an
equivalent diminution of exterior signs of intelligence.   Conditions which simulate idiocy are stupor and different demential
states.   It is incontestable that Esquirol, by the insistence with
which he developed these different points, shows the importance
which they had for him.   We purpose allowing the reader to
be his own judge by making extensive extracts.

Notice in the first place how Esquirol defines idiocy.   It is
he who first used the term idiocy as a substitute for *idiotism*,
the word employed before his time, which has since been reserved
for grammatical use.   He says

Idiocy is not a malady, it is a state in which the faculties are never
manifested, or have never developed sufficiently for the idiot to acquire
the knowledge which other individuals of his age receive when placed
in the same environment.   Idiocy begins either with life, or during that
period which precedes the complete development of the affective and intellectual faculties; idiots are what they must remain during the entire
course of their lives.   Everything in the idiot reveals an organism either
of arrested or of imperfect development.   It is not possible to conceive
of changing this condition.   Nothing can give to these unhappy beings,
even for a moment, more reason or more intelligence.   They do not attain
to an advanced age, seldom living to be over thirty.   When the brain
is examined, defects of structure are nearly always found.

Immediately following this is a passage in which Esquirol distinguishes idiocy from insanity.   This distinction is extremely
important.   It is worth while to quote his own words.

Insanity and idiocy differ essentially, or else the principles of all classification are illusions.   Insanity, like mania or mono-mania does not commence before puberty; it has a period of growth more or less rapid.   Insanity, such as senile dementia, increases from year to year by the wear-
ing away of the organs or by the successive loss of different faculties.   All
the symptoms show physical weakness; all the features are drawn, the
eyes dull, depressed; and if the insane man wishes to act, he is moved by
a fixed idea which has survived the general loss of intelligence.   Insanity
may be cured; one can conceive the possibility of suspending the symptoms;
there is a diminution, or privation of the forces necessary to exercise the

faculties, but the faculties still exist. A shock of the moral nature, medicines, might awaken him or arouse sufficient force to produce the manifestation of some ideas, of some affection; other means, too, might remove the obstacles which suspend their manifestation.

If a man having become insane does not succumb rapidly, he may run through a long course and arrive at a very advanced age.

When an autopsy is performed, one sometimes finds organic lesions but they are accidental, because the thickening of the bones of the skull, or the spreading of the cranial plates ("l'écartement de leur tables,") coincident with senile dementia, do not in the least constitute defects of conformation. It is the same with the alterations and changes in the substance of the brain caused by the progress of age.

The insane man is deprived of possessions which he formerly enjoyed; he is a rich man become poor; the idiot has always been in misery and want. The state of the insane may vary, that of the idiot remains always the same. The one conserves much of the appearance of the complete man, the other retains many traits of infancy. In one case as in the other, there are no sensations or practically none; but the insane man shows in his organization and also in his intelligence something of his past perfection; the idiot is such as he has always been, he is all that he can ever be relative to his primitive organization.

A few lines farther on, Esquirol makes another distinction between idiocy and other mental states which resemble it only in appearance. It seems useful to reproduce this passage also.

But there are individuals who seem to be void of sensibility and intelligence, who are without ideas, without speech, without movement, and who remain where they are placed, who must be dressed and fed. Are they not idiots? No, surely not. These are not the diagnostic symptoms. A single epoch in a malady cannot give an abstract idea of it; on the contrary one must see and study this malady in all its states, each one of which should furnish some factor to the diagnosis. I have previously given the history of a girl who offered all the symptoms which one takes ordinarily for the signs of idiocy. That girl was terrified, and it was fear that chained the exercise of all her faculties. I cared for a young man 27 years of age, who, deceived by a woman and failing to secure the place he wanted, after an attack of insanity, fell into a state of apparent idiocy. The face of the invalid was highly colored, his eyes fixed and uncertain, his countenance without expression; it was necessary to dress and undress him and to put him to bed; he did not eat unless the food was put into his mouth; his arms hung at his sides and his hands were swollen; he always stood but never walked unless someone forced him to do so; he seemed to have neither feeling nor thought. Leeches applied to the temples, tepid baths, cold douches on the head, and above all a general eruption of the skin cured him. This young man told me, after his restoration to health, that a voice within him kept repeating, "Don't move, or you are lost." Fear made him immovable. Intelligence, sensitiveness are therefore not lost, but the manifestation of these faculties is hindered by different motives of which the patients are conscious when they are cured. During my clinical lessons of 1822, we had at the Salpêtrière a young woman, B., who seemed to be in the most profound stupor and in a state of absolute insensibility; she remained sitting by her bed and never spoke. Many times I pinched and struck her without her showing signs of pain. I had a seton placed on her neck and several blisters applied to different parts of the skin, always with the same apparent lack of sensation; the same obstinate silence, the same refusal to walk. One day this young woman did not appear at the clinic, and after that nothing could induce her to return. When she was cured, she told me that one of the pupils had pinched her. This impertinence angered her. What was permissable for me was not for the others and she resolved never again to appear. Certain monomaniacs, dominated by ideas of love or of religion, show the same symptoms. Certainly in all of these cases, the sensuous and intellectual faculties exercise themselves with energy; appearances are deceptive; these are by no means cases of idiocy.

Following Esquirol, there are a great number of authors who, one after the other, have attempted to define idiocy and other inferior states of intelligence, and who have presented a subdivision and sometimes a classification of the different degrees of inferiority of intelligence. To make a complete history it would be necessary to study the attempts of Belhomme, Seguin, Felix Voisin, Morel, Marcé, Griesinger, Luys, Schule, Chambard, Ball, Dagonet, Ireland, Jules Voisin, Magnan, Sollier, Bourneville.

Two principal types of classification have been given; the classification according to symptoms and the anatomo-pathological or etiological classification.

The latter are the less frequent, the less usual. We can cite two examples, one from Ireland, the other from Bourneville.

Ireland,[4] while recognizing that it would be of great interest to take account of the exact intellectual symptoms of idiots, believes that from the point of view of the treatment, and especially for prognosis, the generating cause of idiocy must be taken into account. In his book, he makes a separate study of the following etiological classes:

1. Genetous Idiocy.
2. Microcephalic Idiocy.
3. Hydrocephalic Idiocy.
4. Eclampsic Idiocy.

[4] W. W. Ireland, *The mental affections of children, idocy, imbecility and insanity*, London, 1900, p. 39.

5. Epileptic Idiocy.
6. Paralytic Idiocy.
7. Traumatic Idiocy.
8. Inflammatory Idiocy (the result of Encephalitis).
9. Sclerotic Idiocy.
10. Syphilitic Idiocy.
11. Cretinism (including the Endemic and Sporadic or Myxoedematous Forms).
12. Idiocy by Deprivation.

In spite of the great interest of these distinctions, we cannot find any light for us in this classification, especially from a pedagogic point of view, because the form of inferior mentality with which we most often have to do is what Ireland calls congenital idiocy; it is necessary to know the degrees of this, and Ireland does not furnish us the means of distinguishing them.

We would make the same remark in regard to the pathological classification of Bourneville which differs but little from the preceding. Here it is:

1. Hydrocephalic Idiocy.
2. Microcephalic Idiocy.
3. Idiocy, symptomatic of arrest of development of the convolutions.
4. Idiocy, symptomatic of a congenital malformation of the brain (porencephaly, absence of corpus callosum, etc.).
5. Idiocy, symptomatic of atrophic sclerosis; sclerosis of one hemisphere, or of two hemispheres, sclerosis of one lobe of the brain, sclerosis of isolated convolutions, sclerosis of the brain.
6. Idiocy, due to hypertrophic or tumorous sclerosis.
7. Idiocy, symptomatic of meningitis or chronic meningo-encephalitis.
8. Idiocy, with pachydermic cachexia, myxoedematous idiocy.

Bourneville was the first to study several of the preceding forms, porencephalous and myxedematous idiocy.

In spite of the interest of this classification, it cannot serve as a faithful guide for study during the life of the patient, in whom the nature of the lesions is often very obscure.

We shall therefore set aside the etiologic and anatomo-pathologic, restricting ourselves to symptomatic classifications.

After having carefully examined several of the latter we are now convinced that it will not be necessary to analyze all because all are conceived along the same lines. It is of little import to know that for a certain clinician, there are two orders of inferior intelligence, while for another there are three or four; that is, one uses the terms complete idiocy and incomplete idiocy; that a second proposes the new terms imbecile, feeble-minded, backward; that a third distinguishes the non-social from the non-teachable; or again that one has established the difference between the intellectual idiot and the moral idiot. All this is merely terminology. Questions of terminology are doubtless very important, but only on condition that there be unity of acceptance of the facts and the ideas which the terms indicate. But it seems to us that all the classifications of the authors cited above have the same lack of precision, a fault which consists essentially in this: the symptoms characterizing the different degrees of mental inferiority are not described in such a way that they can be practically recognized and distinguished. In order to justify our remarks it will suffice to cite some of the best known of these classifications.

Dr. Jules Voisin, in his *Lessons on Idiocy*, proposes a classification which places under the title of idiots all degrees of intellectual weakness; it is one of the simplest and best that has been formulated:

I. Complete idiocy, absolute, congenital or acquired, composed of two degrees.

(*a*) The anencephalics, and those who have not even the instinct of self-preservation.

(*b*) These who have the instinct of self-preservation and certain characteristics. These two degrees are incurable.

II. Incomplete idiocy, congenital or acquired, which also includes several degrees, according to the presence, the absence, and the development of certain intellectual faculties, sensory or motor. It is susceptible of amelioration.

III. Imbecility, congenital or acquired: the presence in rudimentary form of all the intellectual, instinctive and moral faculties; perversion or instability of these faculties.

IV. Mental debility, characterized by the weakness or by the lack of balance of the faculties. It is now the motor centers, now the centers of sensation, now the emotional centers which have the supremacy in the excitation. When one of these centers predominates without being counterbalanced by the others, the result is either a "moteur" or a "sensoriel," or a "sensitif."

We also give the classification of Dr. Bourneville, one of the last that has been published. It appeared in the *Treatise on Medicine* by Brouardel and Gilbert.

I. *Idiocy, complete, absolute, or of the first degree:* comprises purely vegetative beings without control over excretory organs and without any intellectual manifestations.

II. *Profound idiocy, or idiocy of the second degree.* Life here is essentially vegetative, and the ideas of relationships very limited. There is a gleam of intelligence, a fugitive attention. Motility, locomotion and prehension exist to a limited extent. Appetite is exaggerated. Inability to retain secretions still absolute.

III. *Imbecility proper;* the intellectual faculties are very incomplete. Attention fleeting ("fugace"). Perversion of instincts. Defective speech, limited language. Will without energy. These creatures are victims of every influence.

IV. *Slight imbecility or intellectual retardation.* The intellectual faculties are retarded, and noticeably below the faculties of children of the same age. The attention may remain fixed, at least for a certain time. Movements, locomotion, prehension, and sensitiveness are generally intact. The stigmata of degeneracy are generally less numerous, and less pronounced than with imbeciles and especially with idiots.

V. *Mental instability.* Sometimes simple, but more often approaching imbecility, intellectual backwardness. Exuberant physical mobility, and intellectual mobility. Sudden impulses.

VI. *Moral imbecility.* Nightmares, tempers, instability and perversion of instincts. Excessive credulity toward those to whom these children abandon themselves, and who dominate them. Egotism. A sexual development beyond their age, or sexual impulses which render them dangerous. Their intellectual faculties may be absolutely intact; intellectual defect is only a secondary characteristic. Stigmata of physical degeneracy are sometimes quite absent.

Let us see some of the principal observations that can be made relative to these classifications; they will bear upon the enumeration of the symptoms and their definition.

Enumeration of symptoms. The authors incorporate into their definitions a great number of motor troubles and disorders of every sort, belonging to the digestive and secretive apparatus, growth, etc. This enumeration would be in place in a clinical record, where all the observable symptoms of a patient are collected; but it has this disadvantage that it misleads the mind, when one attempts a definition where only the essential should be noted. Thus we see the authors laying great stress upon motility, locomotion, prehension and speech in distinguishing the different degrees of idiocy. We admit, that one frequently observes motor troubles with idiots, and that in a general way, the intensity of these troubles is greater in the most profound cases of idiocy. This is not surprising. From the moment that idiocy is admitted to be the result of a number of very different diseases of the brain, it is logical to infer that the diseases which produce an arrested

Esquirol 1st to base diagn on state of intel. primarily ∴ for psychologist to do.

22   DEVELOPMENT OF INTELLIGENCE

or perverted development in the intellectual functions should also
provoke divers disorders in the sphere of motility; as for instance
in the respiratory, circulatory, secretory functions, since all the
functions of the living being are directly or indirectly under the
influence of the nervous system. But it is no less necessary to
establish in the definition of idiocy, a distinction between it and
troubles of a different nature. Idiocy, as Esquirol was the first to
recognize, consists in a weakness of the intelligence. If the
physician gives a child the diagnosis of profound idiocy or of imbecility, it is not because the child does not walk, nor talk, has no
control over secretions, is microcephalic, has the ears badly formed,
or the palate keeled. The child is judged to be an idiot because
he is affected in his intellectual development. This is so strikingly
true that if we suppose a case presented to us where speech, locomotion, prehension were all nil, but which gave evidence of an
intact intelligence, no one would consider that patient an idiot.

It results from these observations that the directing principle of
the preceding classifications does not seem to us correct. The
view is lost that here it is a question of inferior states of intelligence, and that it is only by taking into account this inferiority
that a classification can be established. In other words *a classification of idiocy is a clinical classification to be made by means of
psychology*.

Our conception would be badly understood if it were supposed
that we intend to eliminate from the definition of idiocy all the
purely somatic disorders so frequently observed in these unhappy
cases. On the contrary it is very useful to take note of these
symptoms, especially in cases where by their nature or their
mechanism they reveal to us a mental weakness or insufficiency.
They have less value in themselves than in what they imply.
Hence the necessity for their analysis. Take for example a child
of five years who does not walk. The retardation in locomotion
is not in itself a sign of idiocy, since it might come from a great
number of anatomical or pathological causes which are quite independent of the functioning of the intelligence, for example, Little's
disease, or infantile paralysis. The motility of the lower members must first be examined to see if it is normal and if the members are strong enough to bear the weight of the child and if that
which is lacking is only the psychical factor of locomotion, that is to
say the desire, the will to walk and the intelligent coördination of

the movements of the two limbs. The same analysis must be made in relation to the inability to retain secretions, and in a general manner to all troubles belonging to the sphere of motility, holding firmly in mind the idea that the physical disorders of idiocy have no value except as signs which reveal the intelligence.

The second criticism to the preceding classifications, which is more serious than the first, has to do with the gradation of the symptoms. After one has perused the formulas which the alienists employ, he perceives that very little has been learned, because of their extreme vagueness. They are merely differences of more or less which are pointed out, and these differences, which are declared sufficient to establish the degrees, and consequently diagnostic differences, are not defined at all.

We are told for profound idiocy: "*There is here a fugitive attention.*" What is that—a fugitive attention? In what does it consist? "*Motility exists but a little.*" What does "little" signify? We are assured that imbecility differs from idiocy in this: in idiocy "*there is a gleam of intelligence;*" in imbecility "*the intellectual faculties exist in a very incomplete degree.*" We should like to know what difference must be established between "a gleam" of intelligence and "very incomplete degree" of the intellectual faculties. We are again informed that in profound idiocy "*the attention is fugitive,*" while in imbecility, "*the attention is fleeting.*" We are unable to grasp the distinctive shade of meaning. We are also ignorant of the value of the following symptoms which are noted in the definition of imbecility, "*defective speech,*" "*limited language.*" We admit that we have no idea what precise defect of articulation corresponds to "defective speech." There are people who stammer slightly, and others whose speech is scarcely intelligible. All have defective speech. The same remark is true for "limited language." Very many peasants have a limited language. What extent of vocabulary must one possess in order to have a "limited language?" Again we are told for the diagnosis of imbecility "*Will without energy.*" These are still the same kind of expressions so vague that they might be applied even to normals. What shall we say of the formula for "slight imbecility"—with which we shall close. ". . . . *the intellectual faculties . . . . are noticeably below the faculties of children of the same age.*" "*Noticeably*" is the word which forms the best résumé of the essential character of these classifications.

Even Esquirol himself merits the same criticism when he distinguishes idiocy from imbecility, in writing extraordinary phrases like the following: "with imbeciles the organization is *more or less perfect*," "with idiots *the senses are scarcely outlined—the organization is incomplete, etc.*" Evidently Esquirol has set a bad example and everyone has followed him.

We were therefore right in saying as we did, that it is a fixed basis of differential diagnosis which is lacking with the alienists. The vagueness of their formulas reveals the vagueness of their ideas. They cling to characteristics which are by "more or less," and they permit themselves to be guided by a subjective impression which they do not seem to think necessary to analyze, and which therefore would be impossible to justify. We shall never be able to emphasize sufficiently how far removed from scientific methods are such empirical processes. *Quantitative differences, such as we have noted, are of no value unless they are measured, even if measured but crudely.*

In spite of these objections we willingly recognize that alienists, because of their practice and their medical insight, arrive very quickly at judging and classifying a child. But these judgments and these classifications are made by subjective processes, and no alienist would be able to tell with precision, for example, how many years a certain backward child was behind a normal one of the same age. The distinction between slight mental defect and normality, which is so difficult to trace and yet so interesting, remains therefore completely inaccessible.

Following the symptomatic classifications, we find another type, that of *psychological classifications*.

In these, less attention is paid to somatic symptoms, while the interest is concentrated on the degree of intelligence. The idea is quite recent. Nevertheless it would seem that it already existed in Seguin's book. In that singular work, so remarkable as a practitioner's, so weak as a theorist's, we find the extraordinary idea that idiocy depends on a weakness of the will. The idiot would not be an idiot, if he did not wish to be one. It is useless to stop to discuss this absurd statement, to which several authors—those at least who have had the patience to read the work of Seguin[5]—have given due justice. We have pointed out this error,

[5] E. Seguin, *Traitement moral, hygiène et éducation des idiots et des autres enfants arriérés*, Paris, J.-B. Baillière, 1846, p. 170.

Sollier, weakness of attention
(Followed Ribot's exag. emphasis of attend.)

NECESSITY FOR SCIENTIFIC DIAGNOSIS   25

because Seguin seemed to grasp, very vaguely it is true, that it is
by psychological study that idiots must be classified. We shall
not lay stress upon this.

P. Sollier[6] was the first to propose a psychological classification,
the first, in reality, who attempted to establish a classification of
the degrees of idiocy based on a single psychological characteristic.
That characteristic is the state of the attention. The author,
having formulated this principle, deduces schematically the following division:

> *Absolute idiocy*, characterized by the absolute and complete absence of
> attention.
> *Simple idiocy*, in which there is weakness or difficulty of attention.
> *Imbecility*, in which there is instability of attention.

This curious attempt seems to us to be rightly directed because
it is essentially psychological. It is by a mental quality alone
that Sollier attempts to distinguish idiots. Perhaps, however, he
did not himself realize the value of the principle which directed
him, because he continued to reproduce the definition of his prede-
cessors according to whom idiocy is "an affection of the brain
. . . . characterized by trouble with the intellectual, sensory and motor functions." The expression "motor" which he
uses seems to prove that, in his thought, idiocy is not exclusively
a mental infirmity. As to the intellectual faculty by which Sollier
chose to distinguish different kinds of idiots, he has made an unhappy selection. Why should he have chosen attention before
memory, or imagination, or comprehension, or judgment? This
has very truly the appearance of the *a priori* system. A distinction of this nature ought to be made only from observations taken
from life. The intellectual functions which are the first to develop should be sought out, how they arrange themselves, in what
order they appear, how they coördinate. This is the true, the
only method. To be sure this is laborious enough; very many
patients must be examined, and when one is willing to analyze
concrete facts, he seldom arrives at conclusions that can be ele-
gantly expressed in so brief a formula. These brief formulas belong to literature. The classification of Sollier is more literary
than clinical.

[6] *Psychologie de l'idiot et de l'imbécile*, Paris, Alcan, p. 36.

We see very easily, nevertheless, how the idea came to him of making attention the key to idiocy. Ribot, who recently published an important monograph entitled, "Psychology of Attention," obeyed that quite natural tendency among authors of monographs, to exaggerate the importance of his subject; he insisted especially on the comparison between spontaneous and voluntary attention, concluding that the spontaneous form, which is the primitive, is more important than the other. Sollier, impressed with this argument, which is true only in general psychology, transported it to the clinic, that is to say, into individual psychology, where it is probably false, because individuals seem to differ, not so much by the degree of spontaneous attention, as by the degree of voluntary or deliberate attention. And Sollier has once more followed this preconceived idea, when he supposes that attention, because it is the most important of the faculties of mind (which, by the way, is subject to question), presents necessarily a development parallel to that of all the intellectual faculties, and that its measure will, therefore, serve as the measure of the intelligence. Different observers, Voisin[7] for example, have cited interesting facts which go to prove the contrary.

And now a last objection, Sollier does not indicate by what signs one can recognize the weakness, the difficulty, the instability of the attention, nor how one can measure this so as to make a diagnosis. He contents himself in his chapter on attention with a general and rather vague description in which he makes numerous citations from Ribot, but in which one searches in vain for precise observations upon idiots or imbeciles. The author remains in the realm of general ideas for which his mind has an evident predilection; he never touches ground, never cites a fact. A characteristic sign of this manner is to speak of "the idiot" and "the imbecile," and to describe the states of attention of these abstract entities. We think it worth while to cite several passages which illustrate how the author has grasped his subject.

Here is a passage in which he describes the attention of an idiot:

With the absolute idiot the attention is reduced to its simplest manifestation, one can almost say it does not exist. At times only the sight of nourishment can make him lose his indifference. Sometimes by surprising him, one may catch a gleam of passing attention, which vanishes even

Sollier always vague

---

[7] *Leçons sur l'diotie*, p. 80.

more quickly than it appeared.[8] On hearing a loud harsh noise for instance, the idiot turns about or simply turns his eyes, then falls into the
habitual impassiveness from which nothing can arouse him. He has
no ideas, no perception, scarcely any sensations. With the simple idiot
it is often difficult to arouse the attention of which the subject is capable,
and it is necessary to resort to every expedient which pedagogy can furnish—such as for instance, pictures and colors. Idiots seem to be especially visualists. The attention of the imbecile is primarily, wandering.
With the greatest facility, it passes from one subject to another, with no
connection between the statements. While still young, when questioned,
he will let his gaze wander, will handle objects about him, and make no
reply until after you have repeated the same question many times.
Scarcely has he replied by a few words uttered without thought, before
he recommences his manoeuvres or sets to babbling or to singing. He will
keep repeating that which is said to him of serious matters which in passing have caught his voluntary attention.

These few instances show that the author has observed many
idiots, and that he has familiarized himself with their physiognomy,
their gestures, their manners. There are very many interesting
facts in these rather vague descriptions. But the practitioner
who would take such descriptions as a final guide in classifying
idiots, would be very much hampered. That which he would
need and which Sollier does not give, is a technique capable of
measuring the degrees of attention and of recording the quantitative variations. We cannot, however, reproach Sollier for
having made this important omission in his book. Methods of
measuring attention are still scarcely known; this is one of the least
advanced branches of experimental psychology.

It is unnecessary to add that in spite of these criticisms, the
work of Sollier[9] presents the greatest interest.

We would note as very curious, the distinction which he makes
between "distraction dissipated" and "distraction absorbed."
We shall return to this point at another time when we study the
attention of the feeble-minded.

In closing this history we wish to speak of a recent experiment,
scarcely a year old, due to the efforts of Dr. Blin and his pupil,

[8] Let us emphasize in passing that interesting expression, whose end
is only verbalism; verbalism is the peril of generalizers.

[9] This author proposes another distinction, limited to idiocy and imbecility. Idiocy would be due to certain lesions, while in imbecility there
would be no lesions. Although scarcely practical, this distinction would
be very curious, if it could be demonstrated to be true. Unfortunately,
the author does not insist upon the demonstration.

Dr. Damaye.   It has been explained by Dr. Blin, in a short article upon mental weaknesses.   Dr. Damaye has shown in detail in a thesis how the method of examination, conceived by his master, can be applied to patients; this thesis contains an account, unfortunately rather brief, but very interesting, of the attempt to apply it to 250 idiots, imbeciles, and morons of the Vaucluse Colony. We have not therefore to judge of a purely theoretical idea, but of a method which has really been applied.

Before entering on its exposition, let us say that in precision Dr. Blin's study seems to us superior to anything previously accomplished. The criticisms which we shall make will not cause us to forget that we have here a first attempt to apply a scientific method to the diagnosis of mental debility.

The method consists of a pre-arranged list of questions which are given to all in such a way that, if repeated by different persons on the same individual, constantly identical results will be obtained. The examination is composed of a series of twenty topics. A certain number of questions, graded in several of the series according to their difficulty, are prepared upon each of these topics.

The enumeration of these topics will sufficiently indicate the variety that has been attempted in order to explore in a short time a field of knowledge as vast as possible. We reproduce here not only the list of these twenty topics but also the different questions which are asked apropos of each.

I. Personal Habits

Bearing. Appearance. Cleanliness of body and clothing. (Vest unbuttoned, cravat untied, etc.)

II. Speech

Possibility of emitting sounds. Articulation of sounds. Rudimentary language. Fluent language. As a standard one might cause to be pronounced the words, artillery, artilleryman, polytechnic, constitutional, unconstitutionally.

III. Name

What is your name?	Where do you live?
How old are you?	Date of birth.
What are your given names?	Place of birth.
In what year were you born?	The department.

IV. PARENTS

Are your parents living?
What do they do?
Have you brothers?
How many?
Have you sisters?
How many?
What are your brothers' names?
And your sisters'?
Are your brothers older than you?

Are your sisters older than you?
How old are they?
What is your father's first name?
What is your mother's?
Where does your father work?
And your mother?
Where was your father born?
Where was your mother born?

V. IDEAS OF AGE

Are you young or old?
When will you be a man?
At what age is one a man?
At what age is one a soldier?

Are your father and mother old or
  young?
How old are they?
How do you know when one is old? *{ Dif bet old & young man }*

VI. KNOWLEDGE OF THE BODY

✔ Show me your hands.
✔ Put out your tongue.
  What do you call the place that I
    am touching (cheek)?
✔ Where is your foot?
✔ Where is your leg?
✔ Your thigh?
✔ Your shoulder?
✔ Where are your lips?

∟ Close your eyes.
∟ Put your finger on your right ear.
  Your gums?
  Your eyelids?
  Your eyebrows?
  Your forearm?
  Where is your stomach?
  Where is your brain?
  Close your right eyelid.

VII. MOVEMENTS

✔ Sit down.
✔ Turn around.
✔ Go to the wall and return.
✔ Raise your arms.
✔ Put you finger on your right ear.
✔ Cross your arms.
  Turn up your pantaloons.
✔ Take off your jacket as quickly as
    possible and put it on as quickly
    as possible.

Thread a needle with a woolen
  thread.
Try to make some little stitches.
∟ Sit on the floor, cross your arms,
    and rise with arms crossed. } *3 Commands*
Turn down your pantaloons with-
    out sitting down.

VIII. IDEAS ABOUT OBJECTS

The child is shown different objects which he should name.

Key.

Pin.

Pencil.

Book.

Photograph.

Compass.

Cross-ruled paper.

Table cloth.

Sponge.

Of what use is a pin?

Of what color is this pencil?

Of what color is mine?

Of what can a book cover be made?

What is a photograph?

What can it represent?

IX. INTERNAL SENSATIONS

Did you enjoy your breakfast this morning?

Did you sleep well?

Are you thirsty?

Is your appetite ordinarily good?

What time of the day are you hungriest?

Are you often thirsty?

Are you less thirsty in summer than in winter?

Are you less thirsty when it is hot than when it is cold?

You are never thirsty, are you?

You are never hungry?

What did you dream last night?

What is a dream?

Do you often dream?

X. IDEAS OF TIME

Have you been here long?

What time is it?

Is a day longer than a week?

Is a week longer than a month?

How many hours are there in a day?

How many days are there in a month?

How many months are there in a year?

Is a month longer than a year?

When you get up tomorrow will it be morning or evening?

What day is this?

How many days ago did you come?

How many days is it since you saw your parents?

That makes how many days that you have been going to school?

And day after tomorrow?

And yesterday?

At what hour do you rise in the morning?

How many days are there in a year?

How many weeks are there in a year?

What season is this?

When is it winter?

And summer?

XI. IDEAS OF PLACE

Where are you now?

Where were you before coming here?

Are we far from Paris?

Where in Paris do you live?

Is it far from the Seine? (One might ask the child at this point if his house is far from such or such a street or monument in

order thoroughly to explore his ideas of place.)

In what ward of the city do your parents live?

In what department are we?

What is the principal city of this department.

XII. Patriotic Ideas

From what country are you?
Are you French?
Were your father and mother born in France?
Are there other countries than France?
What are they?

Would you rather belong to another country than to France?
Why do you prefer to be French?
Do you know what it is that one calls his country?
Why should one love his country? ———
Is Brittany in France?
And Normandy?

XIII. Military Service

Would you like to be a soldier?
Was your father a soldier?
Did he ride a horse?
What do soldiers wear on their heads?
What do you call the soldiers who have the cannon?

What soldiers ride horses?
If you were a soldier would you like better to fight on foot or on horse-back?
What is an officer?
What has the officer on his sleeves?
What officer has the highest rank?

XIV. Reading

XV. Writing

Mistakes in spelling of course make the score less according to their gravity and the age of the child.

XVI. Calculation

The child is questioned upon the four operations of arithmetic.

XVII. Drawing

We have adopted the following models—a square, and three varieties of rectangular parallelograms—which the child must reproduce with the pen, to which we have added three lines of varying lengths.

XVIII. Trades

What trade does your father follow?
Is it a good trade?
What is a trade?
What does the baker do?
Are there other religions than yours?

What are they?
What is the difference between the Catholic religion and Protestant religion?
Between the Catholic religion and Jewish religion?

Here, as an example, is part of the examination of a child.

I. The boy F. . . . . of nine years, comes to us with his hands in his pockets, face and hands not very clean, nails bitten, countenance of little intelligence.   = 2

II. Language rudimentary and voice slightly nasal, sometimes unintelligible. He pronounces the standard words badly.   = 2

III. What is your name?—Edmond. (Then after a pause he gives his family name.)

How old are you?—Nine years.

What are your given names?—Emile, Adolphe, Edmond.

In what year were you born?—In 1802.

What month?—In January or February.

What date?—The 9th.

You do not know if it was in January or February?—No.

In what country were you born?—Paris.

Where do your parents live? (He gave the name of the street.)

What number?—No. 9.

In which ward?—Ninth (correct).

In which department of France is it? (Unintelligible reply).   = 3

IV. Your father and mother are living?—Yes.

What does your father do?—He is employed in the gas company. (The child then begins to cry).

What does your mother do?—She sews.

At home?—Yes.

Have you brothers?—Yes. I have four.

What are their names?—Jacques, Yvonne, and Henriette.

You have only three then?—Yes.

Have you sisters?—Two; Marie, Amélie and then my Aunt Petit.

How old are your brothers?—Nine years.

And your sisters, how old are they?—I never asked them; I was not there.

What is your mother's name?—(He gives the family name of his mother.)

But her given name. Is it Henrietta, Jane?—No. (He repeats the family name of his mother.) My father, his name is . . . . (the child gives his name correctly).

In what country was your father born?—At . . . . (unintelligible word).

Where was your mother born?—In Paris.   = 3

V. Are you young or old?—Young.

When is one old?—When one is old.

At what age?—At nine years. My mother is old. My grandfather is dead.

At what age is one a man?—A man is always at least four years old.

At what age does one become a soldier?—Papa, he was a soldier, he was a military man.

Yes, but at what age? . . . .

You do not know?—No.

Is your father young or old?—Young.

How old is he?—Five years old.

And your mother?—She is nine years old.

What is the color of old people's hair?—Red.

How is the face of an old person?—Wrinkled. My mother always has pain in her hands.

How does one walk when one is old?—Like everybody else.

Can old people run?—No.

VI. Put out your tongue. ⎫
Close your eyes. ⎬ Good

Put your fingers on your right ear. (He puts his finger on his left ear.)

What do you call the place (cheek) that I am touching?—Cheek.

Where is your heart? ⎫
And your stomach? ⎬ Good.

And your brain? (He points to his neck.)

Your head? ⎫
Your shoulder? ⎬ Good.

Your forearm? (He points to his arm.)

Your lips? ⎫
Your gums? ⎬ Good.

Your eyelids? (He points to his teeth.)

Close your right eyelid. (He shuts his eyes.)

Where is your foot? (He shows his leg.)

Show me your leg? ⎫
Your thigh. ⎬ Good.

Take off your jacket as quickly as possible. ⎫
Put it on as quickly as possible. ⎬ Passable.   = 3

VII. Sit down here. ⎫
Raise your arm. ⎬ Good.

Put your hands on your head. (He places but one.)

Both of them. ⎫
Cross your arms. ⎪
Stand up. ⎬ Good.
Sit down on the ground. ⎭

Cross your arms and get up with your arms crossed. (He cannot do it.)

He threads the needle and turns up the lower edge of his pantaloons satisfactorily.   = 4

VIII. The child recognizes the inkwell, the apron, the pencil, the sponge, the pin, and table cloth.

What is the color of this pencil?—Yellow. (It is red.)

What color does it write?—Black. (Correct.)

What is this? (cross-ruled paper)—A page.

What is the color of the table cloth?—White.

What do you do with a key?—Open the door.

What do you do with a pin?—Stick.

What do you stick?—Straws to hold them together.

Do you know what a compass is?—No.

You never saw one?—No.

Do you know what a photograph is?—Yes.

What is it?—It is a photograph that one puts little babies in.
What is that a picture of?—That is a picture of a little baby.
Can a photograph represent anything one wishes?—No.   = 3

IX. Did you breakfast well this morning?—Yes.
Did you sleep well?—Yes sir.
Is your appetite ordinarily good?—Yes.
What time of the day are you the hungriest?—At 11 o'clock.
At what hour are you the thirstiest?—At four o'clock.
Are you often thirsty?—Yes.
In summer, are you less thirsty than in winter?—Less thirsty.
When it is hot you are not so thirsty as when it is cold?—Yes.
Do you dream when you sleep?—No sir.
Do you know what a dream is?—Yes.
What is it?—It is to waken in the night.
Of whom did you dream last night?—Of mamma (the child begins to cry).
Did you not have a good breakfast this morning?—Yes sir.
You did not sleep well?—No sir.

We shall not insist upon minute criticism of details. There are questions that seem superfluous, or of mere erudition (what is the chief town of such and such a department). In some the form is unfortunate; for example those which can be answered by yes or no, because such replies do not sufficiently prove whether the question has been thoroughly understood. It would be better to turn the question so as to oblige the child to somewhat develop his thought if he has one. But these are trifles. That which appears to us in most need of criticism is the method employed for grading the replies. The marking is from 0 to 5. How is it given? It is given by the total of the replies to a topic, that is to say according to the bearing of at least 4 replies. There is no special mark for each question. The examiner judges and estimates as a whole: estimation is subjectively made.

The first note is of the more or less intelligent appearance of the face.[10] It seems that for the others, what is considered especially is the more or less intelligent nature of the replies. It is again a synthetic impression. It seems to us that such an estimate is rather too arbitrary. By this means, there enters into the examination that variable element which one so justly wishes to eliminate. When a questioner marks 5 for the total of replies, he is not certain but that another examiner would mark 4. M. Blin

[10] The last, of the attitude during the entire examination.

and M. Damaye could have made some control experiments by asking their colleagues to suggest markings according to the written replies submitted to them.

This same arbitrary spirit is found also in the choice of topics. For each topic the same mark is given, thus making them all of equal rank. One assumes therefore that all the topics present the same amount of difficulty, and that there would be the same reward for a child to answer all the questions about names as to answer all those about religion. Again, in each topic the gradation of difficulty seems to have been made equally arbitrarily; that is to say, it would appear that the author has been guided by his own estimation. Moreover, one has the proof in the fact, that the three series of questions, graded according to their difficulty, (1) for children of 10 years, (2) from 10 to 13 years, and (3) for those above 13 years, are nevertheless answered with the maximum of points by children of from 7 to 8 years. It is the same error that we encounter throughout. Consequently, the whole system constitutes a scale established *a priori*. It is possible, and we very willingly believe that in attempting the application it has been found necessary to mend the system, to correct it in certain points, so that it may harmonize better with practice. But whatever may be the importance of these corrections of detail, they do not in the least take away the schematic character of the plan which seems to us to have sprung fully armed from the brain of a theorist.

Here then is what seems to us the chief defect of this method of examination. Notwithstanding this defect, in practice it must necessarily render a real service, because it creates difficulties which all pupils cannot successfully master, and consequently permits us to make a selection among them. Therefore it is small matter that other tests of intelligence might bring about the same result. Small matter that the themes of others give a result on the whole nearly the same. When one has given examinations he sees that. And the method of M. Blin, fundamentally, is only an examination for scholarship, a new bachelor's degree, or a new certificate of studies, with this advantage we admit, of being a test, whose questions, fixed in advance, do not suffer from the bad humor or the bad digestion of the examiner.

Consequently there is no room for surprise, if we do not find in this collection of questions, any idea upon the gradation of intelligence.   The child who has passed through this rolling mill comes before us with a certain total of marks, 36 for instance, or 70.   We understand that 70 is nearer normal than 36 and that is all.   We have no precise notion of the mental level of these candidates, no notion of what they can or cannot do.   Did the one who obtained 36 have any comprehension of abstract ideas?   We do not know, and cannot divine.   How much is he behind normal children of the same age?   We know this no better."

This brings us very naturally to an exposition of the plan of our work.   It will be seen that our directing idea is different from that of M. Blin although our system of measurement, like his, is essentially psychological.

A. Binet and Th. Simon.

Purp. to diagn. pres. mental state)
Etiology will be neglected

NEW METHODS FOR THE DIAGNOSIS OF THE
INTELLECTUAL LEVEL OF SUBNORMALS

L'Année Psychologique, 1905, Vol. XII, pp. 191–244

Before explaining these methods let us recall exactly the conditions of the problem which we are attempting to solve. Our purpose is to be able to measure the intellectual capacity of a child who is brought to us in order to know whether he is normal or retarded. We should therefore, study his condition at the time and that only. We have nothing to do either with his past history or with his future; consequently we shall neglect his etiology, and we shall make no attempt to distinguish between acquired and congenital idiocy; for a stronger reason we shall set aside all consideration of pathological anatomy which might explain his intellectual deficiency. So much for his past. As to that which concerns his future, we shall exercise the same abstinence; we do not attempt to establish or prepare a prognosis and we leave unanswered the question of whether this retardation is curable, or even improvable. We shall limit ourselves to ascertaining the truth in regard to his present mental state.

Furthermore, in the definition of this state, we should make some restrictions. Most subnormal children, especially those in the schools, are habitually grouped in two categories, those of backward intelligence, and those who are unstable. This latter class, which certain alienists call moral imbeciles, do not necessarily manifest inferiority of intelligence; they are turbulent, vicious, rebellious to all discipline; they lack sequence of ideas, and probably power of attention. It is a matter of great delicacy to make the distinction between children who are unstable, and those who have rebellious dispositions. Elsewhere we have insisted upon the necessity of instructors not treating as unstable, that is as pathological cases, those children whose character is not sympathetic with their own. It would necessitate a long study, and probably a very difficult one, to establish the distinctive signs which separate the unstable from the undisciplined. For the

37

present we shall not take up this study. We shall set the unstable aside, and shall consider only that which bears upon those who are backward in intelligence.

This is not, however, to be the only limitation of our subject because backward states of intelligence present several different types. There is the insane type—or the type of intellectual decay—which consists in a progressive loss of former acquired intelligence. Many epileptics, who suffer from frequent attacks, progress toward insanity. It would be possible and probably very important, to be able to make the distinction between those with decaying intelligence on the one hand, and those of inferior intelligence on the other. But as we have determined to limit on this side also, the domain of our study, we shall rigorously exclude all forms of insanity and decay. Moreover we believe that these are rarely present in the schools, and need not be taken into consideration in the operation of new classes for subnormals.

Another distinction is made between those of inferior intelligence and degenerates. The latter are subjects in whom occur clearly defined, episodical phenomena, such as impulsions, obsessions, deliriums. We shall eliminate the degenerates as well as the insane.

Lastly, we should say a word upon our manner of studying those whom most alienists call idiots but whom we here call of inferior intelligence. The exact nature of this inferiority is not known; and today without other proof, one very prudently refuses to liken this state to that of an arrest of normal development. It certainly seems that the intelligence of these beings has undergone a certain arrest; but it does not follow that the disproportion between the degree of intelligence and the age is the only characteristic of their condition. There is also in many cases, most probably a deviation in the development, a perversion. The idiot of fifteen years, who, like a baby of three, is making his first verbal attempts, can not be completely likened to a three-year old child, because the latter is normal, but the idiot is not. There exists therefore between them, necessarily, differences either apparent or hidden. The careful study of idiots shows, among some of them at least, that whereas certain faculties are almost wanting, others are better developed. They have therefore certain aptitudes. Some have a good auditory or musical memory, and a whole repertoire of songs; others have mechanical ability.

If all were carefully examined, many examples of these partial aptitudes would probably be found.

(Our purpose is in no wise to study, analyze, or set forth the aptitudes of those of inferior intelligence. That will be the object of a later work. Here we shall limit ourselves to the measuring of their general intelligence. We shall determine their intellectual level, and, in order the better to appreciate this level, we shall compare it with that of normal children of the same age or of an analogous level. The reservations previously made as to the true conception of arrested development, will not prevent our finding great advantage in a methodical comparison between those of inferior and those of normal intelligence.")

To what method should we have recourse in making our diagnosis of the intellectual level? No one method exists, but there are a number of different ones which should be used cumulatively, because the question is a very difficult one to solve, and demands rather a collaboration of methods. It is important that the practitioner be equipped in such a manner that he shall use, only as accessory, the information given by the parents of the child, so that he may always be able to verify this information, or, when necessary, dispense with it. In actual practice quite the opposite occurs. When the child is taken to the clinic the physician listens a great deal to the parents and questions the child very little, in fact scarcely looks at him, allowing himself to be influenced by a very strong presumption that the child is intellectually inferior. If, by a chance not likely to occur, but which would be most interesting some time to bring about, the physician were submitted to the test of selecting the subnormals from a mixed group of children, he would certainly find himself in the midst of grave difficulties, and would commit many errors especially in cases of slight defect.

The organization of methods is especially important because, as soon as the schools for subnormals are in operation, one must be on his guard against the attitude of the parents. Their sincerity will be worth very little when it is in conflict with their interests. If the parents wish the child to remain in the regular school, they will not be silent concerning his intelligence. "My child understands everything," they will say, and they will be very careful not to give any significant information in regard to him. If, on the contrary, they wish him to be admitted into an institution where gratuitous board and lodging are furnished, they will change completely. They will be capable even of teaching him how to simulate mental debility. One should, therefore, be on his guard against all possible frauds.

In order to recognize the inferior states of intelligence we believe that three different methods should be employed. We have arrived at this synthetic view only after many years of research, but we are now certain that each of these methods renders some service. These methods are:

1. *The medical method*, which aims to appreciate the anatomical, physiological, and pathological signs of inferior intelligence.

2. *The pedagogical method*, which aims to judge of the intelligence according to the sum of acquired knowledge.

3. *The psychological method*, which makes direct observations and measurements of the degree of intelligence.

From what has gone before it is easy to see the value of each of these methods. The medical method is indirect because it conjectures the mental from the physical. The pedagogical method is more direct; but the psychological is the most direct of all because it aims to measure the state of the intelligence as it is at the present moment. It does this by experiments which oblige the subject to make an effort which shows his capability in the way of comprehension, judgment, reasoning, and invention.

I. THE PSYCHOLOGICAL METHOD

The fundamental idea of this method is the establishment of what we shall call a measuring scale of intelligence. This scale is composed of a series of tests of increasing difficulty, starting from the lowest intellectual level that can be observed, and ending with that of average normal intelligence. Each group in the series corresponds to a different mental level.

This scale properly speaking does not permit the measure of the intelligence,[1] because intellectual qualities are not superposable, and therefore cannot be measured as linear surfaces are measured, but are on the contrary, a classification, a hierarchy among diverse intelligences; and for the necessities of practice

[handwritten margin note: meaning?]

[1] One of us (Binet) has elsewhere insisted that a distinction be made between the measure and the classification. See "Suggestibilite," p. 103, Vol. 11, *L'Année Psychologique.*

this classification is equivalent to a measure. We shall therefore
be able to know, after studying two individuals, if one rises above
the other and to how many degrees, if one rises above the average
level of other individuals considered as normal, or if he remains below.   Understanding the normal progress of intellectual development among normals, we shall be able to determine how many
years such an individual is advanced or retarded.   In a word we
shall be able to determine to what degrees of the scale idiocy, imbecility, and moronity[2] correspond.

The scale that we shall describe is not a theoretical work; it is
the result of long investigations, first at the Salpêtrière, and afterwards in the primary schools of Paris, with both normal and subnormal children.   These short psychological questions have been
given the name of tests.   The use of tests is today very common,
and there are even contemporary authors who have made a spe-
cialty of organizing new tests according to theoretical views, but
who have made no effort to patiently try them out in the schools.
Theirs is an amusing occupation, comparable to a person's making
a colonizing expedition into Algeria, advancing always only upon
the map, without taking off his dressing gown.   We place but
slight confidence in the tests invented by these authors and we
have borrowed nothing from them.   All the tests which we propose have been repeatedly tried, and have been retained from
among many, which after trial have been discarded.   We can cer-
tify that those which are here presented have proved themselves
valuable.

We have aimed to make all our tests simple, rapid, convenient,
precise, heterogeneous, holding the subject in continued contact
with the experimenter, and bearing principally upon the faculty
of judgment.   Rapidity is necessary for this sort of examination.
It is impossible to prolong it beyond twenty minutes without
fatiguing the subject.   During this maximum of twenty minutes,
it must be turned and turned about in every sense, and at least
ten tests must be executed, so that not more than about two
minutes can be given to each.   In spite of their interest, we were
obliged to proscribe long exercises.   For example, it would be

nature of the tests

---

[2] *Editor's note:* Binet's classification of defectives is idiot, imbecile,
and "débile." This seems to correspond closely to our American terminology of idiot, imbecile, and moron. We have accordingly translated
"débile" as moron and "débilité" as moronity.

very instructive to know how a subject learns by heart a series of
sentences. We have often tested the advantage of leaving a person by himself with a lesson of prose or verse after having said to
him, "Try to learn as much as you can of this in five minutes."
Five minutes is too long for our test, because during that time the
subject escapes us; it may be that he becomes distracted or thinks
of other things; the test loses its clinical character and becomes too
scholastic. We have therefore reluctantly been obliged to re-
nounce testing the rapidity and extent of the memory by this
method. Several other equivalent examples of elimination could
be cited. In order to cover rapidly a wide field of observation, it
goes without saying that the tests should be heterogeneous.

Another consideration. Our purpose is to evaluate a level of
intelligence. It is understood that we here separate natural intelligence and instruction. It is the intelligence alone that we seek
to measure, by disregarding in so far as possible, the degree of
instruction which the subject possesses. He should, indeed, be
considered by the examiner as a complete ignoramus knowing
neither how to read nor write. This necessity forces us to forego
a great many exercises having a verbal, literary or scholastic character. These belong to a pedagogical examination. We believe
that we have succeeded in completely disregarding the acquired
information of the subject. We give him nothing to read, nothing to write, and submit him to no test in which he might succeed
by means of rote learning. In fact we do not even notice his inability to read if a case occurs. It is simply the level of his natural intelligence that is taken into account.

But here we must come to an understanding of what meaning
to give to that word so vague and so comprehensive, "the intelligence." Nearly all the phenomena with which psychology concerns itself are phenomena of intelligence; sensation, perception,
are intellectual manifestations as much as reasoning. Should we
therefore bring into our examination the measure of sensation
after the manner of the psycho-physicists? Should we put to the
test all of his psychological processes? A slight reflection has
shown us that this would indeed be wasted time.

It seems to us that in intelligence there is a fundamental faculty,
the alteration or the lack of which, is of the utmost importance for
practical life. This faculty is judgment, otherwise called good
sense, practical sense, initiative, the faculty of adapting one's self

to circumstances. To judge well, to comprehend well, to reason
well, these are the essential activities of intelligence. A person
may be a moron or an imbecile if he is lacking in judgment; but
with good judgment he can never be either. Indeed the rest of
the intellectual faculties seem of little importance in comparison
with judgment. What does it matter, for example, whether the
organs of sense function normally? Of what import that certain
ones are hyperesthetic, or that others are anesthetic or are weakened? Laura Bridgman, Helen Keller and their fellow-unfortu-
nates were blind as well as deaf, but this did not prevent them
from being very intelligent. Certainly this is demonstrative proof
that the total or even partial integrity of the senses does not form
a mental factor equal to judgment. We may measure the acuteness of the sensibility of subjects; nothing could be easier. But
we should do this, not so much to find out the state of their sensibility as to learn the exactitude of their judgment.

The same remark holds good for the study of the memory. At
first glance, memory being a psychological phenomenon of capital
importance, one would be tempted to give it a very conspicuous
part in an examination of intelligence. But memory is distinct
from and independent of judgment. One may have good sense
and lack memory. The reverse is also common. Just at the
present time we are observing a backward girl who is developing
before our astonished eyes a memory very much greater than our
own. We have measured that memory and we are not deceived
regarding it. Nevertheless that girl presents a most beautifully
classic type of imbecility.

As a result of all this investigation, in the scale which we present
we accord the first place to judgment; that which is of importance
to us is not certain errors which the subject commits, but absurd
errors, which prove that he lacks judgment. We have even made
special provision to encourage people to make absurd replies. In
spite of the accuracy of this directing idea, it will be easily understood that it has been impossible to permit of its regulating exclusively our examinations. For example, one can not make tests
of judgment on children of less than two years when one begins to
watch their first gleams of intelligence. Much is gained when one
can discern in them traces of coördination, the first delineation of
attention and memory. We shall therefore bring out in our lists
some tests of memory; but so far as we are able, we shall give these

tests such a turn as to invite the subject to make absurd replies, and thus under cover of a test of memory, we shall have an appreciation of their judgment.

MEASURING SCALE OF INTELLIGENCE

General recommendations. The examination should take place in a quiet room, quite isolated, and the child should be called in alone without other children. It is important that when a child sees the experimenter for the first time, he should be reassured by the presence of someone he knows, a relative, an attendant, or a school superintendent. The witness should be instructed to remain passive and mute, and not to intervene in the examination either by word or gesture.

The experimenter should receive each child with a friendly familiarity to dispel the timidity of early years. Greet him the moment he enters, shake hands with him and seat him comfortably. If he is intelligent enough to understand certain words, awaken his curiosity, his pride. If he refuses to reply to a test, pass to the next one, or perhaps offer him a piece of candy; if his silence continues, send him away until another time. These are little incidents that frequently occur in an examination of the mental state, because in its last analysis, an examination of this kind is based upon the good will of the subject.

We here give the technique of each question. It will not suffice simply to read what we have written in order to be able to conduct examinations. A good experimenter can be produced only by example and imitation, and nothing equals the lesson gained from the thing itself. Every person who wishes to familiarize himself with our method of examination should come to our school. Theoretical instruction is valuable only when it merges into practical experience. Having made these reservations, let us point out the principal errors likely to be committed by inexperienced persons. There are two: the first consists in recording the gross results without making psychological observations, without noticing such little facts as permit one to give to the gross results their true value. The second error, equally frequent, is that of making suggestions. An inexperienced examiner has no idea of the influence of words; he talks too much, he aids his subject, he puts him on the track, unconscious of the help he is thus giving. He plays the part of pedagogue, when he should remain psychologist. Thus his examination is vitiated. It is a difficult art to be able to encourage a subject, to hold his attention, to make him do his best without giving aid in any form by an unskillful suggestion.[3]

THE SERIES OF TESTS

✓ 1. "Le Regard"[4] ✓

In this test the examiner seeks to discover if there exists that coördination in the movement of the head and the eyes which is associated with the act of vision. If such coördination does exist it proves that the subject not only sees but more than that he "regards" (that is he is able to follow with his eyes a moving object).

Procedure. A lighted match is slowly moved before the eyes of the subject in such a way as to provoke a movement of the head or of the eyes to follow the flame. If a first attempt does not succeed the experiment should be tried again after a little while. It is preferable to operate in a quiet place where no kind of distraction is likely to occur. It is not important that the subject follow the movements of the match constantly for any length of time or persistently. The least sign of coördination of the movements of vision is sufficient, if it leaves no doubt in the mind of the examiner.

Additional remarks. The observation of a few spontaneous phenomena may well be noted. Thus it is possible sometimes for the examiner, by fixing his gaze steadily upon the child, to satisfy himself that the child really coördinates for a moment. If the subject is afflicted with or suspected of blindness, the visual stimulus may be replaced by an auditory stimulus. For example, call him loudly, or better, ring a little bell behind his head and notice

---

[3] One of us (Binet) has been for some years the president of "Société libre pour l'étude de l'enfant," and he has striven to spread among his colleagues, mostly teachers, the taste for scientific research. He has found that the two errors mentioned in the text are those which appear most frequently among beginners.

[4] *Editor's note:* We have here retained the word used by Binet, because in the English there is no one word exactly synonymous with it. The word literally translated means "the ability to follow with the eyes a moving object."

if he turns his head toward the sound, or if he has any peculiar facial expression which would indicate that he hears. The reaction of attention to sound seems to develop later than the reaction to light. We have observed children who, when a bell was rung behind the head, would not make a single movement in order to hear better, and yet would follow with their eyes the lighted match. It is scarcely necessary to add that the child who hides his face behind his hand when questioned, or who replies to your smile by a smile, or who walks about the room without knocking against obstacles, stove, chairs, wall, table, proves by his behavior that he coördinates the movements of vision, and thus he has passed the first test.

∨ 2. Prehension Provoked by a Tactile Stimulus

Here the purpose is to discover whether the coördination exists between a tactile stimulus of the hand, and the movement of seizing and carrying to the mouth.

Procedure. A small object, easily handled, for example a piece of wood, is placed in contact with the hand of the child in order to determine if he succeeds in seizing the object, holding it in his hand without letting it fall, and carrying it to his mouth. It is well to stimulate the contact either on the back of the hand or on the palm, and note the results.. It is possible that the subject, after having taken the little object, loosens his fingers and lets it fall. It is necessary in that case to try again with a little patience, in order to learn if the letting go came of a chance distraction, or if the subject is not capable of performing the muscular act which would consist in carrying it to his mouth.

∨ 3. Prehension Provoked by a Visual Perception

Here the purpose is to find whether coördination exists between the sight of an object and its prehension, when the object is not placed in contact with the hand of the subject.

Procedure. The object is presented to his view and within reach of his hand, in a manner to provoke an intentional movement of his hand to take it. This third test is passed when the subject, following a visual perception of the object, makes a movement of the hand towards the object, reaches, seizes and carries it to his mouth. A small cube of white wood, easy to handle is used. In these presentations it is not forbidden to speak and hence the object is offered to the child as follows: "Here is a little object, take it, it is for you—Come now, pay attention, etc." If the subject understands, so much the better for him; if he does not understand the sound of these words has the advantage of attracting his attention. Moreover the examiner makes gestures and makes them more naturally if he talks at the same time.

4. Recognition of Food

Here the purpose is to discover whether the subject can make the distinction by sight between familiar food and what can not be eaten.

Procedure. A piece of chocolate (half a bar) and a little cube of white wood of similar dimensions are successively presented. The test is to see if the subject, by sight alone, makes the distinction between the two objects before carrying them to his mouth. Does he carry only the chocolate to his mouth and begin to eat it? Does he refuse to take the piece of wood, or having taken it does he push it away, or again does he hold it in his hand without putting it to his mouth?

Tests 3 and 4 can be made rapidly as a single experiment. A piece of chocolate is first shown to the child and his attention is drawn to it. Note whether he tries to take it or not. If he makes no effort to attain it, and is not distracted by anything, place the chocolate in the palm of his hand, and note what happens. If on the contrary he takes the chocolate which is shown him and carries it to his mouth, the chocolate is taken from him, and the piece of wood put in its place, to see if he carries this new object also to his mouth.

Although these tests succeed with very many children by appealing to their greediness, it often happens that a willful child, or one frightened by the sight of the examiner whom he does not know, turns away from him and refuses to look at what is shown him. These movements of defense indicate already a mentality that corresponds most likely to the fourth degree. The experimenter must be armed with patience and gentleness. He may have a relative, an attendant, or any other person who knows the child, present the chocolate, but he must carefully note the behavior of the child throughout the operation. If the attack of anger, or tears, or fear lasts too long, the examination is necessarily suspended to be taken up at a more favorable time. These are the disappointments to which alienists are accustomed.

5. Quest of Food Complicated by a Slight Mechanical Difficulty

This test is designed to bring into play a rudiment of memory, an effort of will, and a coördination of movements.

Procedure. First be sure that the child recognizes the candy or bonbon to be used in this experiment. Then while he is watching you, wrap the bonbon in a piece of paper. Present it to him and carefully note his movements. Does he remember that the paper contains a bonbon? Does he reject it as a useless object, or does he try to pull it apart? Does he carry the covered morsel to his mouth? Does he eat the paper or does he make some effort to unfold it? Does he completely succeed in unfolding it, or does he seem satisfied with one attempt? Does he present the covered morsel to some one else as if to ask his aid?

6. Execution of Simple Commands and Imitation of Simple Gestures

This test involves various motor coördinations, and associations between certain movements, and the understanding of the significance of certain gestures. In these tests the subject enters for the first time into social relations with the experimenter and it is therefore necessary that he understand the will and desires of the latter. It is the beginning of inter-psychology.

Procedure. As soon as the subject enters the room say good morning to him with expression, give him your hand with accentuated gesture to see if he understands the salutation and if he knows how to shake hands. In cases where the subject walks in, ask him to be seated; this permits one to see whether he understands the meaning of the invitation and if he knows the use of a chair. Throw some object on the floor and request him by gestures as well as by speech to pick it up and give it back. Make him get up, shut the door, send him away, call him back. So much for commands. Imitation of simple gestures is accomplished by fixing his attention by repeating several times, "Look at me carefully," and when his attention is gained, by saying "Do as I do." The examiner then claps his hands together, puts them in the air, on the shoulders, behind the back; he turns the thumbs one about the other, raises the foot, etc. All this mimicry must be conducted gaily with the air of play. It is sufficient if a single well marked imitation is provoked; the rest is unnecessary. Do not confound the inaptitude for imitation, with bad humor, ill-will, or timidity.

✓ 7. Verbal Knowledge of Objects   *Showing your nose etc*

The object of this test is to discover if associations exist between things and their names. Comprehension and the first possibilities of language are here studied. This test is a continuation of the previous one and represents the second degree of communication between individuals; the first degree is made through imitation, the second through words.

Procedure. This test is composed of two parts. In the first place the examiner names a part of the body and asks the child to point to it. The questions may relate to the head, the hair, the eyes, the feet, the hands, the nose, the ears, the mouth. Ask the child with a smile "Where is your head?" If he seems embarrassed or timid, encourage him by aiding him a little. "There is your head," pointing it out and touching it if the child does not seem to understand what is wanted of him. On the other hand if he replies by a correct designation to the first question go no further, because if he knows where his head is he should know equally well where are his ears and his mouth. Give him therefore some more difficult questions, for example, his cheek, his eyebrow, his heart.

The second part of the experiment consists in making him designate familiar objects, a string, a cup, a key. Bring the child to the table and by means of gestures indicate the objects and turn his attention to them. When his attention is fixed upon the objects tell him to give you the one you name. "Give me the cup. Give me the key, etc." The cup, the key, the string are the three objects asked for. It is of little importance that he shows awkwardness in taking and presenting them. The essential is that by the play of the countenance and gestures, he indicates clearly that he distinguishes these objects by their names. It is preferable to keep these three objects, others less familiar should be rejected, as for instance a box of matches, a cork, etc. The test is made with three objects in order to avoid the right designation by simple chance. With backward children the following facts may present themselves. They do not know the name of the object presented to them, but having understood that they are to designate an object, they point to anything that is on the table. This is a manner of reacting very common among idiots and imbeciles. They make mistakes but they do not realize it, being in fact very well satisfied with their achievements. Here is another source of error to be avoided. In consequence of their extreme docility, many backward children may be bewildered by the least contradiction. When they have handed you a cup, if you ask them "Isn't this a key?" some might make a sign of acquiescence. This is a test of suggestibility of which more will be said further on. To a blind child, give objects to be recognized by the sense of touch.

8. Verbal Knowledge of Pictures

This exercise is the same as the preceding one with this difference only, that the objects are replaced by pictures which, in consequence of the diminished size and the reduction to a plane surface, are a little more difficult to recognize than in nature, and more than this in a picture the objects must be sought for.

Procedure. We make use of a print borrowed from the picture-book of Inspector Lacabe and Mlle. Goergin. This print in colors represents a complex family scene. We show the print to the child and ask him to designate successively the following objects: the window, mamma, big sister, little sister, little girl, cat, broom, basket, bouquet, duster, coffee-mill. The questions are asked in this way: "Where is the window?" or "Tell me where the window is." or "Show me the window," or "Put your finger on the window."

The last suggestion is generally unnecessary because the child has a tendency to place his forefinger, generally a dirty one, upon the detail which is named for him. If he makes an error in designation be careful not to correct it, but make a note of it. In a psychological examination of this kind, one must never point out to a child the errors which he makes. The examiner is not a pedagogue. It is rare that those who take an interest in the picture can not designate the principal details named to them. The incapable ones give no attention to the picture and do not seem to comprehend what is wanted of them. It is interesting to study the attitude of a child during this test. There are two acts to be accomplished, one a search for the object, the other the recognition of the object. At once in the search the aptitudes or inaptitudes betray themselves. Many defective persons show an excess of eagerness to designate the object, which in itself is a sign of faulty attention. They point out at once without waiting to comprehend. They sometimes point out before one has finished the sentence. "Where is the —," said with a suspension in the voice, and already their finger is placed haphazard upon the picture. Such as these do not hunt with care and are incapable of suspending their judgment. This is, it seems to us, a striking characteristic of a weak mind. The child must be closely studied in order to find if, in spite of this special manner, he really knows the names of the objects. A reprimand gently given will sometimes put him on his guard, "No, no, pay attention, you go too fast," and if the question is repeated he will often give a correct answer.

In other cases, errors are sometimes made through suggestibility. The subject seems to imagine that he will commit a fault if he does not designate some object when the question is asked, and out of compliance or of timidity, he makes an erroneous designation for an object whose name he does not know, or which he does not succeed in finding. Notice again, the more reasonable attitude of those who, not knowing the name of the object, refrain from pointing it out but continue the search or reply distinctly, "I do not know." It is rare that an imbecile uses that little phrase. The avowal of ignorance is a proof of judgment and is always a good indication.

9. Naming of Designated Objects *in pictures*

This test is the opposite of the preceding one. It shows the passing from the thing to the word. It also is executed by the use of pictures.

Procedure. Here we make use of another colored print borrowed from the same collection as the preceding. We place it before the eyes of the child and designate with a pencil different objects while asking each time, "What is this?" The objects upon which we place the pencil are the little girl, the dog, the boy, the father, the lamp-lighter, the sky, the advertisement. For the lamp-

Says 7, 8, 9 abt = in diffie.

lighter we ask what he does. Here as elsewhere it is unnecessary
to exhaust the complete series of questions unless the subject fails.
One or two positive replies are sufficient to satisfy the requirements of the test. This test permits us to know the vocabulary
and the pronunciation of the child. Defects of pronunciation, so
frequent in the young, are a serious source of embarrassment. It
often requires a very indulgent ear to recognize the right word in
an indistinct and very brief murmur, and in a case of this sort the
examiner will do well to use an interrogation point. Added to the
difficulties which proceed from faulty pronunciation, are those
brought about by a special vocabulary. Many little children
though normal use a vocabulary invented or deformed by them,
which is understood only by themselves and their parents.

Additional remarks. Tests 7, 8, and 9 do not constitute dif-
fering degrees in the rigorous sense of the word, that is to say they
are not tests corresponding to different levels of intelligence.
We have ascertained that generally with subnormals those who
can pass test 7, pass 8 and also 9. These would therefore be tests
of equal rank. We have kept them, however, because these tests
occupy an important place in our measuring scale of intelligence,
as they constitute a borderline test between imbecility and idiocy.
It is useful to have this borderline solidly placed and all these tests
will serve as buttresses.

Observations, such as one may make every day on those afflicted
with general paralysis, aphasia, or simply people very much
fatigued, show that it is much more difficult to pass from the object to the word than it is to pass from the word to the object, or
we may say, that one recognizes a word more easily than one finds
it. It does not seem clear up to the present that this observation
is also applicable to inferior states of intelligence.

10. Immediate Comparison of Two Lines of Unequal Lengths[5]

As we enter the field of what may properly be called psychological experimentation, we shall find it difficult to define which mental functions are being exercised because they are very numerous.
Here the child must understand that it is a question of comparison, that the comparison is between two lines that are shown to
him; he must understand the meaning of the words, "Show me

[5] Cf. p. 196.

the longer." He must be capable of comparing, that is of bringing together a conception and an image, and of turning his mind in the direction of searching for a difference. We often have illusions as to the simplicity of psychical processes, because we judge them in relation to others, still more complex. In fact here is a test which will seem to show but little mentality in those who are able to execute it; nevertheless when analyzed it reveals a great complexity.

Procedure. The subject is presented successively with three pieces of paper upon each of which two lines, drawn in ink, are to be compared. Each piece of paper measures 15 by 20 cm.; the lines are drawn lengthwise of the paper, on the same level, and separated by a space of 5 mm. The lines are respectively 4 and 3 cm. in length and one-half of a millimeter in width. On the first sheet the longer line is at the right and on the other two at the left. Each sheet is shown to the subject while saying to him, "Which is the longer line?" Note if his reply is correct but do not tell him. In order to eliminate haphazard replies, it is well to repeat the whole series at least twice. The end is not to discover just how far the accuracy of the child's glance may go, but simply to find if he is capable of making a correct comparison between two lines. Many subnormals are incapable of this; but they act as though they were capable; they seem to understand what is said to them and each time put the finger upon one of the lines saying, "This one." It is necessary to recognize those subjects whose errors are not, strictly speaking, faults of comparison but absence of comparison. It often happens that the subject constantly chooses the line on the same side for the longer, for example always the one on the right side. This manner of reacting would be a sign of defect were it not that one encounters the same thing with some normals.

11. Repetition of Three Figures[6]

This is a test of immediate memory and voluntary attention.

Procedure. Looking the subject squarely in the eye to be sure his attention is fixed, one pronounces three figures, after having told him to repeat them. Choose figures that do not follow each other, as for instance 3, 0, 8, or 5, 9, 7, Pronounce the three fig-

[6] Cf. p. 187.

ures in the same voice without accentuating one more than the others and without rhythm, but with a certain energy. The rapidity to be observed is two figures per second. Listen carefully and record the repetition which is made. Often the first attempt is unsuccessful because the subject has not clearly understood and commences to repeat the first figure the moment he hears it; he must be made to be quiet, renew the explanation and commence the pronunciation of another series of figures. There are certain subjects who can not repeat a single figure; in general these are the ones whose mental condition is such that they have not understood anything at all of what is asked of them. Others repeat only a single figure, the first or the last; others pronounce more than three. Special attention must be given to those whose error consists in pronouncing a greater number of figures than that which is said, or in pronouncing a series of figures in their natural order. An individual who, when asked to repeat 3, 0, 8, replies 2, 3, 4, 5, commits a serious error, which would cause one to suspect mental debility. But on the other hand it is true that all feeble-minded and all imbeciles do not commit this error, and that many young normals may commit it. Be careful to notice also if the subject seems satisfied with his reply when this is obviously and grossly false; this indicates an absence of judgment which constitutes an aggravated condition.

Let us say, apropos of this test, that it is important to make a distinction between errors of attention and of adaptation on the one hand, and errors of judgment on the other. When a failure is produced by distraction it is not very important. Thus it may happen that a subject does not repeat the three figures the first time. Begin again and if he succeeds the second time in retaining them he should be considered as having passed the test. A little farther on we shall have to deal with tests of judgment properly so-called, and three or four difficulties will be presented for solution. In this last case, failure will be much more serious, because it can not be due to inattention and the test cannot be considered as passed unless the solutions are given complete.

12. Comparison of Two Weights[7]   3 & 12 grams
                                        Show how

This is a test of attention, of comparison and of the muscular sense.

Procedure. Place side by side on the table before the subject two small cubical boxes having the same dimensions, (23 mm. on a side) and the same color, but of different weights. The boxes, weighted by grains of lead rolled in cotton and not perceptible by shaking, weigh 3 grams and 12 grams respectively. The subject is asked to find out which is the heavier. The operation terminated, two other cubes of 6 and 15 grams respectively are given him to compare, and again 3 grams and 15 grams. If the subject hesitates or seems to be going haphazard, start over again mixing the cubes in order to be sure that he really compares the weights.

At the injunction, "See the two boxes, now tell me which is the heavier," many young subjects designate haphazard one of the two boxes without testing the weights. This error, all the more naïve since the two are exactly alike in appearance, does not prove that the subject is incapable of weighing them in his hand and of judging of the weights while exercising muscular sense. One must then order him to take the boxes in his hand and weigh them. Some are very awkward, and put the two boxes into one hand at the same time to weigh them. One must again interfere and teach him how to put a box in each hand and weigh the two simultaneously.

Additional remarks. Following this weighing of two boxes of different weight and equal volume, one can propose to weigh two boxes of equal weight but different volume. The illusion which is produced under these circumstances is well known. With the weights equal, the larger box will appear lighter; and the apparent difference of weight increases with the difference of volume. Investigations have been made to determine whether this illusion takes place with backward children, and it has been observed by Demoor that there are certain ones who are not affected by it, something which we ourselves have recently verified. We put before the defective children long boxes of white wood, of the same weight, the largest one 24 x 4 x 4 cm., the smallest 12 x 2 x 2 cm., the medium one 18 x 3 x 3 cm. Like many normal children our subnormals, when given two for comparison and asked "Which

[7] Cf. p. 186.

is the heavier," pointed out the larger.   The first naïve response
has but little significance.   If one insists, if one tells the subject
to weigh them in his hand, it sometimes happens that subnormals
either cling to their first designation, or abandon it altogether and
find the smaller one the heavier; in the latter case they are sensitive to the illusion.   It seems to us that before declaring that a
subnormal is not sensitive, one must first find if he can compare
two weights, and whether he is able to judge which is the heavier
of two weights having the same volume.   Having made this preliminary test, one will perceive that very many subnormals are
insensible to the illusion because they are incapable of comparing
weights.   What they lack therefore is a more elementary aptitude.

⊬ 13. Suggestibility

Suggestibility is by no means a test of intelligence, because very
many persons of superior intelligence are susceptible to suggestion,
through distraction, timidity, fear of doing wrong, or some preconceived idea.   Suggestion produces effects which from certain
points of view closely resemble the natural manifestations of
feeble-mindedness; in fact suggestion disturbs the judgment,
paralyzes the critical sense, and forces us to attempt unreasonable or unfitting acts worthy of a defective.   It is therefore necessary, when examining a child suspected of retardation, not to
give a suggestion unconsciously, for thus artificial debility is
produced which might make the diagnosis deceptive.   If a person is forced to give an absurd reply by making use of an alternative pronounced in an authoritative voice, it does not in the
least prove that he is lacking in judgment.   But this source of error
being once recognized and set aside, it is none the less interesting to bring into the examination a precise attempt at suggestion, and note what happens.   It is a means of testing the force
of judgment of a subject and his power of resistance.[3]

Procedure.   The proof of suggestibility which we have devised
does not give rise to a special experiment: it complicates by a
slight addition other exercises which we have already described.

(a) *Designation of objects named by the experimenter.*   When we
ask the child (test 7) to show us the thread, the cup, the thimble,

[3] In a book specially devoted to *Suggestibility* (Paris, Schleicher, 1900)
one of us (Binet) has described several methods of testing for suggestibility which are valuable for application in the schools.

1. bread, cup, thimble, before child
ask him to "show me the buttons"
2. Show feet — then "where is the nitchevo"
3. Snaring lines

SERIES OF TESTS—1905   57

we add, "Show me the button." On the empty table there is no
button, there are only the three preceding objects and yet by
gesture and look we invite the subject to search for the button on
the table. It is a suggestion by personal action, developing obedience. Certain ones obey quickly and easily, presenting to us again
the cup or no matter what other objects. Their suggestibility is
complete. Others resist a little, pout, while feigning to hunt for
it on the table, or in the cup; they do not reply, but cover their
embarrassment by a search which they continue indefinitely if not
interrupted. One should consider this attitude as a sufficient
expression of resistance, and go no further. It would be unnecessary as we are not seeking a victory over them. Lastly, those least
affected by suggestion, reply clearly, "I do not know," or "There
is no button." Some laugh.

(b) *Designation of parts of a picture named by the experimenter.*
When the child has looked at the picture and we have asked him
to point out the window, etc., at the very last say, "Where is the
patapoum?" and then "Where is the nitchevo?" words that have
no sense for him. These demands are made in the same manner
as the preceding ones. Here again we find the three types, children who docilely designate any object whatever, others who
search indefinitely without finding anything, and again others
who declare, "There is none."

(c) *Snare of lines.* Following the three pairs of unequal lines,
which serve to show the correctness of comparison, we place before the subject three other similar sheets each containing two
equal lines. We present them saying, "And here?" Led on by
the former replies he has a tendency, an acquired force, for again
finding one line longer than the other. Some succumb to the
snare completely. Others stop at the first pair and declare, "They
are equal," but at the second and third they say one of the lines
is longer than the other. Others find them all equal but hesitate.
Others again fall into the snare without a shadow of hesitation.

14. *Verbal Definition of Known Objects* Df. of Conc. objs

Vocabulary, some general notions, ability to put a simple idea
into words, are all brought to light by means of this test.
Procedure. Ask the child what is a house, a horse, a fork, a
mamma. This is the conversation that takes place: "Do you

know what a —— is?" If the child answers yes then ask him: "Very well, then tell me what it is." Try to overcome his silence a little and his timidity. Aid him, only when necessary, by giving him an example: "A dog, it barks," and then see if the child understands and approves that definition.

Very young normal children of two or three years, reply to questions of this kind with enthusiasm. They ordinarily reply in terms of use, "A fork is to eat with." This is typical. Record the answer verbatim. Some will keep silent, some give absurd, incomprehensible replies, or again will repeat the word, "A house, it is a house."

15. *Repetition of Sentences of Fifteen Words*[9]

This is a test of immediate memory, so far as it concerns the recollection of words; a proof of voluntary attention, naturally because voluntary attention must accompany all psychological experiments; lastly it is a test of language.

Procedure. First be sure that the child is listening carefully, then, after having warned him that he will have to repeat what is said to him, pronounce slowly, intelligibly, the following sentence: *I get up in the morning, I dine at noon, I go to bed at night.* Then make a sign for him to repeat. Often the child, still not very well adapted, has not fully understood. Never repeat a sentence but go on to another. When the subject repeats it write down verbatim what he says. Many even among normals make absurd repetitions, for example: "I go to bed at noon." Often the child replaces the cultured expression "I dine" for a more familiar form, "I eat." The fact of being able to repeat the sentence correctly after the first hearing is a good sign. The second sentence is easier than the first, *In the summer the weather is beautiful; in winter snow falls.* Here is the third, *Germaine has been bad, she has not worked, she will be scolded.* Now we give five sentences quite difficult to understand:

The horse-chestnut tree in the garden throws upon the ground the faint shade of its new young leaves.

[9] *Editor's note:* Binet's sentences vary in length from thirteen to eighteen words. He has corrected this discrepancy in the 1908 edition by counting the number of syllables given in this and kindred tests. A literal translation of his sentences obviously may not contain the same number of words in English as in French.

*The horse draws the carriage, the road is steep and the carriage
is heavy.*

*It is one o'clock in the afternoon, the house is silent, the cat sleeps
in the shade.*

*One should not say all that he thinks, but he must think all that he
says.*

*The spirit of criticism must not be confounded with the spirit of
contradiction.*

16. Comparison of Known Objects from Memory —

This is an exercise in ideation, in the notion of differences, and
somewhat in powers of observation.

Procedure. One asks what difference there is between paper
and cardboard, between a fly and a butterfly, between a piece of
wood and a piece of glass. First be sure that the subject knows
these objects. Ask him, "Have you seen paper?" "Do you know
what cardboard is?" Thus ask him about all the objects before drawing his attention to the difference between them. It
may happen that little Parisians, even though normal, and eight
or nine years old, have never seen a butterfly. These are examples of astounding ignorance, but we have found, what is still
more extraordinary, Parisians of ten years who have never seen
the Seine.

After being assured that the two objects to be compared are
known, demand their difference. If the word is not understood,
take notice and afterward choose more familiar language. "In
what are they not alike? How are they not alike?" Three
classes of replies may be expected. First, that of the children who
have no comprehension of what is desired of them. When asked
the difference between cardboard and paper, they reply, "The
cardboard." When one has provoked replies of this kind, the
explanation must be renewed with patience to see if there is not
some means of making oneself understood. Second, the absurd
replies, such as, "The fly is larger than the butterfly." "The wood
is thicker than the glass," or "The butterfly flies and so does the
fly." Third, the correct reply.

17. Exercise of Memory on Pictures

This is a test of attention and visual memory.

Procedure. The subject is told that several pictures will be shown to him, which he will be allowed to look at for thirty seconds, and that he must then repeat the names of the objects seen, from memory. There are thirteen pictures, each 6 by 6 centimeters, representing the following objects: clock, key, nail, omnibus, barrel, bed, cherry, rose, mouth of a beast, nose, head of a child, eggs, landscape. These pictures are pasted on two cardboards and are shown simultaneously. Measure the time of exposure with the second hand of the watch. In order that the subject shall not become absorbed in one picture, say to him, "Make haste. Look at all." The thirty seconds passed, the examiner writes from dictation the names of the pictures the subject recalls.

This test does indeed give an idea of the memory of a person, but two subjects may have very unequal memories of the same picture; one of them may recall only one detail while another recalls the whole. Moreover there is a weak point in this test in that it may be affected by failure of attention. It is sufficient that a fly should alight, a door should open, a cock should crow, or for the subject to have a desire to use his handkerchief during the thirty seconds, to disturb the work of memorizing. If the result is altogether lacking, the test should be repeated with another collection of pictures to find whether the first error was the result of distraction.

18. Drawing a Design from Memory

This is a test of attention, visual memory, and a little analysis.

Procedure. The subject is told that two designs will be shown to him, which he will be allowed to look at for ten seconds, and which

DESIGN TO BE DRAWN FROM MEMORY AFTER BEING STUDIED 10 SECONDS

he must then draw from memory. Excite his emulation. The two designs which we reproduce here, are shown to him and left

exposed for ten seconds. (Regulate the time by the second hand
of a watch; the time must be exact within one or two seconds.)
Then see that the subject commences the reproduction of the design without loss of time.

Marking the results of this test, that is the errors committed,
is a delicate operation. Simply note if the reproduction is absolutely correct; or if without being correct it resembles the model;
or if, on the contrary, it bears no resemblance whatever to it.

19. Immediate Repetition of Figures *(number? above 3)*

This is a test of immediate memory and immediate attention

Procedure. This is the same as for the three figures, see above
Here the errors noted for the three figures take on greater proportions. One must be on the watch for errors of judgment. A
normal may fail but the manner is <u>different</u>. ?

20. Resemblances of Several Known Objects Given from Memory — *Similar*

This is a test of memory, conscious recognition of resemblances,
power of observation.

Not in 1908

Procedure. This test closely resembles test 16, except that here
resemblances are to be indicated instead of differences. It may
be surprising to learn that children have a good deal of trouble
noting resemblances; they much more willingly find differences in
the objects given them to compare. One must insist a good deal
and show them that although unlike two objects may be somewhat
similar. Here are the questions to be asked:

In what are a poppy and blood alike?

Similarities

How are a fly, an ant, a butterfly, a flea alike?

In what way are a newspaper, a label, a picture alike?

Under test 16 we have indicated the precautions that must be
taken, notably that of assuring oneself that the child knows the
objects to be compared. There are little Parisians who have
never seen poppies or ants.

21. Comparison of Lengths — *12 pairs of lines*

This is a test in exactness of glance in rapid comparison.

Omitted in 1908

Procedure. In this test one presents a series of pairs of lines.
One line of each pair is 30 mm. long and the other varies from 31
to 35 mm. These lines are drawn on the pages of a blank book,

15 by 30 cm.; there are only two lines on a page. They extend in the same direction, end to end, separated by 5 mm. The longer occupies first the right then the left of the page. There are fifteen pairs. After placing them in order one begins by showing the pair where the difference is greatest. The subject is asked to point out the longer of the two lines.

We then present, in another blank book, a series of pairs of lines very much more difficult to estimate. The pages of this book are 20 by 30 cm.; the constant line is 100 mm. long, the variable ranging from 101 to 103 mm. The exact comparison of such long lines is beyond the ability of many adults. The number of pairs is twelve.

22. Five Weights to be Placed in Order[10]

This test requires a direct concentration of attention, an appreciation of weight, and the memory of judgment.

Procedure. Five little boxes of the same color and volume are placed in a group on the table. They weigh respectively 3, 6, 9, 12, and 15 grams. They are shown to the subject while saying to him: "Look at these little boxes, they have not the same weight; you are going to arrange them here in their right order. Here to the left first the heaviest weight; next, the one a little less heavy; here one a little less heavy; here one a little less heavy, and here the lightest one." This explanation is difficult to give in childish terms. It must be attempted, however, and repeated if one perceives that it is not understood.

The explanation terminated, one must observe with attention the attitude of the child. One child does not understand, puts nothing in order; another arranges the weights very well but does not compare them; he takes one at random and puts it at the left as the heaviest, without comparing it with the others, and places those remaining without weighing them. A third tries them a little, but noticeably goes at it blindly. The reading of the weights which is inscribed on each, shows us the errors.

There are three classes to distinguish. First, the subject who goes at random without comparing, often committing a serious error, four degrees for example. Second, the subject who compares, but makes a slight error of one or two degrees. Third, the

[10] Cf. p. 220.

one who has the order exact. We propose to estimate the errors in this test by taking account of the displacement that must be made to re-establish the correct order. Thus in the following example: 12, 9, 6, 3, 15,—15 is not in its place, and the error is of four degrees because it must make four moves to find the place where it belongs. All the others must be changed one degree. The sum of the changes indicates the total error which is of eight degrees. It is necessary to make a distinction between those who commit slight errors of inattention, and those who by the enormity of an error of 6 or 8 prove that they act at random.

✓ *23. Gap in Weights*

Omitted in 1908

As soon as the subject has correctly arranged the weights and only then, tell him that one of the weights is to be taken away while he closes his eyes, and that he is to discover which has been taken away by weighing them in his hand. The operation demanded of him is delicate. One must note that he does not cheat by reading the marking on the box. If there is any fear of this, wrap the boxes in paper.

✓ *24. Exercise upon Rhymes*[11]

1st expl. what R. is / min. ea.

This exercise requires an ample vocabulary, suppleness of mind, spontaneity, intellectual activity.

Procedure. Begin by asking the subject if he knows what a rhyme is. Then explain by means of examples: "Rhymes are words that end in the same way. Thus 'grenouille' rhymes with 'citrouille,' because it is the same sound 'ouille.' 'Compote' rhymes with 'carotte,' they both end with 'ote.' 'Baton' rhymes with 'macaron,' and with 'citron.' Here the rhyme is on 'on.'[12] Do you now understand what a rhyme is? Very well, you must find all the rhymes you can. The word with which you must find rhymes is 'obéissance.'[13] Come, begin, find

[11] Cf. p. 232.

[12] *Editor's note:* We have here retained the French words because it is obvious that the English equivalents would not rhyme. In using the test one must of course use suitable English rhymes.

[13] *Editor's note:* There are many words in the French which rhyme with "obéissance" and which are perfectly familiar to a French child. This is not true of its English equivalent. One would not think of asking a child to make rhymes with "obedience."

some." In order to accomplish this test, the subject must not only find rhymes, which is partly a matter of imagination, but he must understand the preceding explanation, which is a matter of judgment. There are subjects who remain silent who either have not understood or are unable to find rhymes. Others are more loquacious but the false rhymes they cite prove that they have not comprehended. The minute having elapsed, renew the explanation and try the test again.

✓ 25. Verbal Gaps to be Filled

Omitted in 1908.

This test thought out and proposed by Professor Ebbinghaus of Berlin, varies in significance according to its mode of use. It consists essentially in this: a word of a text is omitted and the subject is asked to replace it. The nature of the intellectual work by which the gap is filled, varies according to the case. This may be a test of memory, a test of style, or a test of judgment. In the sentence: "Louis IX was born in —— " the gap is filled by memory. "The crow —— his feathers with his beak;" in this the idea of the suppressed word is not at all obscure, and the task consists in finding the proper word. We may say in passing, that according to the opinion of several teachers before whom we have tried it, this kind of exercise furnishes excellent scholastic training. Lastly, in sentences of the nature of those we have chosen, the filling of the gaps requires an attentive examination and an appreciation of the facts set forth by the sentence. It is therefore an exercise of judgment.

Procedure. We have simplified it by suppressing all explanations. The words forming the gap are intentionally placed at the end of the sentence. It is sufficient to read the text with expression, then suspend the voice with the tone of interrogation when one arrives at the gap. The subject naturally fills in the gap. If he does not do so spontaneously, urge him a little by saying, "Finish. What must one say?" Once the operation is set going it continues easily.

The operator knows the true words of the text which have been suppressed. He should not yield to the temptation of considering those the only correct ones. He must examine and weigh with care all the words that are given him. Some are good, others altogether bad, nonsensical or absurd. There will be all degrees.

Here is the text with the gaps. The words to be suppressed are in italics.

The weather is clear, the sky is (1) *blue*. The sun has quickly dried the linen which the women have spread on the line. The cloth, white as snow, dazzles the (2) *eyes*. The women gather up the large sheets which are as stiff as though they had been (3) *starched*. They shake them and hold them by the four (4) *corners*. Then they snap the sheets with a (5) *noise*. Meanwhile the housewife irons the fine linen. She takes the irons one after the other and places them on the (6) *stove*. Little Mary who is dressing her doll would like to do some (7) *ironing*, but she has not had permission to touch the (8) *irons*.

26. Synthesis of Three Words in One Sentence[14]

This exercise is a test in spontaneity, facility of invention and combination, aptitude to construct sentences.

Procedure. Three words are proposed: Paris, river, fortune. Ask that a sentence be made using those three words. It is necessary to be very clear, and to explain to those who may not chance to know what a sentence is. Many subjects remain powerless before this difficulty, which is beyond their capacity. Others can make a sentence with a given word but they can not attain to the putting of three words in a single sentence.

27. Reply to an Abstract Question[15]

This test is one of the most important of all, for the diagnosis of mental debility. It is rapid, easily given, sufficiently precise. It consists in placing the subject in a situation presenting a difficulty of an abstract nature. Any mind which is not apt in abstraction succumbs here.

Procedure. This consists in reading the beginning of a sentence and suspending the voice when one arrives at the point, and repeating, "What ought one to do?" The sentences are constructed in such a manner that the slight difficulty of comprehension which they present, comes from the ideas rather than from the words. The child who does not understand, is hindered less by his ignorance of the language than by his lack of ability to seize an abstract idea. There are twenty-five questions. The first are very easy and tend to put the subject at his ease. We do not reproduce them here as they will be found farther on with the results.

[14] Cf. p. 222.
[15] Cf. p. 224.

Here are only four of the sentences. They are among those of medium difficulty.

1. When one has need of good advice—what must one do?

2. Before making a decision about a very important affair—what must one do?

3. When anyone has offended you and asks you to excuse him—what ought you to do?

4. When one asks your opinion of someone whom you know only a little—what ought you to say?

It is often a delicate matter to estimate the value of a reply. Sometimes the subject does not gather all the shades of the question and the reply is too simple, not absolutely adequate to the demand. Nevertheless one must be satisfied if it expresses sense, if it proves that the general bearing of the question has been grasped.

In other cases the reply is equivocal; it would be excellent if it came from a dilletante, or a decadent, because of the double meaning which is ironically evoked. It is of no value in the mouth of a school child. Thus to the first question, "When one has need of good advice—" a child replied, "one says nothing." We suppose he has not understood but if this had been an ironical reply, one might have found in it a curious meaning. As a matter of fact, these uncertainties, which are truly matters of conscience with the examiner, present themselves but rarely. Ordinarily the interpretation is easy because one knows already about what to expect from his subject.

28. Reversal of the Hands of a Clock

This is a test of reasoning, attention, visual imagery.

Procedure. First ask the subject if he knows how to tell time. In case his answer is in the affirmative, put him to the test because it is not best to trust his word. There are imbeciles who say they know how to tell time and give extravagant answers when a watch is given them to read. It is important to note this error in judgment. Having found that the subject knows how to tell time, remind him that the long hand indicates the minutes and the short hand the hours. Then say to him, "Suppose that it is a quarter of three, do you clearly see where the long hand is, and the short hand? Very well, now suppose the long hand is changed to the place where the short hand is, and the short hand to the place of the long, what time is it?" Reverse the hands for the following hours: twenty minutes past six; four minutes of three. The correct solutions are, half past four, and a quarter past eleven.

The subject must not see the face of a watch, nor make the design upon paper, or his cuff or his nail to aid his imagination. As the experiment is made individually, supervision is easy.

When the subject gives the two solutions correctly, one can push him a little further, imposing a question much more difficult. Say to him, "For each of the hours that you have indicated, the reversal of the hands brings about the result that you have found; nevertheless this result is not altogether correct. The transposition indicated is not altogether possible. By analyzing the case with care, tell me why."

This test permits of varying degrees of accuracy in the replies. First, certain ones are not able to make any transposition; they give no solution, or else it is absolutely incorrect. Others who come nearer the truth give a solution which is partially correct; for example, only one of the hands is rightly placed, or perhaps an error of symmetry has been committed, one has put to the right what ought to have been at the left or inversely. The third category is that of subjects who give correct solutions. Finally the fourth is composed of those who give a correct solution and are capable of criticizing the slight inaccuracies.

✓ 29. Paper Cutting[16]

This exercise calls for voluntary attention, reasoning, visual imagery, but not for vocabulary.

Procedure. Take two sheets of white paper of the same dimensions. Call the attention of the subject to their equality. "You see they are alike." Lay the first one on the table, fold the other into two equal parts slowly before the subject, then fold again into two equal parts at right angles to the first fold. The sheet is now folded in four equal divisions. On the edge that presents a single fold, cut out with the scissors, a triangle. Take away the triangular piece of paper without allowing the subject to study it, but show him the folded paper, and say to him: "The sheet of

[16] Cf. p. 234.

paper is now cut. If I were to open it, it would no longer resemble the first sheet of paper here on the table; there will be a hole in it. Draw on this first sheet of paper what I shall see when I unfold this one." It is important that the experimenter say neither more nor less than our text, and that he compel himself to employ the words chosen by us although scarcely exact and accurate. The subject now draws upon the first sheet the result of the cutting which he has just witnessed. He should not be allowed to handle the perforated sheet. Some subjects look a little at the perforation, others rely upon their imagination and begin at once to draw. The less intelligent simply draw an angle placed no matter where on the white page, or perhaps a triangle whose form and dimensions are not those of the cut. A little closer observation causes some to consider the form and dimensions. Somewhat better is the triangle replaced by a diamond drawn in the center of the page. Although better, it is still not the correct result, for to be correct two diamonds must be drawn, one in the center of each half of the paper. This test interests everybody. It requires no development of style. It has nothing literary, and rests upon entirely different faculties than those required by preceding tests. Moreover the correctness of the result is easy to grade.

30. Definitions of Abstract Terms[17]

This test resembles closely those which consist in replying to an abstract question. It differs especially in that it requires a knowledge of vocabulary.

Procedure. Without preliminaries, one asks of the subject, "What difference is there between esteem and affection? What difference is there between weariness and sadness?" Often the subject does not reply. He sometimes gives an absurd or nonsensical answer.

We conclude here the list of tests we have used. It would have been easy to continue them by rendering them more complicated, if one had wished to form a hierarchy among normal children. One could even extend the scale up to the adult normal, the average intelligent, the very intelligent, the hyper-intelligent and measure, or try to measure, talent and genius. We shall postpone for another time this difficult study.

[17] Cf. p. 230.

When a subnormal, or a child suspected of being such, is questioned, it is not necessary to follow the exact order of tests. A little practice enables one to cut short, and put the finger upon the decisive test.

The solutions given by the subjects can be put into four categories:

1. Absence of solution. This is either a case of mutism, or refraining from making an attempt, or an error so great that there is nothing satisfactory in the result. We indicate the absence of result by the algebraic sign minus ($-$).

2. Partial solutions. A part of the truth has been discovered. The reply is passable. This is indicated by a fraction; the fraction in use is $\frac{1}{2}$. When the test permits several degrees one can have $\frac{1}{4}$, or $\frac{3}{4}$, etc.

3. Complete solution. This does not admit of definition. It is indicated by the algebraic sign plus ($+$).

4. Absurdities. We have cited a great number of examples and insist upon their importance; they are indicated by the exclamation sign (!).

The cause for certain defective replies can sometimes be grasped with sufficient clearness to admit of classification.

Besides the failure to comprehend the tests as a whole, we encounter:

1. Ignorance; the subject does not know the sense of a word or has never seen the object of which one speaks. Thus a child does not know a poppy. We write an I.

2. Resistance to the examination because of bad humor, unwillingness, state of nerves, etc. We write an R.

3. Accentuated timidity. We write a T.

4. The failure of attention, distraction. We write a D. The distraction may be of different kinds. There is an accidental distraction, produced by an exterior excitant or an occasional cause. For example, the case of a normal who spoils a memory test because he must use his handkerchief. There is constitutional distraction frequent among subnormals. We have ascertained among them the following types: Distraction from scattered perceptions. Distraction from preoccupation. Distraction from inability to fix the attention.

II. Pedagogical Method

The pedagogical method consists in making an inventory of the total knowledge of a subject, in comparing this total with that of a normal subject, in measuring the difference, and in finding if the difference in the knowledge of a subject is explained by the insufficiency of scholastic training.

The first idea of this method was suggested to us by reading the pamphlets in which Dr. Demoor and his colleagues explain the function of the special school at Brussels. To this school are admitted all children "pedagogically retarded." The pedagogically retarded are those whose instruction puts them two years behind normal children of the same age.

In France, our ministerial commission estimated that these pedagogically retarded, or to speak more accurately, these children lacking education, do not need to be sent to a special class; being normal they ought to remain in the ordinary schools, there to make up their instruction. We have thought that since it is of practical value to make a distinction between the normal who is lacking in school training and the subnormals, this distinction could be made in the type of scholastic knowledge beneficial to each of these classes.

The normal retarded child is one who is not at the level of his comrades of the same age, for causes that have no relation to his intelligence; he has missed school, or he has not attended regularly, or he has had mediocre teachers, who have made him lose time, etc. The subnormal ignoramus is one whose ignorance comes from a personal cause; he does not learn as quickly as his comrades, he comprehends less clearly, in a word, he is more or less impervious to the usual methods of instruction. We now have a method of recognizing subnormal ignoramuses; this consists in estimating at the same time their degree of instruction and their knowledge. Thus the idea of the pedagogical method originated.

Having acknowledged what we owe to Dr. Demoor and to his colleagues, we must nevertheless add that these authors do not seem to appreciate the need of precise methods of evaluating even among normals the amount of retardation in instruction. It is probable that in their practice the amount of this retardation is taken into account. Teachers do not hesitate, however, to make estimates of this nature. They will say without hesitation that

such a child is two years or three years retarded. The value of
these estimates is as yet undetermined.

We have found the following direction of great value to teachers
who are attempting to designate the subnormals in their school.
"Any child is subnormal who, in spite of regular or sufficient
schooling, is two years behind children of the same age." This
criterion fixes the ideas and evades some uncertainties. But even
though it constitutes a great improvement over subjective appreciation, which has no guide, it has still the fault of lacking precision. It remains to be seen what is acquired from school instruction by normal children of different ages; one must to some
extent make a barometer of instruction. On the other hand there
remains to be organized rapid methods which permit one to tell
with precision the degree of instruction which a candidate has attained. These two lines of research can scarcely be followed out
except by persons belonging to the teaching profession. We have
succeeded in interesting different distinguished persons. M.
Lacabe, primary inspector in Paris, has consented to confide to the
instructors of his staff the preparation of a work designed to
measure the knowledge of his pupils in grammar. M. Behr, primary inspector of Fontainebleau, has undertaken to determine
the scholastic attainments of the average child, ideally average,
of neither over nor under intelligence, of average health, and who
has had professors of average merit. The idea is original, the attempt promises to be interesting; it will be laborious. Another
work,[18] entirely different in idea, is due to M. Vaney, school
director of Paris. It is devoted to the measuring of proficiency
acquired in mathematics.

In considering the question as a whole, it is clear that the pedagogical or instruction method, divides into two very distinct
categories:

1. The methods permitting one to evaluate scholastic knowledge including arithmetic, grammar, history, geography—in a
word, all that figures in the curriculums and can be easily
measured.

2. The investigation of knowledge acquired outside the schools.

It is upon this last point that we invite the attention of our
colleagues, the teachers. There is a mass of information that a
child acquires outside of school, which figures on no program. It

[18] See *L'Année Psychologique*, Vol. II, p. 146–162.

is acquired by conversation, reading the paper, observation of all that goes on in the street, in the house, everywhere. It is pre-eminently practical knowledge, part of it is useless, much is very important, quite as important surely as that which has a scholastic character.

We have ourselves recently begun a quest upon this side of the question. We have made collective tests in the school, asking the children to reply in writing to certain questions concerning practical life. More than this, we have asked teachers to put questions individually to the children upon points that we have designated to them. Here is a little sample of the nature of the information which every child is to furnish of himself without the aid of anyone.

1. What is your name? What is your first name?
2. What is your age?
3. What is the exact date of your birth?
4. How long have you attended school?
5. What day is today?
6. What month is it?
7. What year is it?
8. What day of the month is it?
9. What hour is it?
10. Is it morning or afternoon?
11. What is the address of your parents (street, number, apartment)?
12. What is your father's trade, your mother's trade?
13. What are the names of your mother, brothers and sisters if you have any?
14. Which are younger, which are older than you?
15. Count this money. How much is it? (Show 12 sous in 2-sou pieces—1 fr. 80 centimes, one piece of 1 franc; 1 piece of 50 centimes, and the remainder four single sous and a 2-sou piece).
16. Name the colors. (Squares of colored paper, vivid red, pink, light yellow, deep yellow, orange, green, light blue, deep blue, violet, white, grey, black.)
17. Do you read the paper? Which one?
18. Have you learned to ride a bicycle?
19. What is a "correspondance d'omnibus" and what is its use?[19]

[19] *Editor's note:* "Correspondance d'omnibus" cannot be translated into English because the system has no counterpart in this country. But experience would soon teach a resident of Paris the use of this term.

If used in exam of defectives, B. says, we must 1st estab. norms.
Cf Hall etc on "contents of chil. minds"

20. What stamps must one put on a letter sent from Paris to Geneva?
21. How much does a loaf of bread cost?
22. Describe how to fry an egg.
23. How much does a sack of charcoal cost?
24. What do you think is the age of your principal?
25. Did you ever see a cow milked?
26. How much does a street car conductor get a day?
27. Have you ever seen a goat? a frog? a rat? an elephant?
28. Did you ever light a fire?
29. Do you ever do several errands at a time?
30. What is a janitor?
31. What is meant by "le term?" (Obscure for an American but not so for a French child.)

Sommer, the German alienist, well known for his work of pathological psychology, has indicated in a special book the utility of these investigations in determining what he calls orientation in time and space. We do not know what advantages he has been able to draw from them; we are also ignorant of whether or not he has taken the elementary precaution, nearly always neglected, of first establishing how a normal child replies. Here are several examples of the information which we have gathered in the primary schools, upon the extra-scholastic knowledge of normals.

"*Correspondance d'Omnibus.*" In the first class (from 11 to 15 years) there were 16 boys who replied correctly—11 did not know, and 2 replied ambiguously. In the third class (from 9 to 14 years) 4 boys knew, 28 did not know. In the fifth class (from 7 to 12 years) 1 boy knew, 41 did not know. In the sixth class (6 to 9 years) 42 boys did not know. Here is a test that is good for the higher grade because the number of correct replies is proportional to the age.

Frying an egg. In the first class, 15 children described very well the manner, and 15 did not know. In the sixth class 10 described it well, 28 did not know, and 4 had doubtful replies.

Price of a sack of charcoal. In the first class 22 gave a reasonable price (2 fr. 50 to 5 fr.); 3 gave unreasonable prices (25 fr., 50 fr., etc.); 4 did not know. In the sixth class, 7 gave a reasonable price (2 fr., to 5 fr.); 5 gave prices too high (10 fr., 50 fr., 70 fr., etc.); 11 gave too low a price (10 centimes, 1 fr. 80) and 18 did not know.

Know how to ride a bicycle. In the first class 15 knew and 15 did not know. In the sixth class 13 knew, and 29 did not know.

Have you ever seen a goat? a frog? a rat? an elephant? In the first class, all had seen the animals. In the sixth class of 42 pupils, 2 had not seen a goat, 9 had never seen a frog, 8 had never seen a rat and 3 had never seen an elephant. It is curious that the frog should be less known than the elephant.

What is meant by "le terme?" In the first class, 14 knew, and 16 gave ambiguous replies. In the sixth class 3 knew, 3 gave doubtful answers, and 36 did not know.

We hope soon to be able to make out a complete list of items of extra-scholastic knowledge. This is only a sample. It will be necessary to give by ages the percentage of correct replies.

The question is still open as to what extent extra-scholastic knowledge is foreign to subnormals. We can at present only make conjectures on this point. It is probable that the slightly subnormal possess many of these notions of practical life; perhaps their defect manifests itself especially in an inability to assimilate that which is properly scholastic, and on the other hand these may be quite apt in the more concrete facts of every-day life. The absence of this knowledge characterizes especially true imbeciles, those who are more seriously affected. Not to know either the number or names of one's brother or sisters, to be unable to distinguish one's given name and one's family name, ignorance of the address of one's parents, would constitute then a sufficiently serious sign of intellectual inferiority, if this manner of looking at the matter is right, and if there are not extenuating circumstances connected with this ignorance.

To sum up, the pedagogical method is two fold. It consists in establishing as it were the balance sheet of the scholastic knowledge acquired by the child; on the other hand it consists in establishing the balance sheet of extra-scholastic knowledge. The general result will be found, not by a complete inventory—that would take too long—but by tests bearing upon a small number of questions judged to be representative of the whole.

The pedagogical method is somewhat indirect in its manner of arriving at the state and degree of the intelligence; it grasps the intelligence through the memory only. One who is rich in memory may be poor in judgment. One even finds imbeciles who have an amazing memory. It is right to add that in spite of this, these imbeciles are but little instructed, which proves to us that instruction, although it depends principally upon memory, demands also other intellectual faculties, especially judgment. One must not therefore exaggerate the bearing of this theoretic criticism which we here make upon the pedagogical method.

The disadvantages which our use of the method permits us already to suspect, are the following: in the first place it cannot be applied to very young children, of from 3 to 6 years, and it is especially important to point out mental debility at that age; in the second place it requires that one should know the scholastic attainments of each child. It is not always easy to see clearly into the past life of a child. Did he miss his class three years ago? If he followed the class, had he in his temperament, his state of health, his habits, special reasons for relaxation? Was his master a poor one, did he fail to understand the child? The quest may find itself face to face with facts, which from their remoteness and their nature, are very difficult to evaluate. These doubtful cases will not be in the majority, let us hope; but they will present themselves in abundance. M. Vaney has noted several in a statistical study, which is restricted, however. Dr. Demoor[20] finds 50 doubtful in a total of 246 retarded and subnormal children; that is approximately one-fifth doubtful. These facts show that the pedagogical method has its imperfections. It should not be employed exclusively.

III. Medical Method

We speak here of the medical method considered in its narrowest sense; we make the improbable hypothesis of a physician who would judge an idiot simply from medical signs, and without attempting, even in the most empirical form, a psychological appreciation of the intelligence of the patient. We make the supposition in order to better understand the proper field for each method.

What are then the somatic symptoms which the physician can utilize for making a diagnosis of inferior mentality?

There is, we believe, a distinction to be made between two studies, that of the causes and that of the actual condition. When the actual state has been determined, after one has established in

[20] "Les enfants anormaux à Bruxelles," *L'Année Psychologique*, VII, p. 305.

phys. signs and symptoms
of val., but v. inaccurate for diag.
Do not apply to morons

76   DEVELOPMENT OF INTELLIGENCE

a summary manner or by a searching method that a subject has
an inferior degree of intelligence, the physician plays an important
rôle, owing to his special knowledge; it is he, who above everyone
else can throw light upon the etiology of each case, can determine,
for example, that the child suffers from *mal comitial* or is afflicted
with myxoedema or that his respiration is disturbed by adenoids,
that his nutrition is weakened, etc., and that a relation of cause
and effect exists between these diverse maladies and his inferior
intelligence.   The etiology, once determined, serves to guide the
prognosis and the treatment.   It is not a matter of indifference
to know the ill from which the child suffers; if his imbecility is due
to epileptic causes, or rather consists in a state of decadence
brought about by frequent attacks, the prognosis is less hopeful
than if his intellectual weakness is the result of traumatism; in the
latter case, one can hope that the lesion is made once for all and
has not a progressive tendency." But these considerations upon
the etiology, the prognosis and the treatment, remain subordinate
to the study of the actual state of the intelligence; and as it is the
actual state that we wish to study here we shall set aside every
other question no matter how interesting it may be.

It is very evident that for a diagnosis of the actual state of the
intelligence the physician who would rigorously ignore all psychology, would very much diminish his resources.   Nevertheless he
would still have some resources left.   There are many somatic
symptoms that can be considered as indirect and possible signs of
inferior intelligence.

What are these signs?   Here, we must first of all dissipate many
illusions.   The subnormal does not of necessity constantly announce itself by evident anatomical defects.   The physical descriptions of the idiot and the imbecile that one finds in classic
treatises are not always correct; and even if they were, they would
not apply in the least to morons.   But the morons constitute the
majority.   It is the morons that must be recognized in the schools,
where they are confounded with normals; it is they who offer the
greatest obstacle to the work of education.   The diagnosis of
moronity is at the same time the most important and the most
difficult of all.   Let us look therefore into the methods to be employed, to facilitate this diagnosis, from the simple examination of
the body.

Medical literature contains actually a great number of observa-

See p 77

tions which may be helpful if they are first submitted to organization. A great many anomalies of different orders have been
noted among the subnormals; anatomical anomalies, physiological
anomalies and the anomalies of heredity and of growth. In a
recent book, Dr. Ley[21] has made an excellent résumé of what is
known of the diagnostic signs of abnormality, to which he has
added personal observations of his own. We shall present to
the reader in a rapid survey all that scientists have ever thought
to look for, to examine, to analyze and to weigh among subnormals.

We shall take account only of clinical signs, that is to say of
verifiable symptoms upon the living individual; and as we have
already stated, we shall occupy ourselves mainly with the recognition of moronity.

"A complete examination should cover the following points.

Hereditary antecedents.
Development.
Anatomical examination.
Psychological examination."

HEREDITARY INFLUENCES

1. Age of parents at the birth of the child. Nothing special for
the backward. (Ley.)

2. Alcoholism of the parents. 42 per cent of the fathers have
manifested in different ways symptoms of drunkenness and 5.2
per cent of the mothers (Ley). The proportion is strong, but
it is not known what is the proportion for the parents of normals.

3. Tuberculosis. 13.3 per cent of the fathers; 8.1 per cent of
the mothers; 19.7 per cent among the grandparents; 18 per cent
among collaterals (Ley). The proportion is unknown among
normals of analogous social condition.

4. Neuropathic affections. (Especially nervousness, tics, trem-
blings, peculiarities of character, epilepsy, hysteria, migraine,
and accentuated neuralgia). 18 per cent of the fathers; 25 per
cent of the mothers; 11 per cent of the grandparents; 4.5 per cent
of the collaterals (Ley). Nothing is known of the proportion
among normals of the same social conditions. The heredity of
normals is so little known!

5. Consanguinity of the parents. Nothing has been observed.

[21] *L'arriération intellectuelle,* Bruxelles, 1904.

6. The order of the child in the family. Of only children, 8.1 per cent; first born, 15.6 per cent; last born of large families of five children or more, 7.5 per cent; among the last three of families of six and more, 15.6 per cent (Ley). Comparison among normals is also here lacking.

The director of a primary school in Paris, M. Guilbert, at our request consented to measure the height of the children in his school while keeping count of the order of the child in the family. Here is the table:

Height in Meters for Children Classed by Order of Birth in a Family

AGE	ONLY CHILD	FIRST	SECOND	THIRD	FOURTH	FIFTH	SIXTH	SEVENTH
13	1.50	1.49	1.34	1.70	1.44	1.51	1.38	1.70
12	1.44	1.40	1.41	1.40	1.42	1.39	1.53	1.23
11	1.36	1.36	1.38	1.39	1.31	1.35	1.38	1.42
10	1.35	1.33	1.33	1.29	1.29	1.31	1.31	1.30
9	1.30	1.27	1.29	1.30	1.31	1.30	1.22	
8	1.25	1.24	1.23	1.24	1.21	1.26	1.21	
7	1.19	1.19	1.18	1.21	1.21	1.24		
6	1.14	1.16	1.12	1.12	1.10			

There are many irregularities in the figures of this table, which come from the fact that the averages are based upon a rather small number of children. For children higher than the third of the family, the averages bear upon less than ten children. In spite of the resulting incoherencies, one sees vaguely that an only child and those of the third order of birth are the largest children.

We have had the same calculation made for the intelligence, taking for a standard the class to which the pupil belongs, and from this standpoint comparing the pupils of the same age but belonging to a different order in the family. It appears therefrom, clearly enough, that the oldest are the most precocious. To comprehend the following tables, we must understand that the figures express the average of the classes. Thus a child belonging to the first class, a second to the second class, the average of the class for the two is 1.50. The smaller the figure the more precocious the child.

Precocity of Children Relative to their Order in the Family

AGE	ONLY CHILD	FIRST	SECOND	THIRD	FOURTH	FIFTH	SIXTH	SEVENTH	NINTH
14	1.25	1.50	1.50	1.25	2	2	1	2	
13	1.50	2.40	2.21	3.14	1.80	3.50	2	6	6
12	2.50	3.33	3.14	3.66	5.14	4.66	2.50	2	
11	5.45	5.52	4.82	4.36	5.50	5	5	4	
10	6.16	6.92	6.52	5.75	7	6.50	7.50		
9	8.14	7	7.95	7.88	8.4	8.75	10		
8	9.16	9.28	9.30	9.23	8.75	8			
7	9.50	9.87	9.80	9.80	10				

It can be seen that the precocity of the child, (used as the sign of his intelligence) diminishes very slightly as his order rises. It remains to be found if the inferiority of intelligence of the later born does not come partly from social influences such as the poverty and misery of too numerous families; poverty produces poor nourishment, lack of supervision, etc. However that may be, if one does not enter into secondary causes, it seems probable, that, among normal children, being the last of birth is in itself an unfavorable factor.

7. Mortality of brothers and sisters. 33.4 per cent among subnormals (Ley). The proportion is unknown among normals.

8. Unnatural labor. 14.5 among subnormals (Ley). Nothing known among normals.

DEVELOPMENT

1. Pathological history. Convulsions among 28.4 per cent of defectives. Infectious diseases having had an influence over the intelligence, 9.8 per cent of defectives (Ley). The proportion is not known among normals.

2. Retardation of dentition. First tooth appearing after one year, 23.2 per cent (Ley).

3. Retardation of walking. After fifteen months, 50.5 per cent (Ley).

4. Retardation of speech. After fifteen months, 66.4 per cent (Ley).

5. Urinary inferiority. Child wetting the bed at four years and after, 22.6 per cent (Ley).

For all this the proportion is unknown among normal children. The proportion of 50 per cent and of 67 per cent is so strong among defectives, that we ask ourselves whether the speech and the walk not appearing until fifteen months, does not constitute a veritable retardation. The study of normals, unfortunately neglected, would suffice to dissipate all doubt.

ANATOMICAL EXAMINATION

This examination comprises two parts. First, that which can be measured, as the weight, the height, dimensions of the head, the spread of the arms, the biacromial diameter, circumference of the thorax, the vital capacity. Second, that which can be appreciated without measurement: pathological blemishes that are more often called stigmata of degeneracy.

A few words only upon the height, the measure of the head and the stigmata.

Height. Innumerable works have been published upon the height of normal subjects, of all countries, of both sexes, and of all ages;[22] certain measurements have been made upon the height of school children of lesser intelligence and these compared with the measurements of the more intelligent children (Porter-Gilbert); some studies have also been made upon the height of subnormal children.[23]

---

[22] For a view of the whole consult the article *"Croissance,"* of Varigny in the *Dictionnaire de physiologie* of Richet. Several important articles upon normals will be found there. Quetelet, *Anthropométrie*, Brussels, 1871. See also *Mémoires de l'Acad. de Belgique*, Vol. VII. Burk, *"Growth of Children in Height and Weight,"* Amer. Journ. of Psychol., August, 1898. Vitale Vitali, *Studi antropologici in servizio della pedagogia*, Turin. Gilbert, *Researches upon School Children*, Iowa University, 1897. Porter, *The Growth of St. Louis School Children*, Academy of St. Louis, 1894, VI, p. 325.

[23] Quetelet, *op.cit.*, *Mesures faite dans la maison pénitentiaire de Ruysselede*. Berthold, in *Year Book, New York State Reformatory at Elmira*, 1898. *Etudes dans une école de reforme.* Tarbell, *On the Height and Weight and Relative Rate of Growth of Normal and Feeble-Minded Children*, Proc. of the Assoc. of Medic. Off. of Amer. Inst. for Idiot and Feeble-Minded Persons, Frankfort, 1881. Simon, *Recherches Anthropologique sur 223 garçons anormaux*, Année Psychologique, 1900, Vol. VI.

(See also Goddard, *Height and Weight of Feeble-Minded Children in American Institutions*, Journal of Nervous and Mental Diseases, April, 1912. —EDITOR.)

✓ All these documents go to show that less intelligent children do not differ constantly from the most intelligent in their height and bodily development. Gilbert, among others, presents statistics, which prove that there is very little difference between the two categories of children. On the other hand, it has been established in the clearest manner by the investigations of Quetelet, Tarbell, Berthold and one of us (Simon), that there exists a considerable inferiority in height among subnormals when compared with normals of the same age. The average difference of height shown by the figures published by Simon, is sometimes more than three centimeters. It is well understood that one must take the elementary precaution of comparing only children of the same age, of the same race, and of the same social condition.

It remains to be shown how one can utilize these differences for an individual diagnosis. They are average differences, obtained from calculations upon a great number of measures; they are therefore necessary in order to know what modifications must be applied to render them true for the individual. One of us (Binet) has presented an idea in regard to this subject,[24] which it seems ought to take an important place in our medical method; it is the idea of limits. An analysis of the measures shows that there exists a limit of height below which normals are less numerous than subnormals, and above which normals are more numerous than subnormals. This consideration of limits gives place to conclusions more precise than the consideration of the average. Let us cite an example, taking for a standard, the measures which M. Boyer at our request was kind enough to make at the Bicêtre upon the idiots, imbeciles and morons under Dr. Bourneville. For school children of 14 years, the normal height is 1.5 meters; the height of idiots of the same age is found to be 1.37 meters. This is the average obtained. But if one runs over the individual values, he sees that only 5 per cent of normals are to be found below the height of 1.40 meters, while on the contrary, there are 60 per cent of idiots, imbeciles and morons. This is the limit, not impassable but rarely passed, and which in an individual examination, as we shall explain further on, gives a prejudicial presumption. But we can treat this subject at the same time with that of the measurement of the head. It is much more simple.

[24] Bulletin de la Société libre pour l'Étude de l'Enfant, p. 430.

Head measurements. During recent years, a great number of measurements have been undertaken, upon the dimensions and form of the head among normal children of diverse intelligence and among subnormals. Our *L'Année Psychologique* has already published many documents upon this interesting question. A history will there be found (Vol. V, p. 245), a sketch of the technique (Binet, VII, p. 314) and comparative measures upon children of unequal intelligence, (Binet, VII, pp. 369, 375, 403, 412) and upon subnormals (Simon, VII, p. 430), children of different ages, (Binet, VIII, p. 345), upon deaf-mutes (Binet, VIII, p. 385), and the blind (Binet, 368). The learned annual reviews of anthropology of Deniker (*L'Année Psych.*, X, p. 296 and IX) contain the review of several recent articles. From all these investigations it is seen that the dimensions of the head are on an average, a very little greater among the intelligent than among the less intelligent in the schools, and that the more intelligent are grouped more closely around this average than the less intelligent. Among subnormals, the preceding facts are again found with a slight accentuation; the average values of their cephalic development are a little less than among normals; and besides, they do not hold so closely to the average. Certain ones, the microcephalic, separate themselves far below, while others, the macrocephalic are above the average.

In presence of these results, one finds the same difficulty in utilizing them for an individual diagnosis, as in the figures concerning height. The method which we advise is the same: that is to establish a limit. To be below the limit becomes a prejudicial characteristic, or more exactly, an anatomical stigma.

Here are the provisional limits which we propose for subnormals (boys). We have fixed them for the height, the anterior-posterior and the transverse diameters of the head, and the sum of these two diameters. It can be seen that more must be done to make the work complete. One must fix the limit for the other cephalic measurements, their totals, their differences, and repeat this for both sexes.

Here is the method of utilizing this table: of 120 primary school children one finds 3.2 per cent whose height is below the limit; there are 16.3 per cent whose anterior-posterior diameter is below, and 7.5 per cent whose transverse diameter is below; this makes a total of 27 per cent but it must be noted that not one is inferior for two measures at a time.

For a group of 100 subnormals (idiots, imbeciles and morons, children at the Bicêtre, all low types) 34 per cent were found below for height, 40 per cent for anterior-posterior diameter, 27 per cent for transverse diameter; 22 per cent are below for one measure and 33 per cent for more than one measure. It would seem, therefore, that it would be this inferiority considered in relation to two limits, which constitutes the characteristic of subnormals.

We have had the curiosity to apply the same method to the measurement of defectives (probably only morons, and a few ignoramuses) published by Ley. There are 51 out of 187 who are

Limits for Subnormals (Boys)

AGE	HEIGHT	DIAMETER ANT.-POST. CEPHALIC	DIAMETER TRANSVERSE CEPHALIC	SUM OF THE TWO DIAMETERS
	cm.	*mm.*	*mm.*	*mm.*
6	100.0	164	133.0	300
7	105.0	166	135.0	
8	110.0	169	136.0	306
9	115.0	171	137	
10	120.0	172	138	312
11	125.0	173	139	
12	130.0	174	140.0	318
13	135.0	175	141.0	
14	140.0	178	142.0	322
15	142.5	179	143.5	
16	145.0	180	145.0	328
17	147.5	181	146.0	
18	150.0	182	147.0	330

inferior to our limit for anterior-posterior, and 46 for transverse diameter; out of these numbers there are 20 who combine the two stigmata. These results would be significant if M. Ley measures the heads in the way that we do. It would be interesting to know the height of these subjects but it was not given. It has been for other subnormals. The difference is not great; there are 20 per cent of subnormals below the limit for height, and only 17 per cent of normals. The limit is therefore, it would seem, an anatomic stigma less important for morons than for idiots. Finally, among backward children of the primary schools of Paris (mostly morons), measured at our request by Mlle. Sirugue,[25] who used our

[25] We desire here to tender to Mlle. Sirugue our sincere thanks for the zeal and intelligence which she showed in the execution of this work.

technique, we find 11 boys out of 38 who are below the limit for the anterior-posterior diameter, only 4 for the transverse diameter, and among these children, 4 combine the two stigmata. The 7 normal cases are all above the limit. As for the morons of Ley, we find that very few are below the limit for height, only 4 boys out of 38.

We emphasize these last results because of their exceptional importance. It is here a question of subnormals actually found in the schools of Paris. They constitute exactly the category of children that the Commission, charged with the recruiting of the schools for backward children, will have to examine. Therefore by this topical illustration, it may be seen what help may be derived from investigating the height and the cephalic dimensions of these children.

STIGMATA

Great account is made of these stigmata, when anthropometry is practiced in the same office with medicine. If one takes the pains to search systematically for stigmata among defectives, one does not find many more than among normals. Here is a list of those which are most frequently observed:

Adenoidal condition. 15 per cent of subnormals (Ley).

Tubercular. Thorax paralytic among 60 per cent (Ley).

Rachitis. 6.5 per cent (Ley).

Syphilis. 3 per cent (Ley).

Defective nutrition. 60 per cent (Ley). This high figure needs explanation.

Malformations of the cranium. 5 per cent (Ley). One sees that they are rare.

High narrow palate. 60 per cent. Reservation should be made upon such a high figure; it would be necessary to examine the condition of normals in this regard, and above all, to measure the deformity.

Teeth. Absence of incisors, 10 per cent (Ley). Hutchinson teeth 2 per cent.

Ears. The auricle like a handle, 12 per cent. Tubercle of Darwin, 5 per cent. Adherent lobe, 11 per cent. Great simplicity in the folds of the auricle, 18 per cent. Observations lacking among normals.

Hair. Abnormal masses, 1 per cent (Ley).

For the study of these different pathological blemishes, one should: first, measure them, which is possible for at least certain ones; second, find out the frequency of their occurrence among normals, without knowing whether the subjects are normal or not, in order to be free from auto-suggestion.   Until these two points are elucidated, nothing can be drawn from observation of the stigmata; exact measurement is the only check against the arbitrary, the fantastic and the *a priori* methods of experimenters. One could never have advanced the theory regarding the physical type of criminals, if one had measured the stigmata.

PHYSIOLOGICAL EXAMINATION

It must bear upon the following points:
Vision.
Touch.
Other senses.
Sensitivity to pain.

Respiration and
circulatory
functions
$\begin{cases} \text{Respiration.} \\ \text{Quickness of the pulse.} \\ \text{Blood analysis.} \\ \text{Coloration of the skin.} \\ \text{Temperature.} \end{cases}$

Motor functions
$\begin{cases} \text{General gait.} \\ \text{Walking forward and backward, etc.} \\ \text{Expression of the physiognomy.} \\ \text{Strength.} \\ \text{Motor ability.} \\ \text{Tics.} \\ \text{Quickness of movements.} \\ \text{Speech.   Defective articulation.} \end{cases}$

We shall simply say a few words about temperature, the analysis of the blood, and the expression of the physiognomy, regretting that space is lacking to speak of strength and the quickness of movements.

TEMPERATURE

It is known that subnormals have a slackening of the circulation, a less rapid pulse, hands cold and often blue. That would be an interesting sign for the diagnosis, because the taking of the axillary temperature, in tenths of a degree, among normals and subnormals, the same day, at the same hour, and in the same locality, proves that with the slightly subnormals, morons, the thermometric inferiority is about 0.4 of a degree. (Ley, op. cit., p. 77.) There would be opportunity here to establish, just as for height, a limit—the thermometric limit. Care must be taken to avoid causes of error which are numerous, because the circulation is influenced by many slight causes; the hour of the day, the temperature of the place, the state of physical exercise, etc.

EXAMINATION OF THE BLOOD

This test so often made, should probably be rejected. Recent investigation has shown that the number of corpuscles contained in a drop of blood varies with the action of the superficial vaso-motor system, with the constriction or the relaxation of the capillaries affected by pricking; therefore a slight local condition causes variation in the number of corpuscles and from what can be found in a small drop of blood, it is not possible to draw a general conclusion as to the richness in corpuscles for the blood altogether. Let us make a comparison. A permission, a discharge, a holiday, any sort of an order, will cause a variable number of soldiers to leave the barracks; a statistician would commit a great error, if he counted, on any day whatever, or at any hour whatever, the soldiers who passed through the streets, and from that estimated the military force of the country. It is an analogous error which is committed by the counters of corpuscles. In order to render the examination of real value it would seemingly be necessary to provoke a well defined condition of peripheral circulation.

EXPRESSION OF THE PHYSIOGNOMY

Few experimenters can boast of being able to escape the purely instinctive judgment which a physiognomy provokes; we are deeply impressed by fine traits, mobile expressions and intelligent appearances; a vacant look, an open mouth, an immovable countenance, give us an unfavorable impression. It remains to be discovered what is the real value of the expression of the physiognomy, if it is possible to properly estimate it, and in case this is so, if it would be possible to apply it to individual diagnosis.

What do *authors* think of it? Alienists, who have had to do with the gravest forms of mental deficiency, do not hesitate to affirm that the expression of the countenance is deceiving. Here is what Shuttleworth says:[26]

The diagnosis and the prognosis of the different cases of mental defect are so intimately united that they should be examined together. If we consider the great division of congenital and non-congenital cases, we shall be able to note that contrary to the current idea, the prognosis for the former, as a general rule is better than that for the latter. In reality, with the one there is a simple defect of development; with the other, there are lesions more or less irremediable. The superficial appearances are in favor of the non-congenital cases, while the others are judged from their deformed and often repugnant countenances; nevertheless our experience is altogether in accord with that of Dr. Langdon Down (*Obstet. Trans.*, Vol. XVIII) who says that the prognosis—contrary to what one often thinks—is unfavorable if the child is pretty, beautiful to look at, and of seductive aspect.

M. Voisin is of the same opinion. He observes that the congenitally affected are uglier, more deformed than the acquired, and he repeats several times that the latter may have expressions of physiognomy indicating a character of intelligence which is deceptive, because they are the relics of a former period—when the subject had not yet lost his intelligence.[27] M. Bourneville makes the same remark in regard to epileptics, whose numerous attacks put them on the road to decay. Truly, in generalizing this opinion, one would almost say that the more intelligent idiot children appear, the less they are so.

The question would therefore seem to be settled if other scientists had not voiced an opinion diametrically opposite. Dr. Demoor attaches great importance to the study of the play of the countenance in defectives; he believes the expression is very significant and he does not hesitate to say that the diagnosis will have there a much surer support, than in cephalometry. We shall not discuss his opinion regarding cephalometry, since the facts that we have above presented are of a nature to show

[26] *Les enfants anormaux au point de vue mental,* p. 78, Brussels, 1904.
[27] *Leçons sur l'idiotie,* pp. 82 and 83.

whether he was self-deceived. But we believe it is interesting to retain what he has said upon the countenance. Does it seem to disagree with Shuttleworth, Voisin, and Bourneville? In the letter, yes; as to fundamentals, no. It seems possible for us to reconcile all these views as follows. These observers were familiar with different types of subjects. As regards the idiot undoubtedly it is Voisin who is right; the countenance is deceptive. As regards the moron, who forms the majority of the children in the school of Brussels, to which Demoor is attached, it is very probable that the contrary is true; the physiognomy reveals the degree of intelligence.

We do not propose this conciliatory solution, in consequence of a priori reasoning. It has been inspired in us by the results of an investigation which we have recently confided to Mme. Rousson, public school teacher in Paris. At our request, M. Bertillon has been good enough to photograph for us some hundred subnormals, of the primary school taken at random, along with some fifty normals.[28] It was with this collection that Mme. Rousson experimented; she had some seventy persons make the diagnosis, as to whether judged by his photograph the child was normal or subnormal. The teachers gave 80 per cent of correct replies, thus showing in the clearest manner, that the countenance is scarcely deceptive for those who are used to reading it; 20 per cent of errors is a very insignificant proportion, being about the same that Crepieux-Jamin obtains when he searches for intelligence by means of the hand-writing. These results which we give here en gros, and which confirm the opinion of Demoor, show of how great utility would be the precise analysis of physiognomy. There is here a technique to be created. We hope sincerely that we shall be able to bring the question to a conclusion with the collaboration of Mme. Rousson, who is deeply interested in these studies.

In terminating this brief sketch of the medical examination, let us insist upon the method to be followed in such an examination. We have not yet sufficiently developed our ideas on the subject. It is understood that one must force oneself to support

[28] This was a great undertaking, full of all sorts of difficulties; it was successful, thanks to the energy and tact of Inspector Belot, and to the zeal of a great number of instructors.

one's reasoning by objective facts, that can be verified by all and are often measurable. One must guard carefully against intuition, subjectivism, gross empiricism, decorated by the name of medical tact, and behind which ignorance, carelessness, and presumption, hide themselves. Every medical diagnosis which cannot be proved as one proves a sum in addition, is to be rejected.

The diagnosis must rest upon the utilization of different signs, several types of which we have enumerated in the preceding pages. We must in the first place come to an agreement upon the value of these signs; which must be fixed, without any preconceived idea; and the only means of fixing this value is to make a comparative study of the normal state. It is a guiding principle which is too often forgotten in medicine. It is nevertheless so important, so fertile in consequences, that an alienist would certainly distinguish himself, if he did no more than force into the minds of his contemporaries, the idea that the study of the subnormal is not possible except by a comparison with the normal. Here, in our studies upon children, it is not simply a comparison that is necessary, it is a physiological, anatomical and anthropological barometer to which one must return every time with each new subject to find out in what measure this subject is inferior to the normal.

In the second place, there must be established in the series of measurable signs, certain limits, which will demarcate the stigmata. We have already described the stigmata of height, of the head, of the temperature, etc. We shall not repeat ourselves.

In the third place, judging from the comparative frequency of the stigmata among normals and subnormals, a calculation must be devised which will express the presumable amount of retardation which each stigma contains. In other words, we must be able to attach a coefficient of importance to each one of these stigmata. What is the meaning of a height below the limit? What must be inferred from an arched palate? What count must be made of an axillary temperature 0.8 of a degree below normal? What importance is to be given to an alcoholic father and a tuberculous mother?

This is the principle of calculation which we propose.

Suppose that a certain stigma, is to be found always with the subnormal, never with the normal. It would have the value of

100 per cent. Suppose that a second stigma is to be found with all subnormals and with 50 per cent of normals, it will be twice as common with the first, and it would have then the value of 50 per cent. Suppose a third is to be found with 12 subnormals and 6 normals, it will again have the value of 50 per cent although its absolute frequency should be much less. If 100 conventionally represents the certainty, the smaller numbers measure inferior degrees of certainty, down to 0 which represents the complete absence of the indication, and to the negative quantities which represent the indication of the opposite sense.

To sum up, we can utilize three methods for the diagnosis of the intellectual level among subnormals.

1. The *psychological method* which is almost always applicable and which is almost *certain* to reveal the signs of defect; the difficulty being in the execution of the tests which demand in the experimenter a great facility in experimental psychology.

2. The *pedagogical method* which is very frequently applicable, and which reveals *probable* signs of defect.

3. The *medical method* which is applicable only in a restricted number of cases, and which reveals *possible* signs of defect.

A. BINET AND TH. SIMON.

APPLICATION OF THE NEW METHODS TO THE DIAGNOSIS OF THE INTELLECTUAL LEVEL AMONG NORMAL AND SUBNORMAL CHILDREN IN INSTITUTIONS AND IN THE PRIMARY SCHOOLS

The preceding article contains a strictly theoretical exposition of the methods of diagnosis which we have devised for recognizing and measuring intellectual inferiority. It remains to complete the preliminary work, to standardize it, to show how far these methods work out when applied to real facts. After the theory must come the proof.

It will not be a question here of anything but the psychological method. It is the only one which is ripe for complete practical purposes. Other methods can only give accessory indications; but these already permit determinations of intellectual inferiority. This is our conviction; we are now going to give the palpable demonstration.

The psychological examination of a subject lasts on an average 40 minutes. We made in the beginning many useless tests with each child, because we were doing a work of investigation; we were groping; now that one knows what to look for, one can proceed more rapidly, and we believe that a half-hour will suffice to fix the state of the intellectual development of each child.

We shall study successively with our measuring scale of intelligence:

1. Normals.
2. Subnormals in institutions.
3. Subnormals in primary schools.

I. NORMAL DEVELOPMENT OF THE INTELLIGENCE WITH CHILDREN FROM THREE TO TWELVE YEARS OLD

Normals figure here as terms of comparison. We have been obliged to make these lengthy studies, because, up to the present, nothing of the kind existed. So far as we know, there is no work that contains the precise and detailed history of the development of the intelligence of a child. The most complete monographs like those of Allen Gilbert[1] present a series of practical tests, especially upon sensation and the organs of sense, but they almost always leave the intelligence out of the question; there are, nevertheless, very suggestive observations which have been published here and there,[2] but we have not been able to utilize them, preferring to erect a new structure borrowing material from no one.

When the work, which is here only begun, shall have taken its definite character, it will doubtless permit the solution of many pending questions, since we are aiming at nothing less than the measure of the intelligence; one will thus know how to compare the different intellectual levels not only according to age, but according to sex, the social condition, and to race; applications of our method will be found useful to normal anthropology, and also to criminal anthropology, which touches closely upon the study of the subnormal, and will receive the principal conclusion of our study.

These investigations have been made by ourselves personally; in spite of their statistical appearance, they are the results of experiments pursued during long periods upon isolated children. We felt that we could not trust this matter to anyone; and we vouch for all that we report, having been ourselves the constant observers.

We did not know a single child; they appeared to us for the first when they came to the examination. We knew, however, that all were normal. The masters were asked to designate only children of average intelligence, who were neither in advance of nor behind children of their own age, and who attended the grade correct for their years. This prescription was carefully followed in the Primary school; evidently it was less easy to conform to this rule in the Maternal school, because of the tender age of the children; finally, we required that the subjects chosen should have an exact number of years in order that the development should be typical of each age.

[1] Allen Gilbert, *Researches upon School Children and College Students*, University of Iowa, studies in Psychology, edited by G. T. W. Patrick, pp. 1–39.

[2] We know of nothing general, outside the books often cited, of Preyer, Perex, Sully, Shinn, etc., which are either monographs, or collections of anecdotes; there are also scattered notes in special collections like the *Pedagogical Seminary* of Stanley Hall.

The tests took place in the office of the Director or Directress of the school, and in their presence. We have chosen those schools where the office was sufficiently removed from the classes, to enjoy a silence undisturbed by the melodious chants of the children learning to spell. Let us add that we have chosen our Directors and Directresses from among those who best understood that it was a question of making scientific observations, and that it was not wise to intervene during a test to whisper a reply to the pupil.

In our first attempt we were satisfied to make observations upon ten children of the Maternal school, and fifteen of the Primary school, in order to fix the mental capacity of each age. These restricted numbers gave a first estimate. Later we made more numerous observations, which are still being continued. To illustrate our method, we shall simply describe the results obtained from some fifty children. But it must be understood that these results have their special significance which we shall justify in a later publication.

NORMAL CHILDREN OF THREE YEARS

The questionings and the presentation of the tests offered many difficulties. We seated the children beside us at a table. We said good morning to them, making them welcome. Many children of this age remain silent and will not reply, even to a question which they understand. This mutism is partly caused by timidity, the proof of which is that certain children during the examination pull their fingers and roll up their aprons with a rapid motion; the silence of others is partly caused by ill-will, stubbornness or malice. One of this latter class persisted for several minutes in incorrect replies; we showed him a string and asked "Is this string?" He shook his head in sign of negation; and when we asked him regarding other objects, a cup, a button, a thimble, "Is that string?" he nodded affirmation. In spite of these difficulties of psychological examination, it is still possible to accomplish it on condition that one does not offend the children and is willing to wait a little. If the child does not wish to reply to one test we present another; we have always succeeded finally in loosening their tongues. When necessary, if the timidity or bad humor of the child continues, one could put off the

examination to another time; we have not, however, as yet had
to resort to this extreme measure.   Our subjects have never been
loquacious, they showed no spontaneity.   We felt they could have
done better than they did.   The examination makes them in a
certain way seem less intelligent than they are; and this is certainly a general rule.   The simple fact of being put upon the
witness stand, so to speak, in school, by a gentleman who has the
age and appearance of a professor, would naturally inspire an
attitude of reserve, and change very much the apparent attitude
of a child; a fine little fellow of twelve, who sits decently upon
his stool, with tranquil countenance, brows knit, and exchanges
politely his smile with ours, will become, an hour later, a street
urchin making sport of the passers by.   Each one takes, during
the examination, a scholastic attitude, which is slightly artificial;
the moral character, the sentiments of the child are very much
changed, his intellectual capacity is probably less affected except
that he loses much of his spontaneity.

We omit the first tests for normal children of three years.
Since they bring their lunch to the Maternal school, and do not
have to be fed, it is needless to investigate their knowledge of food.
They also understand gestures, simple sentences, since they
reply to our greeting, enter and seat themselves in order.   Let us
mention at once a characteristic of the intellectual development
of a child of three years: it is that he has a verbal knowledge of
things.   First, of the body; all show, when asked, nose, eye,
mouth, ear, foot, forehead.   There is a slight hesitation, at times,
for the eyebrow; and sometimes an abdominal localization for the
heart is given.   Naturally the three objects: cup, string, and
thimble are correctly designated when we call them by their
name.   The test of pictures is the one which interests the children
most; this works equally well, when we name the object and the
child must find it, or when, on the contrary, we point out the
object and the child gives the name.   In the latter case there is
a slight difficulty of interpretation, because one cannot always
understand the word which the child pronounces, either because
it is badly pronounced, or because he uses a special pronunciation
of which we have no key.   Setting this slight difficulty aside,
the test shows clearly that a child of three years passes without
difficulty from the perception of the picture to the name; or from
the name to the picture.

The objects found in the picture, when we name them to the child, are the window, the mother, the little girl, the broom, the feather duster, the pot of flowers, the basket, the coffee pot. When the child names by himself, he designates the little girl, the dog, the boy, the man, the other man; he sometimes names them in his own way; the little girl is called a baby; one child said "Lucy"—the dog is called a "toutou;" the man an "old fellow;" the street lamplighter is recognized as a "gas lighter;" sometimes through error of perspective he is called "a baby" because he is very small. The sky is called "house," and the advertisement a box or a thing "*machin*."

It is worth remarking that children of this age are often eager to name or designate something, no matter what. These errors of designation which are frequent enough, because no one child correctly names or designates all of the series of objects, are due partly to the fact that he is ignorant of the names of certain things, like the coffee pot, for instance, but still more frequently they are due to a lack of attention.

Children of this age show a tendency to point at random. One must at times chide them a little to bring out a correct designation, which proves that they know very well, but are careless.

It will not therefore be surprising to find that they are very susceptible to suggestion. If one asks for the button (which is not on the table) they will indicate another object, book, box, or a distant object which they vaguely point out with the finger. If one asks, when they are looking at the picture, for the "patapoum" or the "nitchevo," none of them say distinctly "I don't know." They always point out something, preferably a small object, like a cup, a candle, a coffee mill, but never a person.

To summarize: the equipment of a child of three years is verbal knowledge of objects, and particularly parts of the body, familiar objects, and objects represented in pictures; correct designation and naming of the majority of objects in a series, but never all; frequent errors through distraction, and a tendency to point at random; finally extreme suggestibility, which manifests itself in the act of pointing out something when one names an object known but absent, or when one pronounces a strange word.

For the other tests, the results are not so good; in exceptional cases certain precocious children succeed but the majority fail. At three years, they do not repeat three figures. We never obtain but one or two figures correctly repeated—occasionally three, but so badly pronounced, so muttered that it requires a very indulgent ear to recognize anything. In no case do they invent a series of figures. The comparison of two unequal lines presents the same difficulty. With the exception of an occasional child, the others do not understand the sense of the experiment, and perhaps not of the words; what they understand is that they must point out a line, and bravely they put their index finger upon one of them; generally they put their finger always to the same side. The comparison of two weights succeeds no better. To the question, "Which is the heavier weight?" they comprehend vaguely, as for the lines, that they must designate something; but they cannot weigh them in their hand, even when shown how. We are no more successful for the definition of common objects, as horse, fork, etc. Without doubt, these children know the objects, but they are prevented by the difficulty of expressing their thought in a sentence. With the exception of a precocious child,—who cannot represent the normal level— they are silent, or else repeat the question, "What is a fork?" "It is a fork."

These first gropings, these mistakes, these infantile forms of reaction, present for psychology the interest of curiosity; all this is similar to what is given by defectives who are older. But so far as our measuring scale is concerned, it is a negligible quantity. All that should be kept in mind is this:

The child of three years, although inattentive and very suggestible, names, or recognizes from the name, the majority of the things that figure in our series of objects and pictures.

At three years a child has then the faculty of naming objects.

CHILDREN OF FIVE YEARS

These children presented fewer difficulties in examination than those of three years. There was one, however, the young R., who began to pout in the midst of the examination and was unwilling to reply to a series of questions. The reflections which we made upon the difficulty of questioning children of three years, can be repeated here, with slight modification. Between three and five years an enormous distance has been traversed. Needless to say that at five years the objects and pictures of the series are correctly named. Nevertheless several errors remain possible. The child may take the street lighter for a small boy, through error of perspective; several cannot name the advertisement. Suggestibility is still great, so that when we name the "*patapoum*" and the "*nitchevo,*" they are shown to us; on the other hand when we ask for the button, no other object is pointed out, they satisfy themselves with hunting, without designating the object.

The characteristic of a child of five years is that it executes the four following experiments: repeats three figures, compares two unequal lines, compares two weights, defines ordinary objects. These are the four characteristic tests of a child of five years because all succeed. From the first attempt they repeat three figures. For the comparison of lines, their attention must be somewhat stimulated by repeating at each new presentation, "Which is the longer?" a useless precaution for children of seven. For the comparison of weights there is a little awkwardness at first. Naïvely, the children reply to the question, "Which is the heavier?" by showing a box without weighing it in the hand. It is necessary to tell them that they must weigh the boxes by taking one in each hand; certain ones weigh only one of them, and others take both in the same hand. We therefore say that in order that the comparison may be correct this lesson must be given; but this done, five year old children make no more mistakes but give correct replies. The fourth test which they successfully pass is that of the definition of objects. They reply to the questions, mostly in terms of use; a fork, it is to eat with; a handkerchief, it is to blow one's nose; occasionally they reply by the composition of things; a house, it is of stone, a horse, it is meat. One child of five years, evidently precocious, gave us the following series, worthy of a child of nine years: "A horse is an animal; a house is of wood; a fork is of iron; a handkerchief is of linen."

This then is the equipment of a child of five. They almost all fail when given higher tests. None repeat exactly the three simple sentences of fifteen words each, and certain ones make, doubtless through inattention, absurd transformations, as: "In summer snow falls." They frequently shorten a sentence or repeat the beginning of it, or remain silent. What they give is generally grammatically correct. Example: One says "I get up in the morning, I go to bed at noon," another says, "Germaine has

been bad, she will be scolded." We have never found that
sentences are given devoid of all grammatical construction,
neither do they give words void of sense. In the test of reasoned
comparisons, they make complete failure. These children cannot
understand in what way different things are unlike. We give
below a bit of dialogue which we exchanged:

Q. You know what paper is? A. Yes.
Q. You know what cardboard is? A. Yes.
Q. Are they alike? A. No, they are not alike.
Q. In what are they not alike? Silence.
Q. Why isn't paper like cardboard? Silence.
Q. Then how do you know that a thing is paper or that it is cardboard?
Silence.
Q. Do you know a fly? A. Yes.
Q. And a butterfly. Do you know that? A. Yes.
Q. Are they alike? A. No, they are not alike.
Q. Well then in what way are they not alike? A. It is paper.

The final answer clearly shows that the child does not understand what is asked of him. Another child replies, "The cardboard is not like paper because it is something else." For the
butterfly he gave a curious reply, "Because the butterfly has
two wings and no head, and because flies have heads and besides a
tail."

This verbiage is the only verbal manifestation in any sense
spontaneous that we have been able to collect from children of
five years. Putting aside the tests which are beyond their
capabilities, we have the following conclusion:

*At five years, a normal child repeats three figures, compares two
lines; after being shown how, he compares two weights; he can also
define ordinary objects.*

NORMAL CHILDREN OF SEVEN TO ELEVEN YEARS

We now leave the Maternal school, and enter the Primary
grades. We examined individually 45 children. For the ages
of seven, nine and eleven years, we shall not note here all the
results, of which several have been obtained by groupings; we
shall simply show what we obtained from 10 children at each age,
chosen not for the quality of their results, but in consequence of
an absolute adjustment of the tests.

We must first trace the boundary line which separates children of five years from those of seven. It is furnished by the series of reasoned comparisons. Because of its importance, let us devote some space to it.

The comparison of two lines, from the point of view of length, is very much easier than the comparison of two objects made from memory. In the first place, the two lines are there under their eyes, while the others must be called to mind; besides when one compares the lines one knows from what point of view to compare them; while in the other test, one does not know and must therefore search for some difference to note. It is a little work of invention, which presents a certain difficulty.

We shall indicate numerically the results of this test, in the table which follows; to render the question clearer we give the results obtained with children of nine years.

Here is the manner of procedure for this test. We first ask concerning each object to be compared, if the child has seen and knows it. All, so far as that goes, know the six objects (fly, butterfly, wood, glass, cardboard, paper), with the exception of one who had never seen a butterfly. Poor child!

The first step taken, the question is put: What is the difference between paper and cardboard? This question is not always understood; one can even say that the majority of children do not reply, do not understand, remain silent, or make absurd statements through a desire to please; for example by repeating "the cardboard." This is what we call the "first time" in our table. We must therefore insist by changing our words and say: "Cardboard and paper are not alike, in what are they not alike?" In this way of asking, the majority of children of seven years, almost all (8 out of 9), could give at least one correct comparison. This test is therefore truly a boundary which they pass, and is an excellent means of distinguishing them, in regard to intellectual level, from the children of five years. Still they do not all always make the three comparisons, and out of 9 children examined, we counted 7 silences out of 27 attempts, therefore about one-fourth. The analysis of the details would show very clearly the infantile character of the replies, and, for instance, the great monotony of repetitions. The child having found a certain difference in the first comparison, reproduces it for the others even when it ceases to be correct by the transfer thus, having found that cardboard is thicker than paper, and that the butter-fly is larger[3] than the fly, they tell us that wood is thicker than glass. Besides these there are absurd comparisons, as for instance, to say that the paper is whiter than the cardboard or smaller than cardboard, or that glass is less hard than wood, or that paper is white and cardboard white also.

The points of view of comparison are also rudimentary: it is the hardness, size (large or small, this is very frequent), strength, solidity, fineness, property of being able to be broken or cut, and finally, less often, the color.

Here are several fragments of replies:

The most awkward of all, Larche —— does not reply at all. He agrees with us that paper and cardboard are not alike, but he can indicate no difference. He remains equally helpless with the other two comparisons.

Let us note in this connection an important point. Children who cannot succeed in this test of comparison do not for that reason alone prove themselves ignorant of the difference of the two objects. Most frequently they do know the difference, but they cannot find or formulate it; one must show it to them. If we ask them, "Which is larger, the butterfly or the fly?" these ignoramuses, these apparent mutes, reply in chorus, "the butter-fly." But this is no longer the test, it is something much easier.

A degree higher than Larche —— is that of Bari ——. When asked the difference between paper and cardboard he replies, "The cardboard." It is then explained to him that they are not alike, and he replies, "Because one is paper, and the other is cardboard." For the second comparison, he says, "The fly is not like the butterfly." *Q*. In what? *A*. Because the fly is not made like the butterfly. Here is a child who appreciates the difference but cannot formulate it. He, however, finds the formula for the last comparison, "Because glass breaks but wood if it falls does not break." He crosses the boundary, but with difficulty.

Pist —— succeeds with the comparison. He does not understand in the beginning and it must be explained to him the fact

---

[3] Thick and large are the same word in French—*gros*.

that they are not alike. His first reply is "the paper." Then when it is explained to him, he says, "Because it is white. *Q.* Which is white? *A.* The paper. *Q.* And the cardboard? *A.* There is cardboard which is white." It is evident that this cannot be counted as a correct reply. Pist —— succeeds better with the other comparisons, "The fly is smaller and the butterfly is larger"—"Because the glass breaks and wood does not break." Let us cite the reply by Vagni —— he does not reply to the questions of difference and when it is explained to him he says: "The cardboard is harder than the paper." He finds nothing for the comparison of the fly and the butterfly. For the third comparison he says: "The wood is harder and the glass is not hard." We do not know the basis of his thought but his sentence is unfortunate.

We have dwelt upon the less clever answers because they are the most interesting. Here is one of the best replies; it is that of Giraud —— "Because paper is finer and much whiter." "Because the butterfly is much larger than the fly." "Because with a piece of glass you can cut yourself, and with a piece of wood you can't cut yourself."

One could make diffuse accessory remarks which are not without interest for pedagogy. Thus a certain child says that a fly has two wings less than a butterfly. This is admirable as erudition; nevertheless this learned child could not tell the difference between wood and glass. Her memory had been stored, but she had not been given the spirit of observation.

We give below the replies arranged in a series. We shall distinguish between responses according to whether the subject replies to the question: "What difference is there?" or to the supplementary question: "Why are they not alike?" We note the number of successful comparisons, the number of repetitions of the same type of reply, and lastly, the number of absurdities. It will be seen that at 7 years a single child Larche —— did not pass the test.

By this method it can be seen how easy it will be to classify any child whatever.

Experiment of Reasoned Comparisons

Boys of Nine Years

NAMES	NO REPLY	REPLY TO SUPPLEMENTARY QUESTION	REPLY TO FIRST QUESTION	ONE CORRECT COMPARISON	TWO CORRECT COMPARISONS	THREE CORRECT COMPARISONS	ONE REPETITION SAME RESPONSE	TWO REPETITIONS SAME RESPONSE	ABSURDITIES
Altmaye......		+		+	+				
Lamarq......		+		+	+	+		+	
Valent.......		+		+	?	+			
Guillerm.....		+		+	+	+			
Baz..........			+	+	+	+	+		
Bonj.........			+	+	+	+			
Dumo........			+	+	+	+			
Brie.........			+	+	+	+			

Boys of Seven Years

NAMES	NO REPLY	REPLY TO SUPPLEMENTARY QUESTION	REPLY TO FIRST QUESTION	ONE CORRECT COMPARISON	TWO CORRECT COMPARISONS	THREE CORRECT COMPARISONS	ONE REPETITION SAME RESPONSE	TWO REPETITIONS SAME RESPONSE	ABSURDITIES
Larche.......	+								
Barr.........		+				+			+
Pist.........		+			+	+			+
Vagn........		+		+		+	+		+
Dast........		+		+	+	+	+		?
Leho........		+		+	+	+	+		?
Vala........		+		+	+	+		+	
Girau.......		+		+	+	+			
Ab..........			+	+	+	+		+	
Dugues......			+	+	+	+		+	

Although the test of reasoned comparisons is truly the boundary of seven years, we have tried it with eight subjects nine years old. Even with them, half do not yet understand what is meant by searching for a difference, and their grasp of the situation must be emphasized by asking, "In what are the two objects not alike?" Out of 24 comparisons (8 subjects made 3 each) there were only two who failed, and the number of repetitions of the same type of reply is not more than 3, while with children of seven years there were 8 repetitions, which shows a noticeable improvement. From all this it results that: At seven years children make the proposed comparison sometimes in response to the first question, oftener to the supplementary question. Mostly they succeed twice out of three times, and often they repeat the same type of reply. The progress between seven and nine years exists but seems too subtle to serve as a line of demarcation; it might be made more apparent by an increase of the difficulty. But our aim is not to employ this test for that distinction. It simply constitutes a boundary between five and seven years; an important boundary, because it is, as we shall see later, the boundary of imbecility and moronity, for those subjects who are twelve years of age.

Before leaving this question of reasoned comparisons, we shall note a curious fact. To some fifteen children of seven, nine and eleven years, we have proposed comparisons, having for their purpose the perception not of the differences of many objects, but of their resemblances, for instance, the resemblance of blood and the poppy, a fly and an ant, a flea and a butterfly, and lastly between a newspaper, a label and a picture. We have been amazed at the difficulty which the child finds in seeing a similarity in two objects which they know to be different. "In what are they alike!" we ask, and the almost constant reply is, "They are not alike?" The child is dominated by a spirit of differentiation. Perhaps the needs of practical life turn their attention more towards the perception of differences than of resemblances, which only become apparent in scientific studies. It would be worth while to investigate in this direction.[4]

After having thus marked the limits between five and seven years, that is to say between the Maternal and Primary schools, we shall show the tests which mark the limits between the ages above seven years, and which will consequently permit us to distinguish between the different children of the Primary schools. The tests upon which we shall depend seem to fall into three distinct categories.

1. Tests of memory.

2. Tests of intelligence which are partly made by the help of language.

3. Tests of sensorial intelligence.

Although there is no clear demarcation between the three categories of tests and though all require the intervention of the senses, of memory and of language, it is by the proportion and the importance of these elements that we characterize them.

---

[4] Since these lines have been written we have methodically made use of the comparison of similar objects as a test of mental debility.

MEMORY

We shall study three forms of memory: verbal memory of sentences, memory of pictures, memory of figures.

Verbal memory of sentences. Between twelve and seven years there is not only a difference of four years, but there is an acquisition of scholastic culture which may be considered enormous. Still, in spite of this increase of instruction, in spite of the development of the faculty of acquiring knowledge which this presupposes, children of nine years and even those of eleven years have not a power of memory very much greater than their younger companions of seven. We had 15 children of seven years repeat individually the 8 sentences which we indicated in a preceding chapter, and which we reproduce here to save the trouble of looking back.

First sentence. I get up in the morning, I dine at noon, and I go to bed at night.

Second sentence. In summer the weather is beautiful. In winter it snows.

Third sentence. Germaine was naughty, she would not work; she will be scolded.

Fourth sentence. The chestnut tree in the garden, throws upon the ground the shadow still faint, of its new leaves.

Fifth sentence. One must not say all that one thinks, but one must think all that one says.

Sixth sentence. It is one o'clock in the afternoon, the house is silent, the cat sleeps in the shade.

Seventh sentence. One must not confound the critical spirit with the spirit of contradiction.

Eighth sentence. The horse draws the carriage, the road ascends, and the carriage is heavy.

Each sentence is slowly and energetically pronounced with the required intonation, in the silence of the examination room. Nothing distracts the child; and when he repeats we note all the words he pronounces, his time of hesitation, his self corrections, his remarks, and the play of his countenance which sometimes shows that he is not satisfied with his effort; this last is what we call the *mimique de jugement.* Besides when we ask him if he is satisfied with his repetition, he should say, "Yes," if the repetition seems to him correct, "No," if it seems to him incorrect.[5]

---

[5] We now keep a systematic count of the grading which the child makes by his answer. This aids us to classify him.

If he repeats nothing, or if he only repeats the first words of the sentence, we say "Well now? ——" but without urging. We avoid too great a suggestion which would force the memory of the child and lead him to reply by an absurdity. This example shows, let it be said in passing, how delicate a psychological experiment is. We should never finish if we enumerated all the precautions that should be taken.

Averages Obtained in an Experiment of Verbal Memory of Immediate Repetition with Ten Children Each, of Seven, Nine and Eleven Years

SENTENCES TO REPEAT	NUMBER OF EXACT REPETITIONS			More than half			Less than half			Absurdities and obscurities		
	7 yrs.	9 yrs.	11 yrs.	7 yrs.	9 yrs.	11 yrs.	7 yrs.	9 yrs.	11 yrs.	7 yrs.	9 yrs.	11 yrs.
"I get up.................	8	9	9	2	2	3	0	0	0	2	1	1
"In summer.................	8	10	10	2	0	1	0	1	0	2		
"Germaine.................	8	10	8	2	0	2	0	0	0			
"The horse.................	3	7	5	6	2	5	0	0	0	2		
"It is one.................	0	1	3	4	5	4	6	4	3	5	1	
"The chestnut tree...........	0	0	0	0	0	5	10	10	5	2		1
"One must not say...........	4	3	9	5	4	1	1	2	0	3	4	1
"One must not confound......	0	5	6	2	3	4	8	4	0	8	5	2
Total.................	31	46	50	23	16	25	25	21	8	24	11	5

In the above table, we write the results in figures which we analyze in the following manner: first, in the columns 1, 2, 3, we note how many children at the different ages made an exact repetition. It is a gross result, but one of the most important; the six following columns contain details upon the quantity of incorrect repetitions; they are noted under three heads according as the child had repeated less than half or the half and more, of the original sentence. Finally the last three columns show in detail the quality of the incorrect replies. These may contain either another sense, though reasonable, or an absurd sense, or finally verbal obscurities, that is to say, sounds that are not known words.

It seems to us interesting to make this distinction, because the first nine columns, on the one hand, and the last three on the other, express results which correspond to different faculties;

not to repeat the whole is a lack of memory; to make absurd changes is an error of judgment.

Out of 8 sentences which were given them, the children of seven years made a total of 31 correct replies, that is about three for each child. In examining the number of errors according to the nature of the sentences, one sees that these errors are readily explained. They are least for the first three sentences, whose sense and vocabulary are within reach of the children of seven years; in the two sentences —— "One must not say" —— "The horse draws" —— the sense still is clear, so that nearly half of the children succeed. On the contrary, the 3 other sentences, "The chestnut tree —— ", "It is one o'clock —— " and, "One must not confound —— " offer by their style and subtle meaning a difficulty which these young intelligences have not been able to master; to the task of memory is added the task of comprehension.

We evaluate in the same way the results for the nine year old children. Obviously, it is a little better; their exact reproductions are 46 instead of 31, but the progress has been in the more difficult sentences, as "The horse" and "One must not confound." If one notes that these children of nine years certainly add to the advantage of better comprehension that of greater control over their voluntary attention, one recognizes that the slight superiority of the results which they here furnish can scarcely be imputed to the growth of memory.

For children of eleven years, there is again a slight improvement; the exact reproduction of the children of this age is 50; but there again the study of detail shows that the gain operates almost exclusively upon the more difficult sentences, "One must not confound, etc." The three simple sentences, given first, have the same number of errors as at nine years.

We do not wish to force the significance of these results, which do not astonish us especially, because we had foreseen them elsewhere;[6] nor shall we go so far as to say that verbal memory does not increase with age, from seven to nine years. We maintain simply that this growth seems slight when completely isolated from certain factors which complicate it, such as control of voluntary attention, power of comprehension, the force of habit, etc.

6 *Experimental Study of the Intelligence*, Paris, 1903, p. 260.

If now we examine the data in the last three columns of our table, that which is due to errors of judgment, we find a considerable difference between children of the three different ages indicated. The number of absurd errors (such as, "I go to bed at noon," "In summer snow falls," "One must think all that one thinks," etc.) is considerable among the youngest children; there being 14. The number of times they mutilated a word or uttered unintelligible sounds was 10, which makes a total of 24 errors of judgment; there are only 11 at nine years and only 5 at eleven years. One can thus clearly see that this test classifies the children as to age, better by the absurdities of their replies than by what they forget, properly speaking, which proves once more that if the memory increases little from seven to eleven years, the judgment on the contrary increases greatly. One gets an impression of this fact without the aid of any calculation, when one has examined the attitude of the children during tests of memory. The child of seven years seems to give himself little trouble. He is less attentive, because he regards the experimenter less when he pronounces the sentence; he makes visibly less effort to repeat, renounces more easily the pursuit of a fleeting memory; and above all when he makes a mistake in repeating he has less often that semblance of judgment which signifies "I realize that I am wrong."

For the individual diagnosis the following conclusions should be borne in mind:

At seven years, a child repeats an average of 3 sentences out of 8 given him, and he commits an average of 3 errors through absurdities and obscurities.

At nine years, a child repeats an average of 4 sentences, and commits only 1 error through absurdities or obscurities.

At eleven years, a child repeats an average of 5 sentences and commits but a half error through absurdities or obscurities.

To utilize these solutions in an individual diagnosis we must use a seriation. Here is the one that these results give us.

Seriation of Results Obtained by the Immediate Repetition of Sentences of 14 to 15 Words Each

Children of Seven Years

NAMES	NUMBER OF SENTENCES EXACTLY REPEATED	NUMBER OF THE SENTENCE EXACTLY REPEATED	IN WHICH SENTENCE THE ABSURDITY MANIFESTS ITSELF
Leho...............	1	2	1, 5, 7
Vala...............	2	1, 3	2, 4, 5, 6, 7, 8
Dugues.............	2	2, 5	1, 7, 8
Dast...............	3	1, 2, 3,	5, 6
Ab.................	3	1, 2, 3	7
Larch..............	3	1, 2, 3	7
Pist...............	3	1, 3, 8	2, 4, 6
Barr...............	4	1, 2, 3, 5	7
Girau..............	5	1, 2, 3, 5, 8	6, 7
Vagni..............	5	1, 2, 3, 5, 8	6, 7

Children of Nine Years

NAMES	NUMBER OF SENTENCES EXACTLY REPEATED	NUMBER OF THE SENTENCE EXACTLY REPEATED	IN WHICH SENTENCE THE ABSURDITY MANIFESTS ITSELF
Bonj...............	2	2, 3	1, 5, 7
Dum...............	4	1, 2, 3, 8	5, 7
Altma..............	4	1, 2, 3, 8	7
Valent.............	4	1, 2, 3, 8	5, 7
Guillerm...........	4	1, 2, 3, 8	7
Brie...............	5	1, 2, 3, 6, 7	5
Berque.............	5	1, 2, 3, 5, 7	
Lamar..............	5	1, 2, 3, 7, 8	6
Bazi...............	6	1, 2, 3, 5, 7, 8	
Gros...............	7	1, 2, 3, 5, 6, 7, 8	

Children of Eleven Years

NAMES	NUMBER OF SENTENCES EXACTLY REPEATED	NUMBER OF THE SENTENCE EXACTLY REPEATED	IN WHICH SENTENCE THE ABSURDITY MANIFESTS ITSELF
Corn...............	3	1, 2, 3	5, 7
Lecle..............	3	1, 2, 5	4, 7
Taudi..............	4	2, 3, 5, 7	1
Bertra.............	4	1, 2, 3, 5	
Calif..............	5	1, 2, 3, 5, 8	
Lev................	5	1, 2, 5, 6, 7	
Gorgi..............	6	1, 2, 3, 5, 7, 8	
Leno...............	6	1, 2, 3, 5, 7, 8	
Barr...............	7	1, 2, 3, 5, 6, 7, 8	
Vign...............	7	1, 2, 3, 5, 6, 7, 8	

Memory for pictures. This is a test which we describe while giving the technique. Let us see in a very brief way the number of pictures which a child of seven can retain, compared to a child of nine or eleven years.

Apparently the memory for pictures grows rapidly with years. We admit that it grows, but it must be less rapid than the preceding numbers would lead us to believe; because the child has need of a certain power to direct his attention, to distribute it equally among the pictures, and it is this which naturally gives a great superiority to the older ones, who know better how to look than the younger ones.

Seriation of the results obtained by the Memory for 13 Pictures

CHILDREN OF 7 YEARS		Number of pictures	CHILDREN OF 9 YEARS		Number of pictures	CHILDREN OF 11 YEARS		Number of pictures
Leho....	3		Bergue..	2		Lecle....	4	
Vala....	3		Altma...	4		Lév......	5	
Dugues.	3		Bonfi....	5		Taudi...	6	
Larch...	3	Aver-	Lamar...	5		Barri....	6	
Dast....	4	age,	Dumo...	6	Average,...	Bertra...	7	Average,
Barri...	4	4.3	Valen...	6	6.2	Debr..	7	7.2
Vagn....	5		Guillerm	8		Gorgi....	8	
Abt.....	6		Brie.....	8		Calif....	9	
Pist.....	6		Gros.....	8		Vign.....	10	
Gira....	6		Bazi.....	10		Ga......	10	

We remark in relation to this last seriation that which would be applicable to every series which we publish; it is that the very great difference, which is noticeable between the first and last terms of each series, comes from the fact that the series is the result of a first test. If one repeated it two or three times, it would disclose the following fact which we have often observed in psychology; each pupil would present a slight gain as a result of practice from the re-examination, with an equal improvement for all, but proportionately larger for those whose results were poorest in the first trial; it would result from this that the seriation at each repetition would condense itself; there would be less individual difference, and the change would be especially marked among the weakest terms. It is therefore the lowest which gain

Probably contrary to fact,

most by the repetition; this seems paradoxical, because one thinks of the ability to adapt oneself as a sign of intelligence; and here it would rather be a sign of mediocrity. But it is easy to understand the reason; the intelligent adapt themselves quickly from the start, and they are thus almost immediately at their limit of adaptibility; on the contrary the mediocre children adapt themselves less quickly, and consequently their progress is more visible.

Memory for figures. This is an exercise which tests a particular sort of memory, the immediate auditive memory for figures, and at the same time the force of voluntary attention.

Every subject was asked to repeat a series of figures of increasing lengths, commencing with three figures. Three attempts were made for the series of 3 figures, then three for the series of 4 figures and so on, until one arrived at a series, for which after three attempts, he obtained no correct reproduction. The figures were written beforehand, and read by the experimenter without the subject seeing them. We make the seriation by making use of the highest series which had been well retained. In spite of the brevity of this indication, it merits complete confidence, having been obtained as the result of many attempts. Experience has shown that in connection with the maximum series, one must note the number of times that the subject invents figures which have not been pronounced, as well as the giving of figures in their natural order (as 1, 2, 3, 4, etc.), and finally by the false appreciation of the subject as indicated by his manner of replying. Certain ones believe that they have replied correctly, when they have really committed errors; if one overlooks a slight inversion, let it pass, but if one slips 2 or 3 new figures into a series without perceiving it, that is a much graver fault. It is therefore important to ask each time for the judgment of the subject upon his repetition. A slight difficulty arises in asking him for a judgment of himself; the least imprudent word forms a suggestion. If one asks: "Have you repeated that correctly?" the subjects often reply "yes" or "no" according to the very slight intonation or scepticism which one puts into the voice. The best procedure is to make in advance this arrangement; as soon as a series has been repeated, the subject shall say, according to the case: "It is correct" or "It is not correct"—or more simply "That's right" or "That's not right." We regret not to have thought in time to have made this arrangement with all our pupils; it is an omission to be corrected another time.

Seriation obtained from the memory for figures

CHILDREN OF 7 YEARS		CHILDREN OF 9 YEARS		CHILDREN OF 11 YEARS	
Names	Maximum series	Names	Maximum series	Names	Maximum series
Pist.....	3	Dumo...	4	Bertra...	5
Leho....	4	Bonfi....	5	Calif....	5
Dugues.	5	Altma...	5	Lecle....	6
Girau...	5	Guillerm	6	Levy....	6
Larch...	5	Valen ...	6	Vign	6
Vagni...	6	Berque..	6	Gorgi....	6
Alt......	6	Bazi.....	7	Gano....	6
Barri....	6	Lamar...	7	Taudi...	7
Vala....	6	Gross....	7	Debre....	7
Dast....	7	Brie.....	7		

Average, 5.3 (7 years); Average, 6.0 (9 years); Average, 6.0 (11 years)

These three series seem to us good because the weakest subjects have not had very different results from those of the average. There is scarcely an exception, save only Pist —— seven years, and Dumo —— in the nine year group.

This group of tests upon memory was rapidly made; it took scarcely more than 4 or 5 minutes. In general we interrupted it by other tests of a slightly different character, in order to rest the child. Our tests of memory, notwithstanding their number, must not be considered as covering all the forms of memory; they concern more particularly the memory for immediate repetition which is essentially a sensorial memory. The memory for ideas is ignored almost entirely. This is an omission which we note is passing, and which it would be easy to fill.

One of us indicated long ago[7] the best means of studying the memory for ideas; it does not consist in the repetition of sentences difficult of comprehension, because those who have a good memory can repeat quickly and exactly that which they have not even understood; it consists in causing a delay between the hearing and the repetition, and obliging the subject to think of other things during that interval; then all that is sensorial, the echo

[7] Binet and Henri, Treatise upon Sensation and Memory of Ideas, *Année Psychologique, I*, 1894, p. 1.

of auditive memory, disappears and scarcely anything but the idea remains. We therefore propose to make again the immediate repetition of the 8 sentences, by a general repetition. It is probable that the work which we announce will be completed by the time the present article is printed.

TESTS OF SENSORIAL INTELLIGENCE

These are made independently of the development of language, of the abstract idea, and have an extra-scholastic character. They are important from many points of view. The manifestations of sensorial intelligence are frequent among defectives, who cannot adapt themselves to the teaching in the schools, and these facts are interesting for the pedagogy of subnormals; they prove that one would succeed better in their education if, instead of obstinately imposing upon them scholastic knowledge, which is not made for them, one taught them other things.

We divide our tests of sensorial intelligence into 2 groups.

1. Those which appeal almost wholly to the elementary processes of sensation, perception, and sensorial attention. These are the comparison of lines.

2. Those which require a particular intervention of judgment and reflection; these are putting weights in order, and paper cutting.

Comparison of Lines. It will be recalled that the booklet of short lines to be compared, contains lines one of which measures constantly 30 mm. and the other varies between 31 and 35 mm. There are 15 comparisons. Children, even when very young, have shown the accuracy of their glance. The number of tests was 15, chance might have produced rather more than 7 errors. No subject gave replies due to chance, that is to inattention pure and simple, because the incorrect replies are, without a single exception, comprised between the numbers 9 and 15; that is to say, it is for the lines where the difficulty of perception of difference is the greatest, that the mistakes are made. Where the pupils failed therefore was before the difficulty of comparison.

They are generally very rapid in their designations; and the test lasts scarcely a minute for the designation of the 15 lines. We did not find among them that automatic tendency to es dig-nate constantly the same side. The automatism could easily be seen from the figures which we give. Thus the longest line in the series which we give is constantly to the right for the numbers 1, 3, 4, 6, 9, 10, 11, 13, 15 and to the left for the other numbers, 2, 5, 7, 8, 12, 14. Consequently a person, who by automatism would always designate the right side, would make errors exclusively of the second series, and on the contrary, a person who designated always the left side, would make exclusively errors of the first series. There is to be noted in the case of Larch —— the rudiment of automatism, starting with the 11th line, and in the case of Barri——starting with the 12th, but this is not very significant.

Test of the Short Lines. Seriation of the Number of Errors

CHILDREN OF 7 YEARS			CHILDREN OF 9 YEARS			CHILDREN OF 11 YEARS		
Names	No. of errors	Number of the line where the error is made	Names	No. of errors	Number of the line where the error is made	Names	No. of errors	Number of the line where the error is made
Vala....	4	10, 13, 14, 15	Berqu..	2	12, 14	Lévy ...	2	9, 12
Dast....	3	9, 13, 15	Guill...	2	11, 15	Taudi..	0	
Larch...	3	11, 13, 15	Dumo..	1	15	Barri...	0	
Barri...	2	12, 14	Lamar..	1	11	Lecle...	0	
Abt.....	1	14	Bazi....	1	15	Calif...	0	
Leho ...	1	11	Altma..	1	9	Debr ...	0	
Girau...	1	13	Bonfi...	1	14	Ganon..	0	
Vagni...	1	15	Valent..	1	14	Bertra..	0	
Dugues	1	13	Brie....	0	0	Vign....	0	
Pist	0	0	Bazi....	0	0	Gorgi...	0	
			Gros....	0	0			

The booklet of the long lines offers sufficiently great difficulties which are apparently of a different order; the lines are long and it is not easy to include both at a single glance; one must pass from one to the other, consequently the attention is directed from one to the other in succession; perhaps even memory must intervene. It is an operation which requires a little art. It will be useful to us if it enables us to select the children according to age; but in interpreting it, one must remember that it does not measure simply the sensorial faculty of perception, but something more refined.

There are a dozen pairs of lines to compare. The series of comparison is rapidly made; it takes little more than a minute.

Comparison of Long Lines. Seriation of Number of Errors

Children of Seven Years

NAMES	NUMBER OF ERRORS	NUMBER OF LINE WHERE ERROR OCCURRED
Barri	7	3, 5, 7, 8, 9, 10, 11
Vala	6	3, 5, 6, 8, 9, 11
Dugues	6	2, 6, 7, 8, 10, 11
Leho	6	2, 6, 7, 8, 10, 11
Dast	5	1, 4, 5, 9, 12
Larch	5	3, 4, 7, 8, 11
Pist	4	6, 8, 9, 12
Abt	4	3, 6, 10, 11
Vagn	4	1, 5, 9, 12
Girau	3	6, 7, 10

(5.0)

Children of Nine Years

NAMES	NUMBER OF ERRORS	NUMBER OF LINE WHERE ERROR OCCURRED
Valent	6	1, 2, 3, 5, 7, 10
Dumo	6	4, 6, 7, 8, 10, 11
Altma	6	2, 4, 6, 8, 10, 11
Gross	5	3, 6, 8, 10, 11
Berqu	5	2, 3, 6, 9, 12
Bonfi	3	7, 8, 12
Guillerm	3	5, 8, 12
Lamar	3	4, 7, 9
Berqu	2	3, 11
Bazi	2	5, 12
Brie	1	9

(4.2)

Children of Eleven Years

NAMES	NUMBER OF ERRORS	NUMBER OF LINE WHERE ERROR OCCURRED
Bertra	7	3, 7, 8,9, 10,11,12
Lévy	6	2, 4, 6, 7, 8, 10
Vign	5	2, 6, 7, 8, 10
Barri	4	3, 6, 8, 12
Gorgi	3	2, 6, 10
Taudi	3	6, 10, 11
Lecle	2	7, 11
Calif	2	7, 10
Gano	2	2, 3
Debra	1	3

(3.5)

If one examines what underlies these figures, it will be found very interesting. These children of eleven years have a remarkably accurate glance; certain ones who make only 2 or 3 errors are more clever than some intelligent adults. It is rare to find a test which will show the superiority of a child of eleven over an adult.[8] This comes from the fact that the glance is a natural quality which cannot be cultivated at school; probably it is one of those aptitudes which makes part of the psychology of the savage, and it would be interesting to know how much it is worth with the defective.

The consideration of the nature of the errors permits us to eliminate the element of chance. To judge hastily, one might say that if chance gives 6 correct replies out of 12, every child whose correct replies number 6 has a glance no more accurate than blind chance. But in reality, the systematic distribution of the errors in the second part, from 7 to 12, shows that they are due to the difficulty of comparison. The errors from 1 to 6 are those which should be ascribed to inattention, especially in the case of children, who like Debra —— and Gano —— have committed no error with the pairs of lines from 7 to 12.

A word, in passing, upon automatism. The longest line is to the right, for the numbers 1, 4, 5, 9, 12 and to the left for the numbers 2, 3, 6, 7, 8, 10, 11. This points out Dast —— immediately as an automaton to the left, and also Vagni; the automatisms to the right are more numerous, which is quite natural as one employs the right hand for making the designation; it is to be found in the case of Vala ——, Bertra, Leho ——, Abt ——, Dumo ——, Altma ——, Gross ——, Levy ——, Vign ——, etc. For almost all there is a slight inclination to point to the right; that is easily understood; when there is a doubt, automatism triumphs. By actual count there are found among the youngest children 33 errors to the right and 16 to the left, that is to say, less than half. Those of nine years commit 27 errors by designating to the right and 14 errors by designating to the left; lastly, at eleven years there are 31 errors of the first class and 4 of the second; it seems in the last case that the right-handedness which develops with age, influences the automatism to the right. There would be reason then to think that if the automatism is a sign of the lack of intelligence, the right-handed form of automatism is a sign of the development of voluntary motor power.

---

[8] We give some examples of results obtained with adults. A school director commits two errors with the long lines; a lady, two errors, also. An adult (Binet), 3 errors. A teacher, 5 errors. Young ladies of twenty, 4, 5 and 6 errors.

Seriation of the Results Furnished by the Arrangement of Weights

Children of Seven Years

NAMES	TOTAL NUMBER OF ERRORS	ORDER GIVEN TO THE WEIGHTS	ERRORS BY TEST
Vagni......................	22	15, 6, 3, 9, 12 15, 9, 6, 3, 12 15, 3, 6, 9, 12	8 6 } 22 8
Valad......................	20	15, 3, 12, 9, 6 12, 15, 6, 3, 9 3, 15, 9, 6, 12	6 6 } 20 8
Dast.......................	20	15, 3, 6, 9, 12 15, 6, 12, 9, 3 15, 3, 6, 9, 12	8 4 } 20 8
Larch......................	14	15, 12, 9, 3, 6 15, 9, 3, 6, 12 15, 6, 12, 3, 9	2 6 } 14 6
Dugue......................	13	15, 9, 12, 6, 3 12, 15, 9, 3, 6 9, 12, 6, 15, 3	2 4 } 13 7
Pist.......................	10	15, 9, 12, 3, 6 15, 6, 12, 9, 3 15, 12, 9, 3, 6	4 4 } 10 2
Leho.......................	6	15, 9, 12, 6, 3 15, 9, 12, 6, 3 15, 12, 6, 9, 3	2 2 } 6 2
Abt........................	6	12, 15, 9, 6, 3 12, 15, 9, 6, 3 15, 9, 12, 6, 3	2 2 } 6 2
Barri......................	2	15, 12, 9, 3, 6 15, 12, 9, 6, 3 15, 12, 9, 6, 3	2 0 } 2 0
Girau......................	0	15, 12, 9, 6, 3 15, 12, 9, 6, 3 15, 12, 9, 6, 3	0 0 } 0 0

Children of Nine Years

NAMES	TOTAL NUMBER OF ERRORS	ORDER GIVEN TO THE WEIGHTS	ERRORS BY TEST	
Altma	12	15, 12, 6, 9, 3 15, 3, 9, 6, 12 15, 9, 6, 12, 3	2 6 4	12
Lamar	10	15, 12, 9, 6, 3 15, 12, 3, 6, 9 15, 9, 6, 3, 12	0 4 6	10
Guillerm	6	15, 12, 9, 3, 6 12, 15, 6, 9, 3 15, 12, 9, 6, 3	2 4 0	6
Grapi	4	12, 15, 9, 6, 3 15, 9, 12, 6, 3 15, 12, 9, 6, 3	2 2 0	4
Berqui	2	15, 12, 9, 6, 3 15, 12, 9, 6, 3 15, 12, 6, 9, 3	0 0 2	2
Dumo	2	15, 12, 9, 6, 3 15, 12, 6, 9, 3 15, 12, 9, 6, 3	0 2 0	2
Bazi	2	15, 12, 9, 3, 6 15, 12, 9, 6, 3 15, 12, 9, 6, 3	2 0 0	2
Brie	2	15, 12, 9, 6, 3 15, 12, 9, 6, 3 12, 15, 9, 6, 3	0 0 2	2
Valent	0	15, 12, 9, 6, 3 15, 12, 9, 6, 3 15, 12, 9, 6, 3	0 0 0	0
Bonfi	0	15, 12, 9, 6, 3 15, 12, 9, 6, 3 15, 12, 9, 6, 3	0 0 0	0
Gros	0	15, 12, 9, 6, 3 15, 12, 9, 6, 3 15, 12, 9, 6, 3	0 0 0	0

Children of Eleven Years

NAMES	TOTAL NUMBER OF ERRORS	ORDER GIVEN TO THE WEIGHTS	ERRORS BY TEST	
Debra......................	10	9, 6, 12, 15, 3 12, 15, 9, 6, 3 15, 12, 9, 6, 3	8 2 0	10
Lecler......................	4	12, 15, 9, 6, 3 15, 12, 9, 3, 6 15, 12, 9, 6, 3	2 2 0	4
Barri......................	4	15, 12, 9, 3, 6 15, 12, 9, 3, 6 15, 12, 9, 6, 3	2 2 0	4
Lévy......................	2	15, 12, 9, 6, 3 15, 12, 9, 6, 3 12, 15, 9, 6, 3	0 0 2	2
Vign......................	2	15, 9, 12, 6, 3 15, 12, 9, 6, 3 15, 12, 9, 6, 3	2 0 0	2
Gorgi......................	2	15, 12, 9, 6, 3 15, 12, 9, 6, 3 12, 15, 9, 6, 3	0 0 2	2
Gan......................	0	15, 12, 9, 6, 3 15, 12, 9, 6, 3 15, 12, 9, 6, 3	0 0 0	0
Tandi......................	0	15, 12, 9, 6, 3 15, 12, 9, 6, 3 15, 12, 9, 6, 3	0 0 0	0
Bertra......................	0	15, 12, 9, 6, 3 15, 12, 9, 6, 3 15, 12, 9, 6, 3	0 0 0	0
Calif......................	0	15, 12, 9, 6, 3 15, 12, 9, 6, 3 15, 12, 9, 6, 3	0 0 0	0

Arrangement of 5 weights. This test may be analyzed in two ways, in watching the child do the test, and in noting the order in which he places the weights. These are two phases of the experiment which have about the same results, and have the advantage of the one confirming the other; they must therefore be separately analyzed to see if they conflict.

An observation of the reaction of the child often shows whether he arranges the weights haphazard, or whether he compares them. When a child puts aside the first weight which comes to his hand without comparing it with the others, one is immediately warned; one should note also those who use only one hand, and those who use two, weighing the different weights at the same time with both hands.

It will be noticed that the youngest children committed very serious mistakes, so serious that one questions if they have understood very much; the maximum error would have been 30 and the mean error near 20. There are 3 that are no better than mere chance. The children rarely corrected themselves; the third attempt is no better as an average than the second; (36 errors for all in the first, 34 in the second and 43 in the third), experience taught them nothing. Children of nine commit infinitely fewer mistakes; all make an arrangement that is better than by chance, but they do not correct themselves any better than the seven year old children (8 mistakes in the first, 18 in the second and 14 in the third). Children of eleven years—leaving out the first, Debra ——, who must have had a curious lack of attention— made fewer mistakes by far (6 for the first, 4 for the second and 4 for the third). We note again that it is the heaviest weight which is the most frequently put in its place. The children of seven years put it 24 times in its place; children of nine 30 times, and of eleven 25 times. It can be seen by the following statistical study how the different children distributed their attention. Here are the details of the exactness of position.

Number of Times Each Weight Was Put in Correct Position

	WEIGHT				
	15	12	9	6	3
For 10 children of 11 years..............	25	24	28	26	27
For 11 children of 9 years..............	29	24	23	24	26
For 10 children of 7 years..............	24	10	12	12	15

While the children of nine and eleven years busy themselves with all the weights, those of seven years fix their attention principally upon the heaviest. The rest are neglected. They therefore do only a part of their work, that which especially appeals to them. Is it because in the explanation which is given them they are told to put the heaviest aside first? It is possible if they were told to put the lightest aside first, that they would make the opposite error. It would be worth investigating. In any case the interesting thing is that their attention remains local, partial, it does not synthesize the whole; and this is a proof of the weakness of attention, or of the weakness of comprehension.

Omission of weights. This test is made immediately following the preceding. Here are the results:

At seven years, the mistakes on the average are so many as to be incalculable.

At nine years, there is an average of 2 errors with a maximum of 5.

At eleven years, there is an average of 2 errors with a maximum of 5.

Paper cutting. This is a very difficult exercise. We have not had time to try it at length. We have ascertained only that at twelve years, few normal children draw a central diamond.

These tests of sensorial intelligence require further development, for they will certainly be a very useful aid in analysing the aptitudes of defectives. It will be advantageous to maintain the distinction which we have proposed between the faculties of sensation and of sensorial perception (comparison of lines), and that of judgment and sensorial reasoning (the arranging of weights and paper cutting).

SUGGESTIBILITY

[handwritten margin note: admits it doesn't dep. on intel]

We do not believe that the study of the manifestations of suggestibility will permit the evaluation of the intellectual level. Without doubt we may lay down the principle that suggestibility in its extreme form requires a suspension of critical sense. But daily observation shows us persons of very keen intelligence who are however not lacking in credulity. On the other hand, when attempting to bring out the suggestibility of a school child, one does not have to take into account simply his judgment; different feelings of reserve, discretion, or propriety enter into the experiment which would make an intelligent adult simulate suggestibility, in order not to offend the experimenter, or even to become really suggestible through a feeling of timidity, which has a certain social value. One of us has shown that defectives are rendered less suggestible, simply through an absence of the feeling of timidity, and this absence is in them a lack of social sense.

These reservations once made, we give the results obtained from the Suggestion Test. We designate with 0 the absence of resistance; H indicates hesitation before the suggestion, and 1-h, 2-h, 3-h, so many hesitations; av. indicates that the suggestion has been avoided and 1 av., 2 av., 3 av., that a corresponding number of the suggestions have been avoided. (See p. 57, for the explanation).

CHILDREN OF 7 YEARS	CHILDREN OF 9 YEARS	CHILDREN OF 11 YEARS
Leho............ 0	Mont............ 0	Bertra.......... 1 h
Daste........... 0	Briet........... 0	Vigné........... 1 h
Barri........... 0	Valent.......... 1 h	Barri........... 1 h
Larch........... 0	Dumo............ 1 h	Taud............ 2 h
Abl............. 1 h	Gross........... 1 h	Lecler.......... 3 h
Dugues.......... 1 h	Lamar........... 2 h	Lévy .... 3 h
Girau........... 2 h	Grap............ 2 h	Debr............ 2 av
Vala............ 3 h	Altma........... 2 h	Gorgi........... 2 av
Vagna .... 3 h..	Bazi............ 3 av	Gano............ 3 av
Pist............ 3 av	Berquin......... 3 av	

INTELLIGENCE WITH DEVELOPMENT OF LANGUAGE

The study of the aptitudes is most important, because it is by their lack, as we shall see later, that mental defect betrays itself the most strikingly; it is the difficulty of comprehending an abstract question, or of replying in such a way as to give proof of judgment, of spontaneity, and of invention. We have used many experiments; there is one that is of chief importance, that of abstract questions; others, of secondary importance, are those of incomplete sentences, concrete and abstract definitions, rhymes, synthesis of three words in a sentence.

Abstract questions. We have already given several examples of abstract questions.

We shall give later (p. 124) a complete list in the form of a table with the results obtained.

Our series of questions presents an order of increasing difficulty.

When the child is brought in to be examined, it is useless to waste time in preliminary explanations; the first question is so easy that it is sufficient to pronounce it in a tone of interrogation, for the child even the one of seven years to understand what is wished of him and to reply. The bait is taken and the sequence of questions elicits naturally the replies. These are written down exactly as given without correction. The hesitancy of the child is noted, his embarrassment, his slowness to speak. If one encounters mutism, one excites the emulation of the child persuading him that he can reply, repeating the question with proper tone and inflection. One should avoid such insinuation as, "You do not know?" or "You do not understand?" Because this encourages indolence and carelessness, and there are very few embarrassed children who would not quickly seize such a subterfuge. The best way is always to encourage in order that every one may do his best. We have here an examination approaching a clinical examination, and one must show much patience and gentleness. There are two errors to be avoided, one of procedure at the moment of the test; the other of interpretation, when later one studies the replies. The error of procedure consists in going too rapidly and not being sufficiently patient in awaiting the reply. Mutism evidently has an enigmatical character; it may signify, "I understand nothing" or else it may come from the fact that the child has a slow mind and does not at once find a suitable answer; or again the child has considerable reflection and judgment, and cannot content himself with the first answer that comes into his mind, but is searching for a better; it is evident that those who reply haphazard are the more alert but not necessarily the more intelligent. One of us has elsewhere[9] insisted upon the necessity of choosing between several interpretations of the slowness of intellect.

In questioning school children, one arrives at a true interpretation by taking into account all of the replies; one can soon determine whether it is a question of the slowness of a judicial mind or of one that does not comprehend; but this work of interpretation upon the sum total of the replies cannot conveniently be made

[9] *Étude expérimentale de l'intelligence*, Paris, Schleicher, 1902, p. 45 and ff.

except when all of them are brought together. During the examination one does not yet know. One must therefore be prudent in selecting the right moment when it is safe to pass to another question. The matter is a very delicate one. It is far better to waste a little time than to throw a slow subject into confusion. We formally call the attention of the experimenter to this source of error. With a little experience one soon sees whether or not the child is hunting for a reply or if he has given up; the expression of his countenance may be a valuable indication.

It remains to interpret the data. We should have wished to eliminate from this interpretation all that is arbitrary, and certainly we are not entirely satisfied with our results. Nevertheless one principle has guided us; we are not forced to search for absolute accuracy in the replies; we take the sentences of the children of 11 as forming the standard by which we compare those of younger children. There is therefore a personal part in our selection; but this personal part consists in selecting from replies which have been really thought out and given, in estimating these replies, and not in making out of whole cloth an ideal form for the correct reply. We have, moreover, attempted to take into consideration the mentality of children. Certain replies might be considered appropriate in a dilettante, and with a grain of irony they might even seem to be witty retorts. To how many difficulties could not one reply, as did a certain child; "One should go to bed," or "One must consult the doctor." Frequently we have encountered these unexpected ideas, which amused us greatly. Certain expressions, by the way, such as, "Ah! Madame!" of Shakespeare, would be appropriate for every possible situation. We have nevertheless concluded that what would be wit in a skeptic of thirty, would be incoherence of thought in a child of 7. Here again, if one is in doubt, a glance at the sum total of the replies of a subject enlightens us. Notwithstanding this there remain replies which are frankly enigmatical, as for example the affirmation "Nothing" which in extreme cases might have a meaning but which again might only be a verbal reflex. We regret having sometimes accepted their replies without explanation. One is always learning. When the reply is ambiguous, one should insist and almost force the child to develop differently his idea. This is not always easy; it should at least be tried.

We give below the series of questions, and the replies with our

QUESTIONS	REPLIES MARKED 1	REPLIES MARKED 2	REPLIES MARKED 3	REPLIES MARKED 4	ABSURD REPLIES
1. When one is sleepy what must one do?	One must sleep.—One must go to bed.—One undresses and goes to bed.	One must undress.			
2. When it is cold what must one do?	One must cover up well.—One must get warm.—Cover up well so as not to take cold.	Get warm near the fire.—Make a fire.—Cover up your face.	Stay home.—Stay in the house.		
3. When one is in danger of being late for school what must one do?	One must hurry.—One must run.—One must go quickly.	Be a little quicker the next day.—Ring the bell.—One will be kept in.—One must get up early.			
4. When one sees that it is raining, when one is going out, what must one do?	One must take an umbrella.—One must take a rain coat.—One must cover up well.	One must not go out.—Stay at home.—Do not go out.—Protect yourself.—One must stay at school.			
5. When one is tired, and has not enough money to take the omnibus, what must one do?	Walk more slowly.—One should rest and then go on.—One must rest so as to be able to walk.	One must sit.—One must rest.—Rest on a bench.	One must go afoot.—One must walk.—Walk.—Go afoot.	One must make money.—One cannot go.—One must start earlier.—One must not go.—One must go home.—Take a taxi.	
6. When one has missed the train what must one do?	Wait for another.—Take the next.—Wait for the second.—One must take the one following.	One must wait.	One must try not to miss it again.—Take the trolley.—Walk.—Take the omnibus.—Go home.		Because one hasn't enough money.
7. When one breaks something belonging to another what must one do?	One must pay and ask to be excused.—You must ask the person to whom it belongs to excuse you.	One must pay.—Replace it.—Pay for it.—Buy another.	Mend it.—Give it back.	We must fight.	Go to the doctor.

8. When one finds that one's copy book has been stolen, what must one do?	Ask it of the teacher.—Take a complaint to the teacher.—Speak to the principal.	Try to find the copy book.—Find the thief.—Hunt for it.	Buy another.—Replace it.—Go take it.—Take it from the person who stole it.—He must pay.	Take care of one's self.—One has nothing to do.—Do nothing.—One must write.
9. When the house is on fire what must one do?	Call the fireman.—Telephone.	Save oneself.—Run into the street.—One must run so as not to be burned.	One must get away.—One must put out the fire.	
10. When one has been struck by a playmate who did not mean to do it, what must one do?	Pardon.	Do not tell it to the teacher.—One must not tell.—One must not complain.—Say nothing.	Do not hit back.—Do him no harm.—Tell him to pay attention.—Tell him like this: don't do it again or you will be told on to the teacher.—You must not do to him, what he did to you.	Tell the teacher.—Defend yourself.
11. When one has need of good advice, what must one do?	Ask it of the teacher.—Ask it of one's parents.—Ask it of some person you can trust.—Ask it of someone older.	One must ask it of someone.	One must listen.—Listen well.	
12. When one is lazy, and does not wish to work, what happens?	Later it will happen that one is wanted nowhere.—One remains ignorant.—One remains always a block-head.—One can do nothing and cannot earn a living.—When one is grown he will repent.	One becomes a tramp.—One is in want.	He will have a fool's cap.—One gets punished by the master.—It soon happens that one is the last of his class.—One gets bad marks. One is given blows with the ruler.—The master punishes him.—One is kept in.	
13. Why should one not spend all his money, but put some aside?	For when you are out of work.—Because if one is sick and has no money one will die.—For old age, or case of sickness.—It is for when one is old.	Because later one may be in need.—Because we are unhappy.—To buy things.—One must not spend everything.—To economize, buy clothes, food.		

QUESTIONS	REPLIES MARKED 1	REPLIES MARKED 2	REPLIES MARKED 3	REPLIES MARKED 4	ABSURD REPLIES
14. When one has received a punishment which one has not deserved, what must one do?	One must do it so as to discuss it afterwards with the teacher.	One must protest.—One must speak.—One must tell his father.—Tell the teacher. You must tell the teacher that it isn't you.—One must try to to have it amended.	One must do it.—One must do it just the same.—One does it just the same.	One must not do it.—One must not go.	You must excuse.—Be good.—Because one has not been good.
15. Before deciding an important matter what must one do?	One must consider.	One must think if one can do it.—Get information.—One must ask if one can do it.—Pay attention.			One must go and see the doctor. — Eat. — One must run after it.
16. What can one do to earn 10 sous which one needs?	One must sell something.—One must sing.	One must work.—Go and work.—Work.			That some one gives it to us.
17. When a person has offended you and comes to ask your pardon, what must one do?	One must forgive.—One must reconcile one's self with them.	One must excuse them.	Thank them.—Receive them well.	Listen to them.—One must go and say to them to pay attention. —one must speak. One must not fight.	
18. If some one asks your opinion of a person whom you know but little what must one do?	One must say that one does not know what they are.—One must say nothing, or say that one does not know them well.—One must not speak without knowing.—One should say, I do not know that person well enough to to give you an opinion. —One might say nothing since one scarcely knows them.	One must say nothing.—That one does not know.—One says nothing.—One does not talk about it.			One must ask.—One does not recognize him any more.—Answer him.

19. When two persons discuss a question before coming to an understanding about the words, what happens?	It will happen that they contradict themselves.—They will talk nonsense.—They will not talk about the same thing.	It will happen that one does not know.	That they dispute.—One will quarrel.—They will get angry.—A quarrel.—They will end in a dispute.		You must stay at home.—Because one quarreled.—Do not tell others.
20. When a person always contradicts you no matter what you say, what must one do?	You must try to make him understand when you are right and when you are wrong.	You must let him say—You must not speak with them.—One must tell one's parents.	One must revenge one's self.		
21. Why must we judge a person by his acts rather than by his words?	Because one is more sure in seeing the acts than the words.—Because one cannot believe the word and if one has seen it one always believes.—Because when one says the words it is not certain that they will be put in action, but when they are put in action one is sure they are done.—Because words can lie but acts cannot.	Because one can tell lies.—Because words are deceitful.—Because they will lie.			Because one does not know.—Because it is to know if one has committed a crime.—No not lie nor steal.
22. Why does one forgive a wrong action committed in anger more easily than a wrong action committed without anger?	Because when one is angry one hardly pays attention.—Because when one is angry one is forced to do the bad action.	Because anger may call itself.	Because it is bad.—Because one is angry.—That makes you angry.—Being angry one might tell.—Because he cries and upsets everything.	It is because one is not angry.	

QUESTIONS	REPLIES MARKED 1	REPLIES MARKED 2	REPLIES MARKED 3	REPLIES MARKED 4	ABSURD REPLIES
23. Why is it better to persevere in what has been commenced than to abandon it to commence something else?	When one has commenced a thing one already knows something about it, while if one begins something else one knows nothing of it and one has lost uselessly one's time.	Because one must not commence two things at once.—If we do not finish the teacher catches us.—One must finish what one does.	Because if one commences it is less hard than at the end.		
24. Why should we not remind a person of the service which we have rendered to him?	One should not because that is unkind.	Because one might easily ask another and perhaps they would do it.—Because a good act is never lost.—Perhaps they will render you one later.			
25. What should one do when one has committed a wrong act that is irreparable?	One must beg pardon.	One must hide.—One should do one's best to repair it.—One should all the same attempt to repair it.—One should avoid committing another.—One must go to another country.			

Cf the 25 compreh. ques.

markings, which are quite conventional and provisional. They may be divided into 3 groups: 1st, the replies having a meaning bearing upon the questions; 2nd, absurd, unintelligible, ambiguous replies, those having a wrong meaning; 3rd, silence. It is chiefly into the first group that we have attempted to introduce degrees. Those which we propose, after having discussed these things at length with all possible care (it requires judgment to appreciate tests of judgment, and we hope not to have been entirely lacking) have the advantage of establishing a uniform system of marking, applicable to all, which, if in certain details it might seem arbitrary, cannot however be accused of favoritism. Furthermore, notwithstanding the interest and even the pleasure, which we have found in making these distinctions, they are not of very great importance in making a diagnosis; because we must above all take into account the silences and the absurd, ambiguous, nonsensical replies.[10]

QUESTIONS

First question. When one is sleepy what must one do? A question so simple that any one might reply, and the reply is nearly always satisfactory. In the answers marked 2 it is simply the *expression* of the thought that is defective.

Second question. When it is cold what must one do? A very easy question. One can scarcely find shades of difference in the value of the answers. Replies marked 2 and 3 indicate a poorer means of protection against the cold, as it is not so general as that indicated by replies marked 1.

Third question. When one is in danger of being late for school what must one do? In order to reply one must comprehend the precise meaning of the demand; many children answered badly because they did not understand. It is easy to see that the replies marked 2 contain a wrong comprehension. We ask what must be done to avoid the menace of actual tardiness. One child understood that it was a question of preventing one's tardiness next day; another described the consequences of actually being late, for example, the punishment inflicted upon the tardy ones, or the necessity for ringing the bell, since the door of the school would be closed.

[10] *Editor's Note:* We have translated these questions and replies literally. But for use with American children we employ a more colloquial form.

Fourth question. When one sees that it is raining when one is going out, what must one do? Very easy question, as easy as 2. In the replies marked 2 the subject indicates an inappropriate solution, too special to respond to the general character of the demand; but it is not serious.

Fifth question. When one is tired and has not enough money to take the omnibus, what must one do? This little problem brings out the differences of comprehension and of judgment. The solution, to be satisfactory, must contain two ideas, that of rest to be taken, and that of the walk to be taken afterwards. The replies marked 2 do not take into consideration the necessity of the walk.

The replies marked 3 do not take into account the fatigue. The replies marked 4 are contradictory to the sense of the question, or are ambiguous expressions.

Sixth question. When one has missed the train what must one do? This question is so simple that it calls up a reply almost automatically. The youngest have nevertheless committed errors of judgment.

In the replies marked 1 the form is of little account. The idea is there and it is correct.

In the replies marked 2 the idea is vague.

The replies marked 3 are badly adapted to the question; take the omnibus or the trolley we are told; but do we know there is one? As to going home, is that natural if one is prepared to take the train? And try not to miss it again is a beautiful suggestion when it is already gone!

Seventh question. When one breaks something belonging to another, what must one do? The idea of paying or replacing the object, and of excusing one's self must be indicated for the reply to be satisfactory.

Eighth question. When one finds that one's copy book has been stolen what must one do? The correct solution is to carry the complaint to one in authority. Then a reply much less appropriate is to reply without giving the authority to which one complains. Then—to hunt for the object; to replace it; are replies still less suitable since they apply to a case where an object has been lost.

The replies marked 4 take it for granted that the thief is known.

Ninth question. When the house is on fire what must one do? Evidently one must call the firemen; several had the idea simply of saving themselves.

Tenth question. When one has been struck by a playmate who did not mean to do it, what must one do? First comes the idea of pardon; then absence of denunciation. Next come the replies where the absence of vengeance is noted.

Eleventh question. When one has need of good advice what must one do? Evidently one must ask it of a person who has had experience; this is the first idea. To say that one must listen to it, is to indicate an idea less important, less adapted to the question.

Several replies are unintelligible, probably because the children have not understood the meaning of the word "advice." Here a lack of vocabulary is responsible.

Twelfth question. When one is lazy and does not wish to work, what happens? The replies are somewhat difficult to classify but they are interesting to analyze. Nearly all the children understood the sense of the question; but they took different points of view. The smallest, in general, thought only of the immediate results; that is, being kept in, bad marks, dunce cap, foot of the class and (we regret to have to register this naïve confession) the blows given by the teacher. The horizon of ideas of the older ones is more extended; they have foreseen the more distant but more important consequences of laziness, that is to say ignorance, the difficulty of earning a living, etc.

Thirteenth question. Why should one not spend all his money, but put some aside? Saving is necessary in view of sickness, age, lack of work. This is what the children explain more or less completely. Others affirm especially the advantage of useful expenditure, like buying necessities, or paying the rent. Others indicate simply the need in which one may later find one's self. In general they have replied well.

Fourteenth question. When one has received a punishment which one has not deserved, what must one do? The best conduct under such circumstances must contain the association of two things: the protest and the execution of the punishment. Furthermore, one might discuss the second point, whether it is a duty to submit to an unmerited punishment. There is more elegance perhaps in submitting first and protesting afterwards; but that is an affair of appreciation. We place lower the refusal to execute the punishment. The child revolts against the unmerited character of the punishment, but he does not comprehend the line of conduct to follow.

Fifteenth question. Before deciding an important matter (prendre parti) what must one do? The little word "think" is the best reply. There were many absurd answers. The children have not understood or thought it was a question of a pleasure party (*partie*).

Sixteenth question. What must one do to earn 10 sous which one needs? The older children especially replied by the commonplace remark: one must work, which they remember from a lesson. We prefer two typical replies, both given by the younger children of seven years whom school had not caused to forget life: "One must sell" says one; "One must sing" says another. This is a curious bit of naïve misery. These are childish words that are truly touching!

Seventeenth question. When a person has offended you and comes to ask your pardon, what must one do? It is the pardon that comes at once into the mind. Those who have comprehended have had this feeling, but often the word has suggested their thought. With intelligences less developed, the altruistic idea effaces itself more and more; there remains only a neutral or negative state.

Eighteenth question. If some one asks your opinion of a person whom you know but little, what must one do? Several succeeded in expressing more or less well that ignorance imposes discretion; others have indicated silence as necessary without giving the motive.

Nineteenth question. When two persons discuss a question before coming to an understanding about the words, what happens? The idea is subtle and the words are not in the vocabulary of a child. The question was poorly understood. The child vaguely divined that there had been a conflict, and it was upon this point that he concentrated his attention. Several replies were marked 1, but with reservation.

Twentieth question. When a person always contradicts you, no matter what you say, what must one do? The replies are very defective.

Twenty-first question. Why must we judge a person by his acts rather than by his words? The reply should contain an indication of the comparative value of words and acts. Rarely understood. In the best cases there is an attempt at a parallel. Lower down merely words are given.

Twenty-second question. Why does one forgive a wrong action committed in anger, more easily than a wrong action committed without anger? Good replies are rare. In general the children have seen in anger an aggravating circumstance, or the only thing to qualify.

Twenty-third question. Why is it better to persevere in what has been commenced, than to abandon it to commence something else? Good replies are rare. Most often (second reply) the thing is affirmed without the motive being given. Several give scholastic motives, indicating that their outlook is limited. There are finally several unintelligible replies.

Twenty-fourth question. Why should we not remind a person of the service which we have rendered him? Badly understood. Children here show their utilitarian tendencies; they say we must not allow the person to do us a service. This is a wrong meaning. These questions invite absurd replies, which is their principal reason for being.

Twenty-fifth question. What should one do when one has committed a wrong act which is irreparable? Like the preceding this question invites absurdities. Defectives often accept the invitation.

The order followed in the preceding list has not been that of the difficulty of the questions. We have made the calculation of all the solutions given for the first 20 questions only, and we have been able to establish the order of difficulty which will be found in the following table. The most difficult question is the 20th; then comes the 7th, 14th, 18th, etc. This order has been established in making a synthesis of the replies given by the three different ages, of seven, nine and eleven years; if one had taken into account only one of these age groups a rather different order would have been given. In this table we have therefore subdivided the questions into three groups, the easiest from 1 to 12, those of medium difficulty from 13 to 19, finally the most difficult from 15 to 20. In the vertical columns is shown the number of the replies, marked 1 or 2, or 3, etc., the silences (S), and the absurdities, ambiguities or nonsense (A). It will be noted that for the easiest questions, children of seven reply as well as those of nine years, but children of eleven distinguish themselves by a larger proportion of excellent replies, marked 1. For the questions of medium difficulty, the three groups are well differentiated; the youngest have 26 silences, and 7 absurdities; the children of nine have 8 silences and only one absurdity; those of 11 years have only 1 silence and no absurdities. That shows us, let it be said in passing, that prolonged silence is not an indication of reflection, but of ignorance, an incapacity of replying. We had

Tables of Replies to Abstract Questions

QUESTIONS	REPLIES																	
	Children of 7 years						Children of 9 years						Children of 11 years					
	1	2	3	4	S	A	1	2	3	4	S	A	1	2	3	4	S	A
Difficult																		
20					2	3	1				7	2	1	3	2		4	
7					8	1	1		4		5		3	1	1	2	4	
14					5	5	1	1			8		4	4			2	
18		2			7	1	2				6	2	5	3			2	1
15		2	1		5	2	3	3			4		1	4	2		2	1
Total..........		4	1		27	12	8	4	4		30	4	14	15	5	2	14	2
Medium																		
19		1			4	2		6			1	1	3	2	6		1	
10				5	5		2	2	1	3	1		2	1	3	5		
5			3	4	2			3	7				3	3	3	2		
11				1	7	2	1	2	3	1	3		5	4	2			
8	2	1		5	3		4	1	4		2		5	1	3	2		
16	6				1	2	2	10					11					
6	3	1	4		1	1	1	4	1	3	1		10	3				
13		4	1		3		2	8					6	5				
Total..........	11	7	8	15	26	7	23	17	20	8	8	1	45	19	17	9	1	
Easy																		
12	1		8			1	3	1	5		1		6	1	3			1
4	4	6					2	7				1	7	3				
9	8	2					3	5	2				5	5	1			
3	6	2				2	8	2					10	2				
2	3	4	3				7	3					9	2				
1	10						9	1					11					
Total..........	32	14	11			3	33	19	7		1	1	48	13	4			1

felt a theoretical doubt in regard to this, which the reading of the table on page 124 dissipates.

The table also shows that absurdities are frequent with children of seven years (there were 19), rare with children of nine years (there

were 6), and exceptional with children of eleven years (2). We
have already noted this fact in connection with the repetition of
sentences. It now remains to arrange these data for the individual
diagnosis. Space is lacking for making all the necessary calculations, and we shall reduce our indications to the minimum. It is
sufficient to reproduce here for each age, two samples of their replies; one given by a normal child who represents the average
accuracy; the other given by a normal child whose reply was the
poorest. These series will serve as terms of provisional comparison when we shall have appreciated the type of reply of the subnormal; we shall see if it is above the average or below, or at least
below the least intelligent of the normals, for the given age.

Le ——— , eleven years, normal, gave the poorest replies. 3
absurdities, 5 silences, 4 replies marked 3 and 4.

1. One must sleep, 1.
2. One must get warm, 1.
3. One must hurry, 2.
5. One must rest, 1.
6. One must take the other, 1.
7. One must replace it, 2.
8. One must replace it, 4.
9. One must escape, 2.
10. One must pardon him, 1.
11. One must listen to it, 3.
12. One must work, 3.
13. For later, 2.
14. (Silence).
15. (Silence.)
16. One must work, 2.
17. (Silence.)
18. One must ask for it. A.
19. It happens that one knows nothing, 2.
20. (Silence.)
21. (Silence.)
22. Because an action without anger, one can forgive it, while an action
with anger one can forgive it, A.
23. Because when one commences it is not so hard as at the end, 3.
24. Because of the service which one has given is better one must keep
it, A.
25. One ought to try to make it all right, 3.

Debra ——— , eleven years, normal, gave replies of average value.
0 absurdities, 0 silence, 5 replies marked 3 and 4.

1. One must go to bed, 1.
2. One must cover one's self well so as to avoid taking cold, 1
3. One must hurry more than usual so as to arrive in time, 1.
4. One must take an umbrella, 1.
5. One must go on foot, 3.
6. One must wait for another train, 1.
7. One must pay for it, 2.
8. One must tell the teacher, 1.
9. One must try to get away, 2.
10. One must not denounce him, 3.
11. One must ask one's parents, 1.
12. One does nothing, and one cannot earn a living, 1.
13. With economy one has something to fall back on when one is old, 1.
14. One must consider it, 1.
15. One must not disobey; one must do it, 3.
16. One must work, 1.
17. One must not fight, 3.
18. One should say: I do not know that person well enough to give you any opinion about him, 1.
19. It happens that they fight, 3.
20. One must let him talk, 2.
21. Because one cannot believe what is said, but when one sees, one believes always, 1.
22. One pardons a bad act committed in anger, because right away he remembers he ought not to have done it, while a wrong act done without anger remains a long time in the hearts, 1.
23. It is better to continue a task begun because in another it will be more difficult to do it, 3.
24. Because one ought not to have done it. That is unkind, 1.
25. One must go into another country, 2.

Altm ——, child of nine years, gave very bad replies. 0 absurdities, 13 silences, 1 reply marked 3.

1. One must go to bed, 1.
2. One must cover up, 1.
3. One must hurry, 1.
4. One must shelter oneself, 2.
5. One must sit down, 2.
6. (Silence).
7. One must buy another, 2.
8. (Silence).
9. Go for the firemen, 1.
10. (Silence).
11. (Silence).
12. One knows nothing, 1.
13. Without that one could not live, 2.
14. (Silence).

15. (Silence).
16. One must work, 1.
17. (Silence).
18. (Silence).
19. They fight, 3.
20. (Silence).
21. (Silence).
22. (Silence).
23. (Silence).
24. (Silence).
25. One should ask pardon, 1.

Barr ——, nine years, gave replies of average value.   0 absurdities, 7 silences, 5 replies marked 3 and 4.

1. One undresses and goes to bed, 1.
2. One must dress up warm, 1.
3. One must hurry all the way, 1.
4. One must find shelter, one must stay at the school so as not to get wet, 2.
5. One must rest on a bench, 2.
6. One must wait and take another train, 1.
7. One must replace it, 2.
8. One must tell the teacher, 1.
9. One must get away so as not to get burned, 2.
10. One must not give him back what he did to us so as not to do evil, 4.
11. One must listen to it, 3.
12. One soon becomes the last of one's class, 3.
13. Because when one is older one cannot work, and will have nothing to live on, 1.
14. (Silence).
15. One must say it, 2.
16. One must work, ·1.
17. One must be reconciled with them, 1.
18. They both get angry, 3.
19. (Silence).
20. (Silence).
21. (Silence).
22. (Silence).
23. (Silence).
24. (Silence).
25. One must correct it, 3.

Another indication may be helpful.   The average number of absurdities among children of 11 years (for the above 25 questions) is 0.5; the maximum number is 2.

For children of nine years, the average number is 1 and the maximum number is 3.

For children of seven years, the average number needs correction; it would be 20, if one admitted in the calculation two children, rather extraordinary, who committed a great many absurdities. If they are eliminated, there are only 6, which makes a trifle less than one absurdity for each pupil, with a maximum of 2. The number of silences varies equally. It is 2 on an average at eleven years with a maximum of 5. It is 5 on an average at nine years, with a maximum of 12. It is 6.5 on an average at seven years, with a maximum of 11.

Tables of Replies to Abstract Questions

	SILENCES		ABSURDITIES	
	Average number	Maximum number	Average number	Maximum number
Seven years..........	6.5	11	1*	2
Nine years............	5.0	12	1	3
Eleven years.........	2.0	5	0.5	2

* This is a corrected average be it remembered.

Search for rhymes. A few words only upon this test, which we tried with only five children of seven years, five of nine and five of eleven years. At seven years, no one can find a word to rhyme "obéissance" and the words they find after much pains have no bearing upon the questions. At nine years they understand better, and after a minute's search, they can find at least one rhyme, sometimes two, three or four. At eleven years, a rather larger number is found.

Abstract definitions. Still another incomplete attempt upon five children of each age. At least we have been able to prove that even at twelve years, a normal cannot express the difference between certain abstract terms. In his desire to give some sort of a reply he says absurdities. Here are some examples, which will suffice to enlighten us, mixed with certain attempts which contain a glimpse of a correct idea. Deron ——, Esteem and affection. Esteem when one speaks well of someone who is not there, and affection, is to love some one. Fleur ——, Weariness and sadness. In sadness, one despairs, but in weariness, one wishes amusement. That distinction is not at all bad. Esteem someone, one almost loves them, and in affection one loves them. Halli ——, Whe

one esteems someone, one loves them.   When one has affection,
one loves also.   Bari ——, Esteem is love; affection one says one
loves.

/   *Combination of three words in the same sentence.* Still another
test which lack of time has not permitted us to perfect.   It is
only at twelve years that we note the first attempts, and they are
very imperfect.   Out of five children there were only three who
were able in two minutes of work to bring out the following sentences.   Halli ——, Paris is a large city where there are gutters;
and where the people have little fortune.

Fleur ——, In Paris, by jumping a *gutter*, I found a little fortune.

Bari ——, In the city of *Paris*, there are gutters, where one can
find his *fortune*.

Remember that no one told them how to go to work.   If a
model sentence had been given, doubtless they could have passed
the test.

Verbal blanks to be filled.   Last test which was tried on only five
children of seven, five of nine, and five of twelve years.   The results were analogous to those which were obtained with abstract
questions.   It is therefore useless to describe them here, as that
would be mere repetition.   But for the examination of a particular
child, these repetitions are very useful; that which is wearisome
in a description renders great service in practice.

We have now established certain demarcations which permit us
to recognize the normal development of intelligence among children, and above all to know when a child who is suspected of retardation, appears really backward as compared with children of
his own age.

We shall not here describe the process to follow for each comparison; we can do it more successfully in the next section, where we
speak of backward children.

Enough of theory, let it give place now to the demonstration.[11]

II. Institution Cases

Before showing how the psychological method permits us to
recognize and in a certain way to classify backward children in the
schools, we wish to show what help it offers to doctors in an institution.   The diagnosis of intellectual inferiority is made in sub-

[11] See page 64.

*Instit.
Cases
Tested 30.*

stantially the same manner in the school as in the institution; only the children in institutions are in general more seriously affected than those in schools; the true idiots are reserved for the institutions as we believe that they will rarely be admitted into a school. Therefore the tests to be submitted to children in an institution are slightly different from those to be used in schools.

In the institution as in the school, two questions are to be solved; first, is the child inferior in intelligence? Second, to what degree is he inferior to the normal?

The first of these questions is most important for the teacher, who must above everything else become expert in making the distinction between normal and subnormal, an extremely delicate task, because many of the morons whom it will be interesting to recognize, closely approach normality. This distinction once made, the operation is almost finished, because the school serves only to conceal the morons. The attention of the clinician is differently directed. The important question for him is not so much whether the child presented to him is normal or subnormal; ordinarily this question is, as it were, settled in advance because of the gravity of the mental defect of the subject. Even parents, or an attendant, would be capable of recognizing that an idiot or an imbecile is not normal; at least this is true in most cases.[12]

What the physician seeks with the greatest care is the differential diagnosis of idiot, imbecile and moron.

Consequently in the following pages we shall specially occupy ourselves in classifying the children in one of these three subdivisions; we shall hope to demonstrate that the application of the psychological method to subnormals in an institution, gives results both rapid and exact.

The children of whom we are about to speak were all examined in the Salpêtrière under the direction of Dr. Voisin, during the months of February and March, 1905. Dr. Voisin was good enough to open his establishment to us, with a liberality and disinterestedness which could only be equalled by his attachment for the inmates of the Salpêtrière, whom he calls with an eloquent

---

[12] There are some exceptions to this rule. It is easy to imagine that some parents, wishing to rid themselves of the care and expense of the education of the child, should seek to have him admitted although normal to the special care for backward children. It is the business of the doctor to know whether or not the child presented to him is normal.

simplicity, "his children." We found the same welcome from Madame Meusy, who directs the school connected with the establishment; she was present at all of our experiments, aiding us by her knowledge of the children, showing always toward them that sweetness, that sensibility without sentimentality which makes her such a sympathetic teacher.

Nearly all of the children were examined in her office. Several, however, belonging to the lowest grades, were seen in the halls where they habitually stay. All the others came to us one by one. Doubtless this is not a faultless clinical method. It would often be interesting to observe the child in the very center where he lives; and in modifying his external surroundings as little as possible, his spontaneity would best display itself. But after all, it is not this that we are looking for; the individual method, freed from all accidental outside distraction, is practically indispensable for a minutely accurate mental analysis. The child when isolated has more timidity and reserve. But on the other hand one obtains a more sustained attention. The office of Madame Meusy was for all these children a familiar place, which they seldom left without a bonbon. Each child was brought by a teacher, or by an attendant with whom the child was familiar. Since Madame Meusy was always present the child remained in familiar territory. Let us note, by the way, that the silence was only relative, because of the proximity of the class room. For certain tests requiring concentrated attention, like that of the repetition of six figures, this might sometimes be a cause of trouble, but in other cases our tests leave the child so little to himself that this fact did not prove a serious inconvenience.

One of us questioned and the other wrote the replies, or noted the attitude, the play of the countenance of the child who was being questioned. The examination took on, by the way, more the air of a game conducted without dry formulas, and the child was always encouraged. It goes without saying that his replies were never ridiculed no matter how incorrect they were; he was given the credit of his willingness to try. For any one who knows these poor beings and realizes to what degree they open out when praised and on the contrary, how quickly they withdraw within themselves at the least reproof, there is no doubt that this indulgent attitude is indispensable to obtain on their part even a small output of effort. With a few exceptions, of which we shall speak as we go along, all have lent themselves with docility, some even with good grace to our investigations. Among some fifty children examined, only one or two offered any obstacle which came from the disposition, that is to say, from ill-will and not from the lack of intelligence; this small number is an important fact; it proves without question that our methods of examination, even though they require the active coöperation of the subject, are nevertheless practically possible. What examination, by the way, would be able to dispense with the coöperation of the one who is its subject? Even a physical examination is rendered impracticable by cries and incessant movements. A *priori* it was to be expected that even more difficulties would present themselves in psychological investigations. Such has not been the case. Subnormal children have submitted themselves willingly to these investigations and those cases of opposition which we did encounter were not significant for we have met and noted similar ones among normal school children. Naturally when such difficulties present themselves, one cannot draw conclusions from a single sitting; one should return at a more favorable moment. But the rarity of these occurrences leaves no doubt that they can be overcome.

In examining the replies of subnormal children of the Salpê- trière, it will be seen that they permit us to separate our subjects into distinct groups and subgroups.[13] But what significance shall we attribute to these? They are only schematic divisions and probably susceptible to further rearrangement. It must not be considered that as they stand we feel they completely delimit moronity, imbecility, and idiocy. Even while taking account only of the development of the intellectual faculties properly so- called and limiting ourselves to a study of the degree of intelligence, from the very first one meets many difficulties, among the principal of which is the following. Here is a child of twelve years, who does not know how to apply to the objects which he sees the words which he hears and which he pronounces; the majority of children of two and three years can already do this; he presents therefore a retardation of ten years. Then here is another child

[13] In spite of the number of children examined our work takes into account only about thirty, as we have been able to use only those upon whom we have made a sufficient number of tests and we did not know this until the work was finished. The grades of others are somewhat uncertain and it will be necessary to test them again.

of the same degree of intelligence who is four years old; he is only
two years behind children of his own age.   Are we not justified
in taking into account this enormous difference of age?   Would it
be right to say that these two children, because they have the same
intellectual level, both belong to the same category, and that the
younger is an idiot in the same way as the older?   Are we not going
to see on the contrary, that the child of four years will later make
progress, and soon no longer merit to be classed with the other,
change his group, and rise to imbecility?

"It will therefore be necessary to introduce two factors: the intellectual level and the age of the subject.   Only, to do this, many
questions must be settled whose solution is today completely in
suspense.   The psychological development of the normal child
had hardly been touched upon; the present work contains the first
attempt in this regard." We have at least seen which tests were
possible at the different ages, and which on the contrary could not
be determined upon. (Nothing as yet has been attempted for the
subnormal states and the difficulty is very great." As to what concerns school children it is possible to determine this development
of the intellectual faculties according to age, by the average results obtained with different groups, chosen from the same social
condition, the same educational environment.   One of the factors,
that of mental capacity—is quite constant.   For subnormals similar to those of the Salpêtrière similar averages would be of no
value, because subnormals differ too much among themselves to
permit of substituting one for the other in taking averages. "It
would be necessary to follow individually very many subjects in
their development, to see if the states of intellectual inferiority
are caused by arrested development, or by very slow evolution
continued irregularly or intermittently, or to see if some essential
faculties could increase while others remained stationary or un-
awakened.   It would be impossible, before these facts are ascertained, to compare these subjects with normal children age for age
year for year, detail for detail." No doubt it is possible—perhaps
even probable—that a child who at five years has scarcely the
intellectual level of a child of two, will be the same at ten or fifteen
years.   Without doubt one can suppose that the cerebral defects
which have thus far prevented the acquisition of ordinary ideas,
would remain a definite obstacle.   But we have no right, without
the facts, to affirm this.   And no actual test can tell us, moreover,

whether an idiot is or is not capable of improvement and to just what point.[14]

It is a pity that the fundamental questions of psycholgeny, so easy to elucidate in institutions where the same defective children are retained ten and twenty years, have never yet been studied except in vague statistics!

All these children have been classified entirely without regard to age. We have supposed, whatever their age, that they have attained their entire development; we have taken into consideration only their actual state, the day on which we saw them, as though it were a fixed thing, and as though we had to take no account of the age they have attained, nor if later they might develop further. But under all these reservations, and although in a manner somewhat arbitrary, relative and partial, it still seems that, the intellectual development being supposed finished, one can propose from this unique point of view to establish categories among them.

How many principal categories must be formulated? *A priori*

[14] A single indication quite confusing seems to come out of a work which we have just finished upon the pedagogical results of the work of M. Bourneville at the Bicêtre. Our learned colleague put at our disposal the records of the years, 1900, '02, '03, '04, containing notes on the dismissals that occurred in his service. In working up these results into tables we arrived at a few interesting points. There is no doubt some optimism in the statements published by M. Bourneville. He does not consider that any boy under his care shows deterioration and the lowest mark that he gives a boy is that of "même état" (no change). He records nothing but conditions of "même état" and conditions of improvement which surprises those a little who know that epilepsy with repeated attacks almost surely brings mental deterioration and there is a great deal of epilepsy at the Bicêtre. This medical optimism appears also in a large number of cases of improvement which are noted among subjects who become adults or are transferred to other institutions. These cannot, however, be more than slight improvements and without social significance since most of the subjects in question are bound to remain confined. Granted that leniency was exercised in counting up the cases, it is of greater significance to acknowledge that the number of socalled improved idiots who are pointed out to us is extremely small; most of them remain unimproved. Here are the proportions. Improved idiots 24; unimproved 52. But on the other hand, notwithstanding the length of time and the evident leniency of the doctor in charge, we are compelled to acknowledge a total absence of improvement among two-thirds of the idiots. It is fair to conclude that the intellectual condition of the idiot does not tend to improve. But we repeat—data of this kind are too vague to become authoritative in science.

it would seem that there is no good reason to form one number of
categories any more than another, and the determination of these
numbers, whatever they be, is open to criticism in about the same
manner and for the same reason that one can criticize the physicist,
who has fixed the number of the colors of the spectrum at seven,
when one could describe ten colors or twenty.   In the same way
one could describe five or ten different degrees or more, of intellectual inferiority.   Every continued series permits an infinite
number of divisions.   But for practical use it becomes necessary
to restrict the number; moreover in medical language the three
terms, idiot, imbecile, and moron, are already in use (refer to
footnote on moron, p. 41); it would be very difficult not only
to reject this classification, but even to simplify it by the suppres-
sion of one of the terms, or to complicate it by the introduction of
a new term.   It is therefore simply for reasons of convenience
that we accept a triplicate division of inferior intelligence.   It
remains to be determined where we shall place our limits separating idiot from imbecile, imbecile from moron, and lastly moron
from normal.   We reserve the term idiot for subjects without a
vocabulary.   We do not wish to say by that, that they do not
pronounce certain words, but they are incapable of passing from
the object to the word, or even from the word to the object.   One
of the best tests upon which to form a judgment, is to ask them to
designate in a picture the objects which one names for them.   The
test is so much the more to be recommended because it has for the
normal child the great attraction of curiosity.   There is also a
great advantage in asking him to point out the objects corresponding to the words which are said to him, rather than to make
him name the objects which he himself sees, because of the defects
of pronunciation which often prevent him from being understood.
This is a test that normal children pass between two and three
years.   Before that, the child has no relations, by language, with
those who surround him.   To reserve the name of idiocy to those
who persist in that state of social isolation is in reality to cling to
the strict etymological sense of the word, for the word *idiot*,
properly speaking means *alone, isolated.*
    We regret that there is no distinction equally precise between
imbecile and moron.   Nevertheless it has seemed to us that, to be
able to appreciate and express a difference existing between two
familiar objects, to compare weights, to find rhymes, and when

asked to repeat six figures, not to repeat a series at random or to say an absurdity—that is to say, anything which requires of the subject, a precise comprehension of what is asked of him and a little judgment—would never accord itself with a state of imbecility. It is therefore these tests which will serve as limits.

Lastly we have noticed that children of twelve years can mostly reply to abstract questions. We limit provisionally mental defect at this point. A moron shows himself by his inability to handle verbal abstractions; he does not understand them sufficiently to reply satisfactorily.

These three groups are not of homogeneous composition and one has often experienced the necessity of subdividing them. We shall therefore push the analysis that far but without inventing new terms. It would seem proper, in order to distinguish each group, to precede the generic name by an adjective designating the subdivision, that is to say, the species. Unfortunately those proposed up to the present time are not suitable. The terms complete idiocy and profound idiocy have been used; but this distinction is lacking in immediate clarity, because one cannot see which is more serious for an idiot to be complete or to be profound. Somewhat clearer terms, complete and incomplete, developed by negation give the insufficient number of two degrees. We prefer to risk some more expressive terms, examples of which will be found farther on.

We shall now pass in review successively, these three different groups of children. We shall sometimes precede the record of the tests given to each child by certain clinical notes. But the reader will be so good as to remember, that we are not giving here complete, or even psychological observations, but simply fragments chosen with the view of illustrating a method. We present nothing but incomplete groups.

IDIOTS

Without Use of Language

In the first group, we must note that the absence of language on the part of the child places the experimenter in a rather difficult situation. The means of producing psychological reaction is necessarily more vague, more undetermined. The technique of each test is less precise; above all else the replies, consisting in gestures, in attitudes, and in acts, require more interpretation. Here especially can be seen how necessary is the word in order to bring out the thought.

We call to mind that the tests which constitute this group are the following: reaction to light and to sound; prehension after tactile excitation; prehension after visual perception; distinction between what is food and what is not; imitations of movements and execution of simple orders through word and mimicry.

All these tests are accomplished by children of two or three years. The average chronological age of the subnormals studied by us and which we place in this group, is about ten years with a variation of seven to twelve. The least retardation is therefore of five years, and consequently enormous.

According to the tests accomplished, it is possible to distinguish among these children four subgroups which seem to correspond equally to the degrees of intelligence.

To find analogies among normals for the several extreme cases which we are going to present, it would be necessary to visit infant hospitals or even to study the child when only a few days old. There are indeed among subnormals whom we have studied, beings eight or ten years old, whose intelligence does not exceed that of a child of eight days.

We shall therefore indicate our degrees, with the qualifications which we consider the most appropriate.

1. Vegetative idiot. We thus name those who show no manifestation of ideas of relationships. We have so far observed none of this type.

2. Idiot with visual coördination. This is the one that looks at an object, follows it with his eyes. One could also have the idiot who hears, smells, etc. We therefore use here the reaction to light and sound.

We have found only one subject whose intellectual manifestations sought for in this manner, are limited to habitual reaction to light and sound.

Gro. is a child of twelve. She has two club feet and cannot move her lower limbs, she holds one hand in the other, the fingers scratching the palms without ceasing, and at the same time she gnaws continuously the back of her right hand.

Let us now see what strictly has to bear upon our examination. When the bell is rung behind her head, no reaction can be noted.

If one passes the hand rapidly before her eyes, she blinks with her eyelids; one can even notice at intervals a short, spontaneous look. She sees the lighted match before her and turns her eyes to follow it; but still it is only for a short time and her attention has little persistence. There is no attempt at prehension either when an object is presented to her or when it is placed in her hand.

Thus there is in this case a single intellectual manifestation, a fugitive attention to something which glitters; without doubt this expression, fugitive attention, remains vague, but its application to a precise fact does not permit us, so it seems, to deceive ourselves upon the conditions under which its use could be authorized.

Finally let us notice the fact that Gro —— reacts only to light and not to sound. Perhaps it would be wise under these circumstances, to still subdivide this first degree, but we have not enough facts to establish this.

3. Idiot with prehension. This is the one who can perform an act of prehension. There are here two degrees. The first is prehension after tactile excitation.

This group is characterized by an acquisition beyond that of the preceding group—namely, the power to seize an object when it comes in contact with the hand. We have found only one child whose ability was limited to this additional test.

Rich —— is a child of seven years. She sucks her thumb, shakes her head, grasps her arm and carries it to her mouth; all these movements indicate that she is not, properly speaking, paralyzed; nevertheless she does not walk.

Let us see how she conducts herself with our tests.

She starts and laughs when we ring a bell behind her ear, but does not turn her head to look.

She follows a lighted match with her eyes.

If an object is presented to her, she does not seem to know how to direct her arms to take it so long as she is guided by sight only; she may strike it accidently; *more frequently she seizes it, as it were by reflex only,* when the thing is placed in her hands.

She carries a piece of wood to her mouth just as naturally as a bonbon.

These are the only tests that can be given her. Her rank is clearly indicated to us as in the third group. Prehension which does not exist in the preceding case is here clearly realized. There is here an act which constitutes a sharp distinction between the two subjects, and whose realization constitutes a progress. We may call Rich —— *an idiot with incomplete prehension.*

Then comes a more intelligent prehension, more spontaneous, which is provoked by visual perception of an object. Two children were found belonging to this degree, and are consequently *idiots with complete prehension.*

Notice first the tests made with Meuh ——, a child of nine years, microcephalic, cross-eyed, with no control over the excretions.

She turns her head when a bell is rung behind her; her eyes follow a lighted match; *she stretches out her hand to take an object offered her,* but these movements are not natural. Her hand seems to grope towards the object, the other does not aid it, prehension is defective; the hand does not know how to let go.

She gluttonously puts the whole piece of chocolate into her mouth at once and adds the wood as though there were no difference between the two.

And that is all—no response to our greeting, etc.

Now see the other idiot.

Lafre —— is eight or nine years old, and seems more active than the preceding children; she walks, laughs, kisses, and knows the persons whom she sees, but she is constantly in motion, and her attention is difficult to fix.

Here is the result of our examination.

She turns her head to try to see the bell that has been rung. She takes or rejects or throws, carries to her mouth or not, whatever is presented to her without examination, even without looking at it, and consequently not because it is wood, cork, sugar or chocolate but simply as the notion takes her. Her attendant says she will eat indiscriminately pebbles or rags. She has, while being examined, curious gestures in this respect; she often asks with her mouth open as another child would hold out her hand. She takes nothing, however, when numerous objects are presented to her in a box.

Lafre —— is one of the children who showed some ill-will in submitting to the examination.

We do not know whether or not we should classify her in this inferior degree of intelligence. Her indifference to food might come from a defect of the sense of taste, as well as from a lack of the small amount of intelligence necessary to make this distinction. Her gustatory sensibility needs to be investigated.

4. *Idiot with recognition of food.* We have examined three subjects whom we place in this group.

Pich —— will be ten in July. She has an almost incessant twitching of the eyelids, and rhythmic movements of the arms as for beating the tambourine, which movements are momentarily suspended when her attention is fixed.

She turns her head when keys are shaken behind her.

She looks at a handkerchief when shaken before her eyes.

If a bonbon is handed to her she eats it; a piece of money she puts in her mouth; but paper she shakes, unfolds it a little and leaves it on the table. Does she begin or not to see what is food? If a piece of chocolate is given her wrapped in paper, she makes an attempt to unfold it. She will not, however, take anything unless it is given her, not even if it is laid on the table. She also obeys the order to come, given by gesture, and when a metal box containing a penny is shaken before her, she seems at first a little frightened, then takes the box and shakes it herself after repeated example, but it amuses her little and she quickly leaves it. She will not pick up an object nor close her eyes when ordered.

This is an instructive observation as is every fault committed. The child has not been studied sufficiently. The test which will indicate her place exactly has not been the object of sufficient investigation. It would be necessary to go over and over until there was no longer any doubt as to the reply. The child profits in consequence from a little indulgence. It is, however, not at all doubtful that she shows a certain progress over the preceding cases.

Marc —— will be nine in August. She has the habit of frequently raising with her index finger the lobules of her ears. She walks, runs, descends stairs easily, mounts them less easily; she caresses, rubs her head against the person who notices her for a moment, or else bites her own hand or her apron without its being possible to recognize a motive for these manifestations of affection or anger.

She often smells what is handed to her before carrying it to her mouth (this is an illustration of the control of one sense by another), and permits less easily the object to be withdrawn if it is chocolate.

She takes spontaneously from the table some cakes which she sees there. This new extension of prehension seems to be associated with a knowledge of the value of things, since we here meet it for the first time. She obeys gestures, but imitates little and seems indolent; if chocolate is given her wrapped in paper she smells it and lets it fall; the paper is then removed and she is made to taste the chocolate, after which it is again wrapped before her eyes and given her. She does not take off the paper but gives it back, as if to ask that it be given her and hunts in the hands; she seems interested and after several demonstrations, ends by opening the paper.

Neither of these children indicates any part of the body or clothing, or any object named to them, and does not even look at a picture.

These two children have therefore knowledge of food. Without doubt the difference between that which can be eaten and that which cannot be eaten is still obscure. It seems, nevertheless, very certain that they make the distinction. It can be seen by what slight stages one advances little by little. We shall soon see, on the contrary, the range of knowledge suddenly enlarge, the moment language appears.

5. An idiot with the power of imitation of gestures. We call by this name the idiot who can say, "good day," who understands gestures, imitates them, can reply to a smile, makes simple imi-

Schematic Table of the Intellectual Development of a Group of Idiot Children

	GRO.	RICH.	MEIT.	LAFR.	PITCH.	MAN.	DEBR.
7. Indicating and naming of certain objects or pictures. Definition of objects by use.......					−	−	−
6. Indicating parts of the body.................					−	−	−
5. Distinction between that which is and is not food. Examination, refusal to give it back.				−	+	+	+
Imitation of movements, and execution of simple orders by word or mimicry..........		−	−	−	+	+	∓
4. Prehension after visual perception...........		−	+	+			
3. Prehension by tactile excitation.............	−	+					
2. Reaction to light and sound.................	+	+	+	+			
1. Nothing.......................................							
	1	2	3	4			

tations, and executes elementary orders, such as to come, to sit, etc.

It is still a question whether this degree of idiocy is distinct from that of the knowledge of food. Constantly we have found the two aptitudes united; there is here a point to be decided and new observations to be made.

Therefore up to this point, there is no manifestation of language. All these children of whom we have spoken are indeed idiots.

We summarize in the foregoing table what we have already explained. It will again be seen how each child has his place marked in a given group by the fact that he passes the test of the preceding group—while he fails in those which follow.

IMBECILES

From the moment language appears, the aid which it brings to the child is enormous. One is now at the level of children of two or three years, perhaps even younger, aged only twelve or fifteen months. We will give later more precise information. We distinguish among imbeciles the following degrees.

Imbecile with faculty of naming.
Imbecile with faculty of comparison.
Imbecile with faculty of repeating a sentence.
It is evident that these terms are brief and need explanation.

1. Imbecile with faculty of naming

This is one who can reply to the question: "What is the name of such and such a thing?"

Here is an example of transition which seems to belong rather to idiocy.

Debr —— epileptic, ten years old, can imitate. Quickly takes what is handed her, examines the object and as soon as she finds it is chocolate, kisses whoever gave it to her, and tries to run away. She unwraps the chocolate quite cleverly from the paper.

When commanded she picks up, starts to hunt, but only with a relative docility; she does not imitate all the simple movements that one tries to get her to reproduce by executing them before her; simply claps her hands but does not close her eyes when commanded.

She does not show any part of her body nor of her garments when told to do so, takes haphazard any object from among different ones on the table when asked to find a certain one, gives, for example, a cup when asked to do so, but gives it again when asked for a thimble, even though this is also on the table at her disposal, etc. Lastly, she does not look at the pictures in an album when shown, simply moistens her fingers and tries to turn the page. Her attention seems constantly distracted, she does not remain in one place, occupies herself with everything she sees about her. In any case she does not seem to succeed in establishing the relation between objects and their names. She does not therefore pass the fourth degree although her response to the test is better than the preceding.

Now we come to true imbeciles with the faculty of naming. We do not think it worth while to make distinctions, as to whether they name and designate real objects and the parts of their bodies, or, going further, name and designate objects in a picture.

Gava —— sixteen years old, microcephalic, cannot blow her nose, drivels and has no control of the excretions. She pronounces only inarticulate cries except the words "mamma" and "bonbon" which can be understood, but she knows her caretaker, a comrade whom she seems to prefer, and is mostly affectionate and smiling.

She successfully passes the first degree, executes commands that refer to simple acts; throws a kiss, comes when she is called, picks up and gives, catches a ball which is thrown to her, takes an object to another person. She imitates a little, claps her hands, crosses her arms, puts them to her head; does not, however, close her eyes when commanded. She shows, however, when asked, her head, her ears, her nose, her apron, her shoes (only however, by lifting her feet), her tongue, her eyes. But she does not pay attention, does not even look at the group of objects from among which she is asked to choose one, nor the pictures in which she is asked to designate such or such a part; she seems timid and withdraws her hand.

She is characterized by the development of her powers of imitation, simple orders accomplished, and above all the designation of certain parts of her body, that is to say, the exact application of a certain number of words heard to definite things.

Forest —— is also of the same degree. She is a child very slow, who seemingly has great trouble in performing any movement whatever. She only recognizes the thimble among the objects shown but she designates exactly different parts of her body and clothing. She therefore belongs with the preceding.

With Pige ——, Amy ——, Trompe ——, another round of the ladder is mounted. Pige —— is nearly twelve. She is strabismic and has no control of the excretions. She articulates badly but has, nevertheless, several words at her command. She unwraps very well a paper in which some one has enveloped before her eyes a bonbon. She imitates well, shakes the box with a penny in it and carries it to her ear to hear better, saying "joujou." She claps her hands, puts her hands upon her hips, turns her arms, dances and even with a certain development when once set going; she picks up objects, etc. She will hold her eyes shut for quite a long time but on condition however that the order is frequently repeated.

Trompe —— born in November, 1895, microcephalic and strabismic, gives her name "Byseter." She recognizes at sight a piece of wood offered her and only hesitates when a brown piece the color of chocolate is proffered, smiles when she sees it, takes it and prepares to eat it, but smells it and declares it is a "plumeau;" when chocolate is given her she takes it and runs off crying "thanks." She resists and grows angry if one tries to take it from her, and will even steal it from the table laughing, blushing and triumphant if she has been able to seize it. She picks up, imitates movements, closes her eyes when ordered, but does not keep them closed.

Amy —— was born in October, 1890. She is therefore nearly fifteen years old. She runs but does not close her eyes at command, puts her finger on one of them, and spontaneously says while pointing to it, "The clock," which indicates at once her lack of attention. The other tests which these children can accomplish are the following:

1. Indication of the parts of the body. Pige —— shows her nose, her ear, her forehead, her hair. Trompe —— the same, and in addition her hands, her feet, her eyes, her thumb. Amy —— shows her hands, ears, etc., but her little finger instead of her thumb.

As to the distinction between the right and left side, the difficulty seems to surpass by far that of the preceding tests. Trompe —— replies just as it happens, sometimes one, sometimes the other. Amy —— is equally unreliable.

2. Indication and naming of objects. Pige —— shows without error cup, button, cork, candle and ribbon. Names a watch "tic-tac," a chapeau, "po," ruler, "ru." Thompe —— names the same objects by other inventions of his own.

Amy —— often designates haphazard, she gives for example no matter what when one asks for a cup, a little flask for a box of matches, a nail for a crayon, nevertheless she knows this, also the bell, the thimble, the ribbon. Notice also that she often points out an object—"there!" before anyone has asked her anything; so if anyone asks her to show the "nitchevo" she will point out without hesitation, a bottle, and for the "patapoum," the cup.

She names the thimble, button, thread, does not name a piece of chalk and finally names a feather "plumier" (duster), a necklace "a pearl" and gives "machin" for a whistle and a nail.

3. Indicating parts of a picture which are named. Pige —— points out certain things, the "dada," "mama," the doll, but she goes fast, often points out haphazard, the duster for the broom, the coffee-pot for the plates, etc. Finally when we say to her, "show the mama" she designates another object; and the table, she touches the table where we are working.

Trompe —— points out the table, the mama, the cat, the big sister, the doll, the football, etc. Her manner of proceeding is singular enough. She sticks the finger rapidly upon an object before the question has been entirely formulated. Sometimes however she hunts, for example, the boquet, and ends by discovering it or else she makes a mistake. She may show the duster for the broom, the soup bowl for the coffee-mill. "Where is the patapoum?" she laughs and shows the broom; the "nitchevo?" she points out anything no matter what, but always points out something.

Amy —— shows the table, the big sister, after having first designated her for the mama, the bouquet after a like error but she knows the window, and shows the stool for the broom, etc., then she tries to turn the page; she has but little power of attention.

4. Naming of objects in a picture. Pige —— names in a picture, a horse, bird, dog, girl (names are all more or less deformed). She imitates more or less well, the cries of a cat, dog, little bird, but not of a sheep. But when asked what the gentleman, holding a cane, has in his hand she replies "he holds a cake." Amy ——

names the "lady," etc.   She knows the use of objects a little.   A pencil, for example is "to write."

However primitive may be these tests which we have just passed in review, they are nevertheless the first experiments properly so called.   This is an important fact.   It even shows, on the part of the subject who submits to them, a faculty of adaptation already quite developed.   In the previous cases where it was a question only of prehension and imitation, we have scarcely been able to do more than choose from among the habitual conditions of their ordinary life those conditions from which we could draw the conclusions which we sought, and to which we were reduced from lack of method.   Now, on the contrary, we begin to obtain from the child a certain sort of response made with the direct intention of replying.

The examples which we have given permit other remarks.   We sometimes ask the child where in the picture such and such imaginary objects are to be found.   And always something was shown us.   This is the result of an extreme suggestibility.   But why? The explanation is to be found in the habit so common among them of replying at random, and also in their evident satisfaction in any kind of a reply.   It is as though the quality of fitness escapes them. Without doubt they learn from experience but without grasping its whole significance.   Therefore they are always proud of the result whatever it be.   We have not found a single one who replies, "I do not know."

We may also note that if several objects are recognized and named, nevertheless the language is often defective; the word employed is a childish one and not the proper term; moreover there is scarcely an unfamiliar object which does not represent an insurmountable difficulty.   The vocabulary thus shows itself to be extremely limited.

2. Imbecile with faculty of comparison.[15]   This is one who can compare two lines or two weights; who can also repeat three figures, but can go no further.

We found five children belonging to this class: Ruz——, Temple ——, Bouth ——, Bona ——, Delai.

Ruz — said "Good day."   Her replies are lively.   She can give some information about her family but very childish.   Her sister is named Nini.

[15] We believe, without being certain, that there exists an intermediate degree, that of imbeciles with faculty of comprehension.

What does your father do? "He works—At what? "He sews." And
your mother? "She walks." Temple —— born in 1894 has been in the
institution since 1897. She says "Good day," gives her name and can also
give the name and address of her parents. She is serious, attentive and
docile; for example, she held her eyes closed for $1\frac{3}{4}$ minutes even though
without warning a bell was rung behind her ear. Bouth —— born the 14th
of September, 1897, says "Good day," gives her name, but says indiffer-
ently she is twenty or twelve years old, but her replies are slow and her
language indistinct. Bona —— is a child of twelve, somewhat sleepy
and slow; she is beginning to read. Delai —— is ten years old.

We shall pass rapidly over the tests, already accomplished by
the preceding children and consequently easy for these. Temple ——, Ruz ——, Bouth ——, show correctly the different parts
of the body, but Temple alone seems to distinguish her right from
her left hand; the others do not seem to attribute any sense to
these words, because they sometimes show both sides at once
when asked for one or the other.

Naming of objects seems equally easy with the eyes closed, the
objects consequently being identified only by feeling. Without
doubt Bouth —— knows neither a cork nor a candle, Ruz —— by
feeling mistook a paint brush for a pencil. Temple however
gave proof of more knowledge, and knows "safety-pin", "two
sous." If one objects to this last reply by saying that only one
is there, she persists in her opinion saying, "that makes two
sous—one big one." It is not difficult however, to bring out a
certain curious confusion of words "code" for "cord"—(Ruz ——)
"soufflet" (box on the ear) for "sifflet" (whistle). Le Temple in
pointing out the freckles on her cheeks, called them "taches de
doucer" (sweetness) for "taches de *rousseur*" (brown, the French
expression for freckles).

Definitions by use are here still very poor, matches are to "light
the candle"; a cork, "to place near a bottle"—a nail, "to hang
things on."

In the picture, the advertisement, the sky and the lamp-
lighter, puzzle her still; the advertisement is "a book, a copy book;"
the sky is "water" and as for the lamp-lighter "he goes up the
ladder" or "makes smoke," or finally "lights a candle."

The mental inferiority revealed by the replies to "patapoum"
and "nitchevo" is a little less. Ruz—— does not hesitate to indicate at random. Bouth —— shows something for the first, but
hunts vainly for the second with her finger. Temple says at first,
"I do not know" but shows a stool, and replies for the other—

"Le Nit — I do not see it." In spite of all defects, one feels
at every step an advance over the children of preceding groups.

There are two tests, characteristic of the group, which show
the difference more clearly. One of them consists in indicating
the longer of two unequal lines, the other the immediate repetition of three figures that have been repeated to the child.

The children of the preceding group could not pass the test
of comparison of lines. Pige —— always showed both lines
when it was necessary to point out the longer, the one on the
left. Trompe —— pointed to the one on the right and with the
remainder of the lines was often wrong. Amy —— showed them
both. On the contrary Temple —— generally replied without
hesitation, with an approving nod of her head after each designation, and made no mistake even when asked several times. Bona
——, Delai —— recognized at once the longer lines, Ruz ——,
Bouth —— the same. When there was a catch, none of the
children noticed it. Bouth —— the first, had nevertheless quite
a long period of hesitation. But there is in the question such a
strong suggestion that it dominated all appreciation.

The differences of length between the lines varied greatly,
sometimes being strikingly apparent and again scarcely perceptible. We had thought *a priori* that that which seemed difficult to us would be impossible for these children. The result
obtained was contrary to all expectation. From the moment
they could do the test, they did it perfectly, showing a correctness
of glance that was surprising. To speak correctly, their inferiority was not due to less sensorial acuteness but to less intellectual
acuteness; without doubt it is the act of comparing, a very special
function of the mind, which differentiates the preceding group
from this special group of children.

Amy —— could scarcely repeat two figures. Ruz —— gets
three, but with difficulty.

FIGURES GIVEN	FIGURES REPEATED
2, 8, 7	7
3, 6, 5	7
1, 2, 9	1
6, 1, 4	6, 1, 4
2, 7, 3	7, 3
4, 0, 2, 8	4, 0
6, 1, 4, 7	no reply

Here is the test of Bouth ——, showing that she succeeded four times.

FIGURES GIVEN	FIGURES REPEATED
2, 8, 7	2, 8, 7
3, 6, 5	3, 5
1, 2, 9	1, 2, 9
6, 1, 4	6, 1, 4
2, 7, 3	2, 7, 3
4, 0, 2, 8	4. 0, 8
6, 1, 4, 7	1, 2, 4, 5
3, 2, 9, 5	3, 2, 5 . . . 8
6, 4, 4, 9	6, 9, 4

Bounam —— always succeeded, and Le Temple —— can repeat as many as four figures:

FIGURES GIVEN	FIGURES REPEATED
3, 2, 8	3, 2, 8
4, 5, 9	5. 4, 9
6, 2, 1, 8	2, 3, 4, 5, 8
1, 0, 9, 7	1, 0, 9, 7

Several inversions were noted besides a tendency to give the numbers in their natural order 1, 2, 4, 5 (Bouth), 2, 3, 4, 5, (Le Temple). This characteristic tendency of intellectual weakness, is better brought out when six figures are to be repeated. Thus it often happens that a subject gives the whole series of figures from one to ten. This is very rare among young normals, although examples can be found.

Let us examine Delai —— born February 28, 1895.

Asked to pick a particular one from a group of objects, she takes one at random. She indicates exactly the longer of two lines of unequal length. She succeeds at the second trial in repeating three figures:

$$3, 2, 8, \qquad 3, 8$$
$$5, 1, 4, \qquad 5, 1, 4$$

She cannot repeat a single sentence nor indicate the difference between two objects. One sees at once her place. Her intellectual level is the same as the preceding. The simple enumeration of her replies suffices to satisfy us as to this.

3. *Imbeciles with ability to repeat sentences.* The repetition of simple sentences was not possible among the children of the preceding group. This test was a barrier for them; it presented a difficulty which they could not overcome. This incapacity presents all degrees. Ruz —— could not repeat even a part of any sentence that was given her. Bouth ——, Delai —— repeated only isolated words. Bouth —— asked to repeat, "I get up in the morning, I dine at noon and I go to bed at night," said, "I bed —— and bed —— breakfast, etc."

Q. In the summer the weather is fine, in the winter snow falls. *A.* Summer. . . . and . . . . winter.

Delaigne. *Q.* I get up, etc. *A.* I get up at night and I go to bed.

Q. In summer, etc. *A.* Summer . . . . it falls.

Q. Germaine, etc. *A.* Germaine has been ba . . . . .

Among four sentences given to her, Bonamy only once formulated a sentence more or less correct: "I get up in the morning I go to bed at night . . . . and at noon, one eats."

Le Temple —— Among six sentences given there were two very much abbreviated to be sure but which nevertheless made sense. In summer it is fine. In winter it rains. Germaine has been bad — scolded. Twice on the contrary she only muttered words almost without connection. Once she avowed her inability "I don't know how to say that."

Thus none of them was successful. On the contrary, here are new subjects who succeeded: Vaubr —— twelve years, microcephalic with slight goitre, who knows her age but not her date of birth. Tilma —— thirteen years. Vasie —— a victim of myxoedemia, twenty years, always smiling, executed very well the repetition of simple sentences.

Here are the individual replies to this test. Vaubr —— "I get up, etc. . . ." no reply, even partial.—"In summer, etc. . . . ." Repetition entirely correct.

Tilma —— "I get up, etc., no reply, even partial. "In summer, etc." Repetition entirely correct.

Vasie ——, "I get up . . . . etc.", "I dine at noon, I go to bed at night, I breakfast in the morning," "In summer, etc." Repetition correct.

It can thus be seen that among the children who cannot succeed in this test, several of them pronounce only incoherent,

words. It would not do to attribute to this incoherence alone
a prejudicial value because it is sometimes found among normals
—although much younger it is true.

There remain the children who repeat correctly the sentences
and who therefore belong to the group we are studying at this
time. It is interesting to observe that this test which marks
the culmination of their faculties, is readily passed by normal
children of five years. But the youngest of this group is twelve,
and the oldest twenty years of age.

*Schematic Table of the Intellectual Development of a Group of Imbecile
Children*

	GAV	PIG	AMY	TROMPE	RUZ	LE TEMPLE	BOUTH	DELAI	BONA	VAU	TIL	VAS
14. Answers to abstract sentences												
13. Rhymes												
12. Placing 5 weights in order												
11. Concrete differences									−	−	−	−
10. Repetition of simple sentences					−	−	−	−	−	+	+	+
9. Comparison of lines	−	−	−	+	+	+	+	+	+	+	+	+
8. Repetition of 3 figures			−	−	+	+	+	+	+	+	+	+
7. Indicating and naming of certain objects or pictures	−	+	+	+	+	+	+	+				
6. Indicating parts of the body	+	+	+	+	+	+	+					
5. Distinction between what is food and what is not					+							
Imitation and execution of simple orders	+	+	+									
	1	2			3				4			

MORONS (DÉBILES) *(no def. differential sign)*

Our third group is composed of children who succeed with
tests more difficult than the preceding.

A differentiating sign is lacking for this group. Language
distinguishes the idiot from the imbecile; it seems that our next

tests should require more intellectual initiative than the preceding ones, should presuppose more invention, or a judgment in which ideas play a preponderant rôle. But in reality we do not know whether it is a question of a complication of elementary processes, or whether new faculties are required. Five tests, as for the preceding groups, will suffice to establish subdivisions which though of less importance at least will facilitate the exposition. We shall pass them successively in review.

Morons with faculty of reasoned comparison. The first advance seems to be realized by the possibility of recognizing and stating the difference between two given things. Etel —— , eighteen years old, is the representative type of the group. Her replies were correct for the lines; she had no difficulty in repeating three figures; the repetition of simple sentences produced indeed one error, but she was correct in her other attempt. Finally this child distinguished herself clearly over the preceding when she was asked to indicate the difference between two things.

Bon —— , Van —— , Till —— , Vas —— , children of the preceding groups, either did not reply or simply repeated the words of the question, "cardboard," "paper," "fly," etc. or defined more or less one of two things, "A fly can fly—the cardboard— one cuts things," etc., but did not indicate a single difference. These are similar to the replies of normal children who do not comprehend, but who nevertheless wish to satisfy the questioner, but they are the replies of very much younger normal children. In contrast to these are the replies of Etel —— .

Q. What difference is there between paper and cardboard?
A. The paper is finer and the cardboard harder.
Q. The difference between a butterfly and fly?
A. A butterfly is much larger than a fly.
Q. The difference between glass and wood?
A. Glass is thicker.

Certainly the last reply is not brilliant, but the whole forces us to recognize that the consciousness of difference is not foreign to this child, since she makes several correct applications.

Morons with the faculty of seriation. The arranging in order of five weights of the same volume, requires a prolonged effort, a series of operations performed in a determined direction, the conception of an end to be attained, and the means of arriving there. The child is given over to his own powers; he must hold in his mind what is to be done, and this directing idea which has been given him must serve to coördinate his different acts. Three children examined, succeeded. But here it is interesting first to see how those of the imbecile group fail. Til —— for instance when asked to arrange the five weights in order beginning with the lightest, contents herself by placing them side by side; when urged to weigh them, she takes three in one hand, two in the other, balances them a little as if to judge better, then places them at random. Etel —— whom we have placed among the morons, already seemed to handle them more skillfully, but the idea of a serial order escaped her. Notice on the contrary the following:

Liss —— is full of life, her acts seem more intelligent, she makes only one mistake. Here is the order which she found 15, 12, 9, 3, 6. She is a child of seventeen.

Lebos —— (sixteen years) exclaims on seeing them, "Oh yes, they are all the same," but having weighed them in her hand, arranges them correctly.

Janss —— (sixteen years) does the same in spite of her timidity.

The same children were able to give reasoned comparisons, and do successfully all that precedes. The test of weights then seems indeed a new degree.

Other tests. To comprehend what a rhyme is seems more subtle than arranging weights. Lebos —— , Janss —— , after the explanation thought that *bouton* and *mouton* did not rhyme, and Lisse —— , who seemed to understand better, could only find "obéissant" and "obéir" to rhyme with "obéissance." On the other hand Gouven —— (fourteen years) gave in one minute the following rhymes; "souciance" "negligence" "intelligence," "elegance," But we add that this child had obtained her certificate (certificat d'études). We are approaching more and more the normal. What is the degree which separates us from the normal? Principally abstract questions.

No child of the preceding group to whom we gave the abstract questions was able to reply correctly if the sentence was a little complicated. Etel —— finished haphazard.

Q. When one has need of good advice?
A. You must take care of yourself.

Lisse —— is scarcely more capable.

Q. If one has offended you and comes to beg your pardon?
A. "One listens." She answers simply.

Jansee ——, before giving your opinion, etc. *A*. One must hunt for it.

Lebos —— at least says squarely; "I do not know," but with a tone of bad humor, as though vexed to be found in complete ignorance.

Without doubt the foregoing answers are not wholly devoid of sense, one could even find a certain cleverness about some of them. But then almost any reply might be forced to make sense—it is a matter of interpretation. But it is evident that the child is incapable of the subtlety which one would suspect if his words came from someone else.

Gouv —— sometimes succeeds.

Q. When one has need of good advice?
A. One must ask one's superiors.
Q. Instead of crying over an accident that has happened?
A. One must try to avoid it.

She too has misunderstood the situation.

We have, however, two children who surpass this . Romer —— and Perrous ——. Here are the replies of Romer:

Q. Before giving advice, etc.?
A. One must reflect.
Q. When someone has offended you and comes to ask your pardon?
A. One must forgive him.

This child has already passed the other test, having found rhymes. The reply to this abstract question places her at once in a higher group.

The ideas of Perrous —— are still more active, as is shown by her replies to abstract questions:

Q. When anyone asks your opinion of a person of whom you know little?
A. Faith, I hardly know what I would say. I would say that I did not know his character.
Q. Instead of crying, etc.?
A. One repairs it if possible.

In conclusion she was the only child who put three words in a sentence: "I was in Paris and I saw a gutter; I gained a fortune."

Here are two children who may rank with normal children of twelve years. They themselves are seventeen. It would be necessary to give other tests in order to compare them with normal children of their own age. They are therefore above the series.

Table of the Intellectual Development of a Group of Morons

	ETE	LEBO	JANN	LIZZE	GOUVE	ROMO	PEROUS
17. Abstract differences..................					−	−	−
16. Cutting out.........................					−		−
15. Sentence with three words...........						−	+
14. Answering abstract questions........	−	−	−	−	−	+	+
13. Rhymes............................		−	−	−	+	+	+
12. Arranging five weights..............	−	+	+	+	+	+	+
11. Concrete differences.................	+	+	+	+	+	+	+
10. Repetition of simple sentences.......	+	+	+	+	+	+	+
9. Repetition of three figures...........	+	+	+	+	+	+	+
8. Comparison of lines.................	+	+	+	+	+	+	+
	1		2		3	4	5

In order to characterize the morons they must be separated both from imbeciles and normals. The boundary on the side of imbecility, we have already indicated. That on the side of normality, seems to us to consist especially in the ability to answer abstract questions; but it must be understood that that limit is especially devised for children of school age, not over fourteen for instance; this test would be insufficient to distinguish morons of twenty years and over from normals.

"In concluding with these children of Dr. Voisin's institution, we note that it would almost always be possible to compare them with normal children very much younger. We have often been struck with the resemblance which exists, and which can be called out in the reactions of normals and subnormals of a different age. It is possible that certain differences are hidden under these resemblances, and that some day we shall succeed in differentiating them so clearly that we shall be able to find signs of psychological retardation, altogether independent of age. Evidently it would be of great value to know these signs. But for the moment, that which especially strikes us is the resemblance between young normals, and subnormals very much older. These resemblances are so numerous, and so striking that truly, one could not tell by reading the reactions of a child whose age is not given, whether he were normal or subnormal. Furthermore it is easy to point out that certain clever remarks of precocious children, if they came from adults would stamp the latter as morons."

In conclusion, it seems to us that if our divisions and tests are adopted, the rank and intellectual development of each subject can be fixed with great precision.

Here is one, for example, whom according to our classification we consider an idiot. It would be impossible for him to be designated by M. Magnan a moron and by M. Bourneville an imbecile, if they took our divisions for a guide, because we discover that the subject does not recognize nor name the different parts of his body. If one adds "idiot with prehension," one distinguishes him at the same time from the idiot who has only visual coördination and the one that knows food, which gives a distinct idea of his aptitudes. There would be no uncertainties or contradictions of nomenclature.

Let us again recall our classification:

Idiocy
(Incapacity for naming, or recognizing familiar objects when named, or parts of the body, or objects in a picture. Aptitudes of normal children from 0 to 2 years.)

Vegetative idiot. No trace of ideas of relationships.
Idiot with visual coördination. Follows with his eyes a moving object (lighted match).
Idiot with Prehension — Takes an object that touches his hand. Takes an object that he sees.
Idiot who knows food. Can distinguish between what is and what is not food.
Idiot who can imitate simple gestures. Understands gestures, mimics, imitates and obeys.

Imbecility
(Capability for verbal naming. Incapacity of finding the difference between known objects. Aptitude of normal children from 2 to 5 years).

Imbeciles with faculty of naming. Names and recognizes the principal parts of his body, familiar objects, pictures.
Imbeciles with faculty of comparison. Compares two weights of 3 and 15 grams, two lines of 5 and 8 centimeters.
Imbeciles with faculty of repetition. Repeats an easy sentence of 15 words.

The study of moronity will be better made in the schools.

Morons 8-13 yrs.
(abt 15 N)

III. SUBNORMALS OF THE PRIMARY SCHOOLS

In the institution we have studied the idiot and the imbecile; the subnormals that we shall study in the primary schools are the morons.

Let it be well understood in the beginning that we do not propose a general method of diagnosis for all morons, whatever their age. This would be beyond our pretensions. We have studied only the morons of from eight to thirteen years, such as one finds in the schools. It is to these alone that our process applies.

At the time when we write these lines, every primary school in France has replied to a questionnaire sent out by the Ministerial Commission on subnormals in which each school was asked to give the number of deaf mutes, blind, of medically subnormals, of the backward and the unstable.[16] These lists, filled out by the teachers, were collected at the Bureau of Public Instruction in Paris, and were placed at the disposal of the ministerial commission, of which one of us (Binet) was a member. It would therefore be easy for us to know exactly how many subnormals could be found in the schools of Paris, and thanks to the kindly authorization of M. Bedorez, and his predecessor M. Carriot, who opened wide for us all the schools of the city of Paris, we could apply our method to the diagnosis of many hundreds of subjects.

We are still ignorant whether the Ministerial Commission intends to proceed to a scientific examination in the primary schools—of course by the delegation of its power to certain of

[16] These distinctions have an administrative value, but very little if any, scientific value. We do not know what the medical subnormal means, which is here distinguished from the backward and the "unstable." It is probable that by medical subnormal we must understand idiot, and by the others we must understand imbeciles and morons. One of us (Binet) was able to take note, with the Minister of Public Instruction, of the answers made by the provinces to the ministerial questionnaire. The figures shown are lower than it was supposed; sometimes, indeed too low to be exact. Certain Departments indicate as unstable only two or three subjects. The average figures for 21 Departments, would be 64 backward boys, and 38 girls; 78.3 unstables for boys, and 45.2 for girls, or a total of 123.5 for each Department, and a total a little over 10,000 for all France, exclusive of Paris. Very likely the figures for Paris will be higher than these, which show but 2 backward for 1000, a proportion that pleases us but leaves us skeptical. The total number of subnormals who are at present in the primary public schools of Paris would be about 3000.

its members—in order to discover the truly subnormal children, and submit them to tests that would indicate their subnormal character. They would have very many motives for making this investigation: (1). The motive of control over the statistics which they are going to arrange. It would be well to know exactly in a certain proportion of the schools, how far the scientific diagnosis would accord with the judgment of the teachers; (2) An educational motive for the teachers; to show them in this way if they deceive themselves, where they have committed errors, and what are the criteria which they should henceforth employ in order to be more exact; (3) An educational motive for future inspectors who will be charged with the examination of subnormals, and who will have to decide upon their admission to the special classes.

An examination of the subnormal children in the schools, should on general principles be made without the aid of the teachers. These might take during the examination different attitudes that would be somewhat disconcerting. Without doubt the majority of them are too enlightened to misunderstand not only the scientific but the social interest of these questions, and one has the right to expect from them much zeal and readiness to give to the investigators all useful information at their disposal. But certain ones of them will commit—and have already committed as we have proved—errors of many kinds.

Certain ones are absolutely hostile to an investigation of subnormals. These are the timid ones who fear to have trouble with the parents, behind whose discontent they always fear to see the shadow of a municipal officer or a newspaper reporter. There are also the proud who feel that to admit having a subnormal would prove their pedagogical incompetence. There are also those gentle philosophers who imagine that the ideal school is the one where one never raises the voice, and which functions in the perfect stillness of routine. There are also the skeptics who are tired of waiting for a reform in the matter of subnormals and who no longer believe reform possible. Such minds will reply to the investigators what they have already replied to the questionnaire: "We have no subnormals!" or again, "We do not know how to recognize them; that belongs to the doctors."

Others would be lead by an exaggerated zeal to make errors in the opposite direction. Some have already stated that they have

50 subnormals in a school of 300. They seem to reason in the following way: "Here is an excellent opportunity for getting rid of all the children who trouble us," and without the true critical spirit, they designate all who are unruly, or disinterested in the school.

For these and many other reasons, it is better that the investigator prepare himself to dispense with the help of the director, or at least that he be sufficiently sure of his method of procedure, to control and, when necessary to put to the test the information received from the director. The practical question which presents itself does not lack elegance in its simplicity; here it is: being given any school, whose population numbers from 100 to 800 pupils, visit the classes and discover the subnormals scattered among them. Must we examine one by one all the pupils in a school? No, certainly not! That would be altogether useless. One should consider as suspicious only those children, who are the oldest in their class, but whose marks are almost constantly the lowest. One should ask the ages of the children by a collective appeal; then one should look at their reports. We ourselves have not had the opportunity of making this summary selection; but it certainly would be easy and rapid. Suppose that it is made. It remains to proceed to an individual examination of only a small number of children.

It is this individual examination which we are now preparing and hope to make easy by setting forth the investigations that we have already undertaken. We write the following lines with the conscious intention of rendering a service to future examining commissions who will have to pronounce upon the scholastic fate of subnormals.

We voluntarily forego the help which the pedagogical and medical method may furnish, when those methods are completely organized. We shall content ourselves with employing exclusively the psychological method. We have used it ourselves in several schools of Paris to recognize subnormals, and it seems to have given us the beginnings of vital results. We first went to those schools whose directors are among the most intelligent and the most competent. Among these we note M. Vaney, the author of a work published in this volume, upon the measure of the instruction in arithmetic. M. Vaney is particularly interested in the question of subnormals and we had every reason to believe *a priori* that the selection of subnormals which he made in his *mixed with normals* ✓

school would be excellent. We, however, were eager to examine those whom he had chosen. We did examine them, begging him at the same time to mingle them with normals so that their identity would not be known to us. This ignorance is the indispensable condition of any just examination. It is really too easy to discover signs of backwardness in an individual when one is forewarned. This would be to operate as the graphologists did who, when Dreyfus was believed to be guilty, discovered in his handwriting signs of a traitor or a spy. Saganarelle also, in *le Médecin malgré lui* found the pulse of the man bad whom he thought to be sick. The doctor in an institution to whom the parents bring a supposedly defective child, does not need to show very much critical sense, because as a matter of fact under such conditions he never sends any child back, nor declares it to be normal. A little irony is the most salutary thing in the world in a case like this, and we disdain the opinion of those whom it could hurt. ✓

We have pursued our inquiries in other schools where there was a difference of opinion between the director and the teacher who had the child in her class; the director judged the child normal, the teacher judged it subnormal; sometimes there was a difference of opinion between the actual teacher and the teacher of the previous year. Such cases generally are difficult to decide upon, because the defect is slight and the retardation is not very evident; or it may be that it is a question of a child whose disposition is difficult; that is to say an unstable rather than a retarded child. The process which we recommend consists in applying to the child, without any preconceived idea, all of the tests and comparing the results with those obtained from normals, without regard to his age. Since we possess a nearly complete series of the results of the tests for each age of normal children, it is easy to find the place of the candidate in such a series. The subsequent consideration of his age permits us then to know if he is backward, and how much below the average; and one establishes also, at the same time, in what faculties the retardation is most marked. This is the complete method; it is minute and naturally takes some time, possibly a half hour. Under other circumstances one can resort to a more rapid method, which consists in starting the child on the tests appropriate for his age; if he fails, his retardation is, in a way, instantly manifest. This investigation takes only five minutes.

We indicate this to show how rapid the psychological method may be; but we disapprove of this rapidity. The matter is too serious to the child for us to wish to economize a few minutes of his time. On the contrary if the examination should last an hour, for instance, but given at different times, we should not think it too long—quite the contrary.

When our series, a portion of which we have given in this article, is completed; when instead of resting upon the examination of only 10 or 15 subjects, it rests upon 100, we shall proceed by comparing the supposed subnormal with the average normal of each age, and we shall thus see to what average age he corresponds for each kind of test. This method is certainly the best and the most sure, because the average value represents the most fixed value, the ideal value. Unfortunately our data are still far from numerous, and we do not possess averages for each age, but only meager averages distributed over two years. Thus, provisionally, we shall make use of the results given, not only by the average normal, but by the most mediocre normal child. The latter, for different reasons, is often an exceptional type. It must be understood that if we use this as a standard, it is in a wholly provisional manner, in order to offset the insufficiency of our data.

FIRST OBSERVATION

Here is a child of twelve years, Martin, who presents himself to us without our knowing to what class he belongs. He is sent to us without other information than his age. During our examination we willingly deprive ourselves of all the indications, often very valuable, which the pedagogical method could furnish. We do not ask him to read or write and when he leaves us we do not even know if he can do so. In the same way we systematically neglect the information, always somewhat indirect but sometimes significant, of the medical method. Martin has a small head, narrow brow, and ears like handles. It is probable that the careful measurements of his cephalic development would indicate some stigmata.[17] Since he is past twelve years old it would be

[17] Let us note here a few interesting results which we gathered when the psychological test was finished. By the development of his head, and by his height, Martin is subnormal; his height is 1.27 m., and the volume of his head is that of a 2 year old child.

proper to commence his examination, if one wished to be rapid, by the series of abstract questions. But we prefer to take the longer route and to study the child in a more complete fashion.

Let us begin by reasoned comparisons. Here are Martin's replies.

Differences: (1) The wood is larger and the glass is thinner.
(2) The butterfly is larger and the fly is smaller.
(3) The cardboard is thicker and the paper is thinner.

Strictly speaking, with a good deal of indulgence one could allow these replies to pass, although we must note two defects; first the repetition of the same point of view, that of size, which by indolence or mental limitation is applied to three comparisons; and lastly an absurdity committed in comparison of wood and glass. We have observed a normal child of nine years, who twice repeated the same point of view, but committed no absurdity. Nevertheless Martin is twelve years old. He is therefore by that simple experiment placed below children of nine years.

Although we have not published at any length comparisons of resemblances, we give those of Martin. They are very poor.

(1) The poppy is smaller than blood.
(2) The label is smaller, the picture is square, the newspaper is long.

Q. But no. You must tell me how these things are alike!
A. They are not alike.

(3) Fly, flea, butterfly. They are alike in the head. The flea, it has the head of a fly.

All these remarks of our subject give a first impression. Martin shows himself at least capable of making reasoned comparisons; he makes them more or less well, but he does make them; therefore he is superior to children of five years; and further if the criterion is adopted which we have already indicated, and which consists in distinguishing imbecility from moronity by the test of reasoned comparisons, he is not an imbecile. But is he a moron? A methodical examination will answer for us. Let us study separately his memory, his sensorial intelligence, and his abstract intelligence.

Memory. Martin is a child who has a sufficiently good memory to be normal. Twice at ten days interval, he repeated for us 8 sentences. Each time he repeated exactly and rapidly the first three, the easiest. At the first examination he repeated very well the 8th sentence, failed in the others and committed an absurdity for the 5th. "One must not say all that one thinks, but one must . . . . (hesitation) say all that one thinks."

At the second examination the 5th sentence is repeated exactly but trouble occurs in the 8th sentence. "The horse draws the carriage, the wheel is heavy and the carriage is low." This is not very intelligible.

To summarize, at each one of the examinations Martin succeeds in repeating four sentences and he commits an absurdity. Certain normals of eleven years have done no better. So it is not through lack of memory that he is subnormal. There exists, however, a distinctive characteristic in the manner of his repetition, speed. If anything stops him, and prevents him from repeating immediately, he is lost, and can no longer give a word of what has been said to him. This proves that he uses only the memory of sound in repeating sentences, not the memory of ideas. This latter would be more lasting.

The memory of pictures is more than good, it is really excellent. He succeeds in retaining 8 out of 13 pictures; he belongs to the average level of children of eleven years, is even a little in advance of them. This is worthy of note because we shall see that on the whole Martin is certainly a moron. It is therefore important to remark that for one psychological test a moron may make fewer mistakes than certain normals. We believe that this fact is of great pedagogical importance.[18]

His memory for figures has two characteristics: in appearance it is normal, because he succeeds in repeating exactly, a series of 5 figures, as do certain children of eleven years; he is therefore from this point of view almost normal, slightly inferior, however, because the normal repeats 6. But it is characteristic of him that he judges very poorly the corrections of his reproductions. We require him to say, "That is right" when the repetition has been correct, and "That is not right" when it has been incorrect. In the first place—a fact that is important—he does not submit to this convention, and he must be reminded of it about 8 times before he begins to give the signal spontaneously-

[18] Let us say right here that Martin is not an exception to the rule concerning the morons; all the morons have a visual memory as good as the normals of their age.

and again he often fails. These lapses prove to us the difficulty he has in learning. In the second place we learn that he is truly an optimist. He believes that he has correctly replied in many cases where he has deceived himself. Six times he declares "That is right," when he was wrong and only 4 times did he admit he was wrong, and in 3 of these he had said nothing at all. These are indeed characteristic errors, where the absence of attention borders closely on absence of judgment. Such curious cases require careful study. We suppose that by a strong appeal to the attention, by long training one might succeed in arousing this lagging judgment. But that would no longer be an examination, it would be education.

Let us note again with Martin, many inventions of figures and sometimes, though rarely, a tendency to follow the natural order in the invention. Thus one gives him the series 5, 1, 4, 8, 2, 7, and he announces the series 5, 1, 2, 3, 7.

It can thus be seen that in this test so far as it goes the memory is sufficient. It is not through absence of memory but through weakness of judgment that Martin fails. These examples show how necessary it is to carefully analyse results. A hasty examination would have recognized in Martin a reasonable memory, nothing more.

Sensorial intelligence. Martin conducts himself here in a very interesting manner, which needs close examination. Let us begin by the comparison of lines. This test is of the desired simplicity. We have the intention of grasping, if possible, an elementary fact of sensation; but from the moment of making this experiment we demand also something of the judgment. An attentive study of Martin will show the part intelligence plays in the affair. Although that part is hidden, Martin reveals it to us; because the little slips which he makes are errors of judgment and all the more curious since his sensorial faculties seem good and, to be just, normal.

Bending over the little lines he makes but a single error. That is excellent, and that error is without doubt due to a moment of distraction. He is therefore at the level of children of eleven years, only a little trait in his manner of proceeding is worth notice. He shows himself eager to designate something and begins by pointing out haphazard any one at all. Then he corrects himself quickly, spontaneously, in a way to show that his glance is true, in a word, normal.

For the long lines he shows the same surety of glance. He makes only four errors, for the lines 6, 8, 10, 11. Children of eleven years make on an average from 3 to 5 mistakes, and some make 6 and even 7. He is therefore normal. More than this, starting with the 6th line, when he begins to make mistakes, he is seized by automatism and indicates five times in succession the line to the right. We rarely find with children eleven years old an equally prolonged automatism. And even, on taking up the test at another time, we obtain from Martin a complete series of twelve automatic replies, that is to say twelve times in succession he indicates the line on the right. This is truly a sign of weakness of intellect. No normal child of eleven years so far as we know has conducted himself in this way.

Putting in order five weights—another test of sensorial intelligence—contains also some perceptions, but it implies that the weights are arranged, and that consequently the perceptions are directed and grouped under the influence of a judgment of the whole. Here again, and perhaps in a still more characteristic manner, Martin furnishes for us a distinction between sensorial perception and judgment. Considering only the errors which he commits, this test definitely shows his mental inferiority. See his manner of arranging:

$$\left.\begin{array}{ccccc} 9 & 3 & 6 & 12 & 15 \\ 15 & 9 & 3 & 6 & 12 \\ 15 & 9 & 3 & 6 & 12 \end{array}\right\} 24 \text{ errors}$$

This total of 24 errors is not made by any child of eleven years, nor of nine years nor of seven although certain ones of the latter group approach this. Martin would therefore be below a child of seven years. And interpreting his error it is certain that it is not through inattention, or through fault of our explanation, for at different times we went over our explanation of what was necessary. Furthermore, Martin is satisfied with his results, he thinks them correct, and manifests his satisfaction with that naïveté of *amour propre* which characterizes morons.

We considered it wise to have him continue his arrangements, in order to see if through repetition he would manifest any progress. There has been none. Here are his successive arrangements.

$$
\left.\begin{array}{ccccc}
15 & 3 & 6 & 9 & 12 \\
15 & 12 & 3 & 9 & 6 \\
15 & 9 & 12 & 6 & 3
\end{array}\right\} \text{14 errors}
$$

$$
\left.\begin{array}{ccccc}
15 & 3 & 12 & 6 & 9 \\
15 & 6 & 9 & 12 & 3 \\
15 & 3 & 12 & 6 & 9
\end{array}\right\} \text{14 errors}
$$

Martin uses only one hand, the right. He scarcely compares the two weights. He seems only to hunt for one, the heaviest. In fact, the box of 15 grams is now always correctly placed. This is curious enough. The errors with the other boxes are erratic enough, but an error with 15 is never committed. It is even with great cleverness that Martin discovers this box of 15 grams. He goes at it with the surety of instinct. In order to prevent him from recognizing the boxes by sight we have enveloped all in paper which makes them exactly similar. With the boxes wrapped in paper, Martin has made the following arrangements:

$$
\left.\begin{array}{ccccc}
15 & 9 & 6 & 12 & 3 \\
15 & 12 & 6 & 9 & 3 \\
15 & 6 & 9 & 3 & 12
\end{array}\right\} \text{12 errors}
$$

$$
\left.\begin{array}{ccccc}
12 & 6 & 15 & 3 & 9 \\
15 & 6 & 12 & 9 & 3 \\
15 & 9 & 3 & 6 & 12
\end{array}\right\} \text{18 errors}
$$

No progress has been made and the box numbered 15 remains in correct position. There is nevertheless with Martin a very good sensorial function, since he succeeds in recognizing the heaviest of 5 weights but this judgment does not permit him to understand the order of the other four. This is precisely the type of error made by children seven years old, and it is interesting to see that mental state retained by a child of eleven years. It is a striking proof of the fact that the sensorial faculty may be good but the judgment poor. Let us finish by the test of paper cutting, the last of those upon sensorial intelligence. He draws an angle, not closed, small and not in the center of the paper; he is therefore very inferior to children of eleven years.

Abstract intelligence and language. His inferiority to children of his own age is pronounced in these respects. He fails in the rhymes; he gives the following words as rhyming with obéissance; öbéi, obéissante, sage, dissipé. After a minute we renew the explanation which has no other result than to make him pronounce the word, "obéi." Scarcely any child of nine years would commit a similar absurdity.

But it is chiefly in the series of abstract questions that his deficiency shows itself. This series alone would be sufficient to characterize him, and so definitely that other tests seem superfluous. We shall now give the exact replies, generally very brief, and we shall follow them with our marks as for normal children.

There are no less than 8 absurdities, 3 silences and 4 replies marked 3 or 4.

By the number of these absurdities he is very much inferior to the worst children of nine and eleven years. There were only two children of seven years who committed a number of absurdities approaching his, that is to say seven.

1. Go to bed, 1.
2. Cover up well, 1.
3. One must hurry, 1.
4. Put on a raincoat, 1.
5. Go on foot, 3.
6. One must wait, 2.
7. One must pay, 2.
8. One must tell the teacher, 1.
9. Get the firemen, 1.
10. Silence.
11. Listen, 3.
12. One does not know, 2.
13. To pay the rent, 1.
14. Silence.
15. Must not go, 4.
16. One must work, 2.
17. One must not listen, A.
18. One must do nothing, A.
19. A fight, 3.
20. Nothing, A.
21. Because he has done harm, A.
22. Because he is worse and then he is not so bad, A.
23. Because he wishes to quit, A.
24. Because it was a good thing, A.
25. One does not do it, A.

To recapitulate, Martin is a child whose sensorial faculties and memory for immediate repetition are normal; but even in the most elementary experiments slight details already betray his lack of judgment. He lacks judgment first in certain tests of sensorial intelligence (like arranging weights) and especially in verbal tests implying abstract ideas. For all these points he has scarcely the level of children of seven years so that he is retarded five years, since he is twelve years old. This case is interesting because of the evidence of mental inferiority. In the school, one meets with morons, but they are seldom of as profound a character as Martin. He represents one of the lowest grades above imbecility.[19]

We shall now study more rapidly a second type of mental inferiority much more frequent than the preceding.

SECOND OBSERVATION

Raynaud is a young boy of eleven years with fine regular features. He has nothing subnormal in his physique nor in his manners. The impression which he makes is much more favorable than that of Martin. Nevertheless when examined closely, one finds he has a rather weak cephalic development. His head is the size of that of a child of 5 years, a retardation of six years, which without being unknown among normals, is nevertheless rare. We did not take the measurement, be it well understood, until after the psychological examination was ended. His height is normal, 1.4 meters.

During the examination there is a marked contrast of manner with that of Martin. In proportion as Martin is quick, Raynaud is slow. He can scarcely make up his mind to reply; he is undecided, pained almost, and contracts his brows as if in distress.

The test of reasoned comparisons is favorable.

He gives concrete differences.

> The paper is light, and the cardboard is heavy.
> The fly is smaller.
> Wood is less heavy than *lead*.

He is therefore not an imbecile.

We shall not give in detail all the tests—that would be tedious and useless. We give a summary.

Memory. Raynaud is weak, weaker than Martin, although superior in judgment, as will hereafter appear. He correctly repeats only three out of 8 sentences, which is few. His memory is therefore defective, although not below some normals of eleven

---

[19] According to M. Vaney, this subject is 4 grades backward in figures. It is only in the last year that he has been able to read well.

memory, Sensorial intel, abstract intel

years. Moreover his trouble comes from his slowness in replying. So also for numbers, he does not exceed four; on the whole he does not go so far as Martin, nor as normals of his age; on the other hand he never deceives himself, or very seldom, and at once corrects the error that he commits. Thus he has a poor memory, this is one of his weak points. This is probably a particular form of memory, the slow form as though benumbed.

Sensorial intelligence. He succeeds very well in all the tests and commits only one error with the short lines and only two for the long. He is therefore in this respect superior to normals of his age.

For the arrangement of weights, he makes no mistake, uses both hands, weighs with care, five times in succession he makes not a single error.

For the paper cutting he draws a central diamond.

Here is a child who in spite of his moronity, as we shall observe in an instant, has a good, an excellent sensorial intelligence. Without doubt it is this which should be cultivated in him rather than yoking him to abstract notions.

Abstract intelligence. Several preliminary tests show his weakness; he cannot find a single rhyme, and he cannot make a synthesis of three words in a sentence. But it is chiefly in his manner of replying to abstract sentences that he reveals himself. He has 6 absurd replies, 5 silences and only 4 replies marked 3 or better. This places him on a level with children of seven years and he is but slightly superior to Martin.

Here then is the opinion which one must form of this pupil. He is a moron; and represents a type which we believe quite common, the moron with sensorial intelligence. One frequently encounters this combination. The sensorial intelligence of Raynaud is better than that of Martin, and the proof is the skill with which he arranges the weights, and draws the cut in the paper. If Martin is low grade moron type, Raynaud represents a type of intellect a little higher.

Let us recall as a particular trait of Raynaud, his indolence of memory.

It seems to us that intelligent pedagogy could gain much from these facts.[20]

[20] M. Vaney says that Raynaud is retarded. This child has been in school for 5 years; he is only in the second grade in arithmetic. He was not able to read until $9\frac{1}{2}$ years old.

THIRD OBSERVATION

A few words will suffice to characterize young Ernest. The director of the school and the child's teacher do not agree in regard to him. The teacher thinks he understands, and believes him to be normal. The director insists that he has only attained the third grade in arithmetic in spite of his 5 years in school, and that he had difficulty in learning to read; therefore he is disposed to consider him retarded. Who is right?

Assuredly the director. It is not out of respect for those in authority that we agree with him, it is because the psychological method proves it.

The error of the teacher comes no doubt from the fact that he compares him with very much younger pupils, aged from seven to nine years, who are in the same class, and does not take into account the difference in age; this is one of the reasons why teachers so often give defective reports of their pupils.

One might also make allowance for this child because he suffers from a malady which occasions absence from school, but the psychological examination removes all doubt. Ernest is mediocre but not below normal for the memory of sentences (3 sentences repeated, and 2 absurdities) and for the memory of figures (4 figures only; here is evident retardation, but not lack of judgment). His memory is weak.

Sensorial intelligence is normal; 6 errors for the long lines, 2, 7, 8, 10, 11, and none for the short; he arranges the weights 3 times without error and completes the gaps with one error in three attempts. He draws a central diamond.

So far Ernest would be normal but abstract intelligence is deficient in him as in Raynaud and most other defectives. He is in the same class as Raynaud only slightly less marked. For abstract questions he has 5 absurdities, 1 silence, and 10 replies marked 3 or better. This is a little better than Raynaud gave us. But one sees at the same time that this is the level of children of seven years; and moreover normal children of seven years are more prudent; when they do not understand, they keep silence and here is truly a condition where silence is golden.

These three little psychological biographies show clearly what is most lacking in morons. It is abstract intelligence. In a rapid examination one might be satisfied to give them 7 or 8 of these abstract questions. They would serve immediately to classify them.

We may be excused from developing here a long conclusion. One word will suffice. "We have only wished to prove that it is possible to find in a precise and truly scientific way, the level of intelligence, to compare that level with a normal level, and consequently to conclude how many years a child is retarded. In spite of the inevitable errors of an initial work, which is mere groping, we believe we have made our demonstration."

A. Binet and Th. Simon.

THE DEVELOPMENT OF INTELLIGENCE IN THE CHILD

L'Année Psychologique 1908

"The Measurement of Intelligence" is, perhaps, the most oft repeated expression in psychology during these last few years. Some psychologists affirm that intelligence can be measured; others declare that it is impossible to measure intelligence. But there are still others,[1] better informed, who ignore these theoretical discussions and apply themselves to the actual solving of the problem. The readers of *L'Année*[2] know that for some time we have been trying approximations, but they were not so well thought out as are those which we now present.

We have constantly kept in mind the point of view of pedagogy, normal as well as pathological. For several years we have tried to gather all the data and material capable of shedding light upon the intellectual and moral character of children. This is by no means the minor part of pedagogy, the least important, nor the least difficult. We set for ourselves the following program: first, to determine the law of the intellectual development of children and to devise a method of measuring their intelligence; and, second, to study the diversity of their intellectual aptitudes.

We hope that we shall be able to keep faithfully to this rather extensive program, and especially that we shall have the time and the strength to realize it, but already we see that the subject is far richer than we at first imagined. Our minds always tend to simplify nature. It had seemed to us sufficient to learn how to

---

[1] We have sometimes been accused of being opposed with blind infatuation, to all theory and to the *a priori* method. It is an unjust reproach. We admit the use of theory before the experimental researches, in order to prepare them and afterwards to interpret them; what we strongly reject, are theoretical discussions which are either intended to take the place of an exploration of facts or which are established upon obscure, equivocal and legendary facts, such as are gathered from books, for this is what certain people call observing; it is reading. In our opinions, the ideal of the scientific method must be a combination of theory and of experimentation. Such a combination is well defined in the following formula: prolonged meditation upon facts gathered at first hand.

[2] See *Année*, XI, p. 163 and ff.

182

measure the child's intelligence. This method of measurement we now set forth, which if not complete is at least established upon correct lines, and already usable. But our experience has taught us that there are other problems equally important connected with this. The child differs from the adult not only in the degree and quantity of his intelligence, but also in its form. What this childish form of intelligence is, we do not yet know. In our actual experiments we have only caught glimpses of it. It certainly demands careful study." Moreover, in trying to trace the lines of development of the child's intelligence, we naturally were led to cast a glance at the program of studies, and we have found that certain of these studies are premature, that is to say poorly adapted to the mental receptivity of young children. In other words, the relation between the child's intellectual development and the course of study constitutes a new problem, engrafted upon the first, the practical interest of which is very great. Therefore, before studying the intellectual aptitudes of children we shall be obliged to stop a while at these two stages: (1) special characteristics of the child mind, and (2) the relation between the intellectual development of children and the instruction which they receive. In the present article will be found some attempts to solve these interesting questions.

For the moment we must content ourselves with studying what pertains to intellectual development and the processes to be used in measuring it. It will be seen that these researches will interest not only the dilettanti in psychology but certainly will render great service to psychiatry and to medico-legal surveys.

Let us limit our subject still further. In previous publications we have shown that it is possible to divide the methods of measuring intelligence into three groups: (1) the anatomical method, (measurement of the cranium, of the face, of corporeal development; observation and interpretation of stigmata of degeneracy, etc.); (2) the pedagogical method (measurement of knowledge acquired at school, principally in spelling and arithmetic); (3) the psychological method (measurement of the uncultured intelligence). All these phases of the same study are rapidly being developed thanks to the collaboration of a few persons whom we have succeeded in interesting in them, but we shall present elsewhere the anatomical and pedagogical study. Here we shall consider only the psychological measurement of intelligence.

This measurement is taken by means of a series of tests, the gradation of which constitutes what we call a "Measuring Scale of Intelligence." It is important, above all, to set forth these tests with sufficient precision to enable any one to repeat them correctly who will take the trouble to assimilate them.[3]

To avoid making our description a monotonous methodology, we shall describe and discuss many of the replies obtained from children by these tests, and we shall try through all our experiments to let the reader form a picture of the child in the course of its development.

CHILDREN OF THREE YEARS OF AGE

Pointing to nose, eyes, and mouth. One of the clearest signs of awakening intelligence among young children is their understanding of spoken language. For a long time the young child understands only gestures, and our speech has affected him only by the intonation of the voice. Idiots are beings who remain all their lives in this elementary stage unable to communicate with their fellows through language. The first step toward acquiring a language is its comprehension. We understand the thoughts of others expressed in speech before we are able to express our own. Consequently, the first test is given to show that the child understands the meaning of ordinary words; the simplest way that he can prove this without speech is to execute a spoken command in the fashion of the mute; our test consists therefore in ordering him to touch the parts of his face which he knows best, the nose, the mouth, the eyes. One could equally well show him a picture containing familiar objects, and when his attention became fixed upon the picture one could ask him some very

---

[3] The work that we here publish is so long and minute that to shorten it we omit an historical sketch; it will be found however in a previous volume, of *l'Année psychologique* (Vol. XI, p. 163). Let us recall also that M. Decroly and Mlle. Degand have been kind enough to take up and verify our first investigations with a care for which we congratulate them, and that the Société de pédologie de Bruxelles has put these investigations in their schedule of work. All our successive experiments and certain new ones have been made either at l'Asile Sainte-Anne, or at la Salpêtrière, or in the primary and maternal schools of Paris. They bear therefore always upon children of the so-called working class. This is a fact to be emphasized.

simple questions inviting an analysis. One might ask, for example, "Where is the chair?" "Show me the baby," "Show me the window," etc. *A priori*, it might be thought that the child would have more trouble in recognizing an object in a picture, than a real object. Our drawings and pictures are on flat surfaces, and by the artifice of perspective represent the three dimensions of real things. They are, moreover, very much reduced in size. One might conclude that for these reasons it is more difficult to recognize a pictured object than a real object which is before one and which has color, relief, and its actual size, but this is only an *a priori* objection.

In fact, every child who finds his mouth and nose, when they are named to him, finds equally well the objects which he is asked to look for in a picture, on condition of course that these objects are familiar to him and are drawn with sufficient correctness.

To conduct this test, one must look closely at the child, attract his attention, and repeat several times, "Show me your nose," or, "Put your finger on your nose," and repeat the same order for the eyes and the mouth. Sometimes the child does not execute the movement because he is distracted or because he is bashful and is ashamed of what is requested of him. But, as a rule, with a little insistence he is readily made to obey. Sometimes a child shows his nose by thrusting his face forward, without making any movement with his hand, or indicates his mouth by opening it, as an animal would do. There is, indeed, an animal period when the hand is still a paw and not an organ serving to make signs and expressive gestures. Since this test and those following are intended especially for the children of the Maternal School it is necessary that whoever makes the experiment know beforehand that many among the very young children, especially those three or four years old, remain silent and motionless when they are asked questions. Some decide to perform little acts such as pointing to the nose but do not want to speak; speech seems to be harder to them than gestures. The directresses of the Maternal School can always point out children who in the classroom *never* answer the teacher, sometimes even after two years of acquaintance. The greater number of these silent children speak and prattle with their companions, and are mute only in the class-room. Others, indeed, speak to no one—neither teacher nor school companions, but do speak in their homes, at least so their parents assure us. The teachers have great trouble in training them. We recall a charming directress of the Maternal School at Fontainebleau who told us that for two years she could not succeed in making a little four-year-old boy talk, but finally succeeded with the help of a cat. One day she left the child in a room with the animal, and, little by little, the child spoke to the cat and said "Good morning, pussy." From that moment the miracle had taken place, his tongue had been loosened.

One may easily imagine the difficulty attending such an experiment when such cases of silence are met with. What is to be done? It is often useful to ask the teacher to interfere. If she is intelligent enough, she will know how to talk to the little folk, to reassure them and make them respond. A little caress to one, a little chiding to another, and all goes well. Sometimes we have seen children declare they could not perform what was requested of them, and remain obstinate in their refusal. For instance, upon being asked to make a bow with some ribbons, they not only would not do it, but even refused to touch the ribbons; yet after having been rather severely reprimanded they would consent and would then make an attractive bow.

Repetition of sentences.[4] After the comprehension of words, the most simple manifestation of language consists not, as might be believed, in expressing a thought, in giving the name of an object, but in the repetition of a word spoken before him. We have discovered that it is easier to repeat a word than to take the initiative in speaking, that is to say to pass from the idea to the word. We have found proof of this among imbeciles, and it helps us in the study of the normal child. The repetition of a word or a sentence is rather easily obtained from young children, say three years of age, if the child is willing to try. But it is sometimes difficult to know if the repetition is correct, for the young child has a natural defect in pronunciation, which we call "*bafouillage*" and which consists in mutilating the words or in articulating them indistinctly. These mumblings are not due to a definite defect of pronunciation which might be caused by an anatomical defect nor to an imperfect functioning of the phonetic organs. It is due simply and wholly to awkwardness and not only affects the articulation of the words, but also modifies their

See also p. 58, 1905 scale.

intellectual value; thus, instead of saying, "*J'ai donné deux sous au mendiant*" (I gave two sous to the beggar), he will say, "*à la mendiant;*" and instead of saying "*Il ne faut pas faire de mal aux oiseaux,*" (You must not hurt the birds) he will say "*à les oiseaux.*" Moreover other errors, very much like these, consist in replacing the language of adults by childish language. Instead of saying, "*Nous irons à la campagne*" (We are going to the country) they say, "*On ira à la campagne*" (One will go to the country).

For this test the following sentences are to be used which have been purposely composed of words easily understood.

"*It rains. I am hungry.*" (6 syllables.)

"*They call me Gaston. Oh! the naughty dog.*" (10 syllables.)

"*We are going for a walk. Mary, let me see your pretty hat.*" (16 syllables.)

These sentences are to be said with expression by the experimenter. Do not tolerate any kind of error in the repetition. If the child remains silent, intimidated, set him going by having him repeat shorter sentences; here we give our whole game:

"*Papa.*" (2 syllables.)

"*My hat. Her shoe.*" (4 syllables.)

"*It rains. I am hungry.*" (6 syllables.)

"*I have a handkerchief. I have clean hands.*" (8 syllables.)

"*They call me Gaston. Oh! the naughty dog.*" (10 syllables.)

"*It rains in the garden. Joseph does his lessons. We are having a pleasant time. I caught a little mouse.*" (14 syllables).

"*We are going for a walk. Mary, let me see your pretty hat.*" "*Charlotte has just torn her pretty dress. I gave two sous to a poor beggar.*" (18 syllables.)

"*My child, it is not right to hurt the birds. It is dark, everyone should be in bed.*" (20 syllables.)

A three-year-old child repeats a sentence of 6 syllables. He can not repeat one of 10.

Repetition of figures.[5] The repetition of figures requires about the same kind of effort as that of sentences, except that the sense of figures is less obvious than that of words; in this case no help is gained from the comprehension of what is said; greater attention is required and the task is more difficult. It is a natural conclusion, therefore, that a child three years old who can repeat

[5] See p. 53, 1905 scale.

a sentence of six words cannot repeat more than 2 figures, which shows that, owing to the suggestion of ideas the power of memory is as it were trebled.

The method of performing this experiment is as follows:

One warns the child that he must listen and then repeat what is said to him. Begin by pronouncing a single figure. The child repeats it. Next pronounce two figures which are not consecutive, for example, 3–7, or 6–4, etc. Pronounce these slowly, at an interval of half a second. If there is any error in the repetition, or if the child has defective speech which prevents the exact understanding of what he has said, begin again. It suffices for the test to be passed if the exact repetition is correct once out of three trials. If the child can repeat two figures, try three, at the same rate of two a second always avoiding intonation. Here again one success out of three trials suffices for the test to be passed. Many young children three years old, who easily repeat two figures, are incapable of repeating three. The addition of one more figure enormously increases the difficulty. If three figures can be repeated, try five, always under the same conditions of speed and pronunciation, accepting one success out of three trials.

Note also how much more difficult it is to repeat five figures than three. The errors made by children in these various repetitions are of several kinds; first, complete silence; second, defective pronunciation, a sort of vagueness or haziness in the pronunciation; third, partial repetition with a tendency to give only the last figures heard, sometimes only the last one; and fourth, a tendency to invent figures which have not been given. This is no haphazard invention. It is an application of the natural order of the figures. For instance, a subject who has been given the series 5, 8, 2, 7, 4 readily says, 5, 8, 2, 3, 4, because the "2" naturally calls up the "3." Sometimes this phenomenon is still more marked, and is so striking that it indicates great weakness of the critical sense. A young child, who has completely forgotten the figures 0, 8, 2, 7, 9, will say 1, 2, 3, 4, 5, 6, etc.

Presentation of a picture. With children pictures render invaluable service. The eyes of even the most inattentive child shine when he is shown a picture. It is an almost certain means of captivating him. Pictures may serve many ends; as we have already said they may be used for the designation of objects. We shall now show how they may be used to make a child talk.

A preceding test has shown us that the child passes from the word to the designation of the object. Now let us try to make him do the reverse, which is infinitely more difficult for him, making him pass from the object to the word. Here the object is a picture, a scene full of meaning, containing a multitude of objects which he knows and at which he likes to look. Let us ask him to tell us what he sees. Not only will he talk and bring all of his vocabulary to bear upon the expression of his ideas, but he is free to look at and to choose what he pleases in the picture; he will, therefore, show us what to him is most striking, and, at the same time, what idea directs him, what is his mentality, how he perceives, how he interprets, how he reasons.

This test has the remarkable advantage of serving in the diagnosis of three different intellectual levels. The replies indicate whether the subject is at the intellectual level of three, seven or twelve years. Very few tests yield so much information as this one. If we add that this test is one which pleases young children the most, and succeeds in overcoming the obstinate silence of the very smallest ones we are justified in concluding that we have found here, by chance, a test of exceptional value. We place it above all the others, and if we were obliged to retain only one, we should not hesitate to select this one.

We used the three pictures which are reproduced in the text. We could, if necessary, substitute other similar pictures, but these are of known difficulty which has been measured, and, therefore should be preferred to others. All of them contain persons and a theme. This is the essential requisite. They are mounted on cardboard. We present them one after the other to the child, asking him, "What is this?" Sometimes if the child is very young, he answers naïvely, "It is a picture," or, "It is a post card." We then ask the question in another form. "Tell me what you see there." It is very rare, altogether exceptional, that the child remains silent. Even a three-year-old child casts a glance of curiosity at the picture, which lends itself to the most childish, as well as to the most learned reflections. The replies obtained are of three distinct types, each of which characterizes a different intellectual level.

1. *Replies by enumeration.* These are the most elementary. The young child simply names the people and the objects which he recognizes in the picture. He enumerates them without

establishing any connection between them. He simply pronounces common nouns. In its most elementary form, this
amounts to saying, "a man, a woman, a papa, a carriage, a little
child." Or, again, some very young children use the definite
article, as "the child," "the man," "the lady." Sometimes
instead of indicating people, objects are singled out, "a bed,"
or perhaps, "a table." Notice that it is the object which is named
and not the action. A child three years old will say, "a man;"
we never have found one who said, looking at the second picture,

FIG. 1

"he is sleeping;" not one who paid attention to the action, or to
the characteristics of the persons. At least a child three years
old who would make such a remark would be far superior to his
age. At three years, therefore, the child is at the stage of *recog-*
nition and identification of objects. This is the important, fundamental work of sensory perception, the one in relation to which all
the other processes of perception are complementary and accessory.

One would suppose the development of this fundamental process of identification might take place in many different ways. In reality it takes place by simple addition, i.e., the number of objects identified increases. For each picture, two, three or four objects are designated instead of one. When there are several identifications, another question arises, that of order. According to our observations a child looking at our three pictures singles out people first, but there are exceptions to this rule, for sometimes an inanimate object is named first. Thus, for the third picture:

FIG. 2

"Two tables, a chair, a bed, a man." For the second picture: "a man, a woman, a bench." For the first: "a cart, a man, a pail, a basket." At times, through suggestion, a curious mistake arises in the examination of the first picture. Looking at the cart the child says, "a cart, a horse."

There is a third stage rather superior to the preceding: the names are no longer given separately, but are connected in a very elementary manner with the conjunctions *and, with, and then,* e.g., "*a man and a woman*" "*a cart and then a man*" "*a man with a woman,"* etc. Occasionally with rather old but backward children, we meet with a type of answer by enumeration, which presents very special characteristics. The enumeration persists but a great number of objects are designated, whereas, on the contrary, the enumeration of a very young normal child is very brief. This difference is easily explained. A backward child, 11

FIG. 3

years old, who has only the intellectual level of a child of 6 or 7 years, has, nevertheless, the advantage over the latter of a larger experience; having lived longer, he has at his command a more extensive vocabulary. For example: Mad ——, a boy ten and a half years, who has the intellectual level of a child of seven years (we shall explain later how we are able to determine the intellectual level so accurately) gives us the following detailed enumeration when looking at the first picture. *"I see an old man, and also a child, there is a flood, there is water, a carriage, a basket, a brush, a pail, two wheels, a carpet."* Another still more characteristic example of enumeration full of details is afforded by Lau——, a child 13 years old, who intellectually is four years retarded. He said, *"A man, a cart, a child, a pail, a basket; back there a piece of wood, back there rocks."* In all these instances we record the type of answer which is given most frequently.

2. Replies by description. This belongs to the level of seven years whereas the answers by enumeration are of the level of three years. One sees that the difference is great. The characteristics of the people and the nature of the things are now pointed out. Moreover, attention is paid to the relation of objects, with the result that instead of simple words, sentences are used. For example:

First picture. *There is a man and a little boy pulling a cart.*

Second picture. *A man and a woman are sleeping on a bench.*

Third picture. *There is a man standing on his bed to look through the window. A man looking in a mirror.*

3. Replies by interpretation. The subject of the scene, or the nature of the people is simply indicated either by a suggesting word, or by comments, and often there is an element of emotion, of sadness or of sympathy. This emotion may have been present in children who gave simpler answers, but they did not know how to express it.

The answers which follow we call answers by interpretation, because the comments go beyond what is visible in the picture; there is a real search for causes, a conjecture. First picture. *A rag picker. There is a poor man moving his household goods. They are people who are moving away without having paid the rent. There is a working man.* Second picture. *It is poverty. An unfortunate. They are unfortunates sitting on a bench who have no home where they can go to sleep. It is night, there are unfortunates.* Third picture. *A prisoner. This shows a prisoner, a man who is in prison, who is standing on his bed to look through the window of his prison, which is barred.* The words *unfortunate, moving away,* and *prisoner* used in the answer warrant us in concluding that the theme of the picture has been interpreted.

We cannot resist making a philosophical remark upon the hierarchy which we have made of these replies. An onlooker who is opposed to this theory, might object that the answers by description are superior to those by interpretation, because they are less liable to error, they state only known facts, adding nothing to them, whereas the interpretation is conjectural and may be simply fancy. *"Hypotheses non fingo,"* this critic observes. We know that this has occasioned many discussions in science. The fact which we have just gleaned from our studies with children, well deserves to be considered as an argument in the debate. Since only older children attempt interpretation we are obliged to conclude that interpretation belongs to an intellectual level superior to that of description. But the question is complicated, for not only must attention be paid to the intellectual level but also to the deviations and errors which may occur in this same level. We recall having shown our pictures to an adult of whose stupidity we were well aware. His interpretations were many and of a peculiar order. For example, the first picture inspired the following reply: *"It is a scene which is taking place in the month of February."* Let us analyze this conjecture. It is evidently an interpretation, but without apparent foundation, and one that is impossible to confirm or to refute. The scene could have taken place equally well in October, November, December, January or even March. Why then this precision which is so useless and unwarranted? The reply of this individual must be ranked among interpretations, and in our classification it is superior to the descriptive reply of a seven year old child; but, besides this, it displays a lack of judgment, and this lack of judgment is independent of the hierarchy of the replies.

Family name. We conclude this brief study of the three year old child by asking him for a bit of information which he should possess—his family name. All children of this age, of course, know their first name, or the diminutive by which they are usually called. But the family name is less familiar to them. Nevertheless, they are asked for it in the school; at the Maternal School they are usually addressed by their family name.

We ask a child therefore, "What is your name?" If he replies only by his first name we insist on knowing his family name "Roger? And then? And what else? etc."

It happens sometimes that the child gives another name than the one by which he is enrolled. To explain these errors one must remember that there are many illegitimate children, and, what is more pitiable, the child's mother has had different husbands, and the name which the child bears in succeeding years is not always the same.

When a child is not able to give his family name one must not ask him for that of his mother, for this question is too difficult for a three year old child, and the reply "She's called Mama" cannot be taken as a bad answer for this age.

CHILDREN FOUR YEARS OF AGE

Sex of the child. "Are you a little boy or a little girl?" Such is the very simple question which we ask. Not all three year old children answer this question. The correct reply is, "A little girl," or "A little boy." Sometimes the child simply says, "Yes," or, "No." Under these circumstances ask two separate questions, "Are you a little boy?" "Are you a little girl?" At this age the least thing distracts a child.

Three year old children may make a mistake, but a normal four year old child will always answer correctly when asked its sex. Besides, it is reasonable to suppose that between the third and fourth years a marked change takes place in the mental state of the child.

Naming familiar objects. This is another exercise of spoken language, but is not at all like the language suggested by the pictures, being much more difficult. In a picture the child named what interested him, or what he could name, whereas in this test the object is shown him and he must tell the name of that object and not of some other. Perhaps at first sight this is a distinction which seems trivial, but in reality it is very significant, the proof of which is that the majority of three year old children succeed in the test with the pictures, but fail at giving the names of objects. Moreover, objects are a little less familiar than men and women, which the child names by preference in the picture.

Show the child three familiar objects one after the other, a key, a closed pen-knife, and a sou, and ask him, "What is this?" "What is it called?" The key is named readily though sometimes with defective enunciation. The pen-knife is usually called a knife, and the sou, sous. We excuse these trifling errors, but the names of the three objects must be correct.

We chose these three objects because any experimenter ordinarily has them in his pocket, and in order to avoid as much as possible the trouble of preparing special materials.

Repeating three figures. This test is given as the test with the two figures. We need not repeat.[6]

Comparing two lines. Here is another test, whose difficulty could not be foreseen. An imbecile who understands when told, "Go shut the door," and who executes the verbal order given without gesture or glance, can not compare the length of two lines placed before him. Does he see that the two lines are of unequal length? It is possible. If he were offered two crackers would he take the longer one to eat? That is yet to be investigated. But he does not understand the words, "the longer;" he does not comprehend that he is required to make a comparison, and so he stupidly puts his finger in the space between the two lines. A three year old child does the same. It is only at four years that they perform the operation correctly.

The test is conducted as follows. On a sheet of white paper draw with ink two straight horizontal lines, one 5 cm. long, the other 6 cm., parallel and 3 cm. apart. Show the lines to the child and say, "You see these lines, tell me which is the longer?" No hesitation is tolerated. Sometimes the child puts his finger between the two lines. If he does not correct himself immediately, this constitutes failure. This test is rapid, easy to execute and easy to interpret.

CHILDREN FIVE YEARS OF AGE

Comparison of two weights.[7] This comparison is the same as that of the lines, except that the lines are compared by a glance, whereas the boxes must be taken in the hand and weighed, often several times in succession. Hardly any children below five years succeed in this test, while a child of four years succeeds in comparing lines.

For this test, use four boxes, all of the same volume, and which weigh respectively, 3 grams and 12 grams, 6 grams and 15 grams. The 3 and 12 gram boxes are shown first. They are placed on a table before the child about 5 or 6 cm. apart. Say to the child, "You see these boxes; tell me which is heavier?"

The most satisfactory reply consists in taking the boxes, weigh-

---

[6] See p. 53, 1905 scale.   [7] See p. 55, 1905 scale.

ing them one after the other in the same hand, or at the same time in both hands, and then indicating the 12 gram box. To be sure that the choice is not the result of chance, the 6 and 15 gram boxes are then shown, and then the first two boxes are again given the child, and he is requested to compare them once more. If there is the slightest doubt the test should be repeated.

A very young child proceeds differently. When he is asked to tell which box is heavier he replies at once by pointing to one of the boxes by chance without weighing them. We are indulgent and readily pass over this naïve blunder, which is explained sometimes by the thoughtlessness of the child, or by suggestibility, or by a desire to please us, and we say to him, "No, that is not right. You must take the two boxes in your hand and weigh them." This supplementary instruction suffices for orienting many subjects; as for the others they are not considered except that we have observed with interest the mistakes they have made. Here are some of them; weighing only one of the boxes and declaring that it is the heavier; putting the two boxes side by side in the same hand and saying that one of them is heavier than the other (in this case the weighing, although much more difficult, is not impossible); finally, placing the two boxes on top of each other and in the same hand; this again is more imperfect as a means of weighing but it is nevertheless possible to make an accurate judgment.

Let us note that this test includes two very distinct operations, one of which consists in understanding that the weights of the two boxes must be compared, and in acting accordingly; another which consists in appreciating the difference between the two weights. The first operation is much more difficult than the second; we may say that it depends on the general intelligence of the child, and presupposes a rather high intellectual level, while the second rests on the much more simple faculty of sensing a difference, which requires a much lower intellectual level, perhaps only of two years. This is proved by the fact that, in spite of all explanation given him, if the child does not succeed by himself in taking the boxes and weighing them, it generally suffices to place the boxes one in each of his hands and to ask him which is the heavier, in order to obtain a correct answer. It is amusing to observe the contrast between the awkwardness with which a little child takes the boxes, weighs them and compares them, and the assurance which he exhibits in sensing the difference in their weight.

Copying a square. This is the first time that we place a pen in the hand of a child.

With ink draw a square, 3 or 4 cm. on a side, and ask the child to copy it using a pen. The use of the pen increases the difficulty and it should not be replaced by a pencil. Young children make the figure smaller, but that does not matter, so long as one can recognize it.

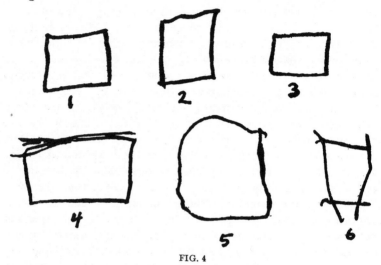

FIG. 4

We give here some reproductions of drawings which we consider satisfactory (1, 2, 3), and others which we consider so imperfect that they constitute failures (4, 5, 6).

"Game of patience." This is a game which amuses children; at the school, children amuse themselves by building things with blocks. It is a game, but at the same time a work of the intelligence, involving materials, sensations and movements. When one analyzes the operation it is found to be composed of the following elements: (1) Consciousness of the end to be attained, that is to say, a figure to be produced; this end must be understood, and kept in mind; (2) the trying of various combinations under the influence of this directing idea, which often unconsciously determines the kind of attempt which should be made; (3) judging the combination formed, comparing it with the model, and deciding if it resembles the other.

This little puzzle at first sight presents the advantage that its difficulty may be increased at will. There are some games easily solved by a five year old child and others so complicated that they severely try the skill of an adult. We began by choosing a very difficult game of patience, and our reason for abandoning it is worth explaining. It was because chance played too great a part in its success.. The game consisted in rearranging a card cut into ten pieces; if by good fortune one combined correctly the first two or three pieces, the rest was easy to guess. On the contrary, if chance were not favorable the problem became much more difficult and the best intelligence might fail. It was proved that in certain cases success was quite independent of age. This objection, suggested by experience, decided us to abandon this type of puzzle.

The one which we have now definitely adopted is so simple that it leaves no room for chance. It is adapted to five year old children and contains only two pieces.

Cut in halves along the diagonal, a card which had the form of an elongated rectangle, thus obtaining two triangles. Place on the table a similar card which is uncut, and put the two triangular pieces in front of the child in such a way that the two hypothenuses are not adjacent and tell the child, "Put these two pieces together; reunite these two fragments so as to make a figure like this one," indicating the uncut card.

Only a third of the four year old children can reconstruct the rectangle. The others do not understand what is wanted; they move the pieces of cardboard about at random, or they refrain from touching them; or, they put them together incorrectly; they place them side by side without connecting them; or they cover one piece with the other; or, finally, they form a figure which has no resemblance to the model. At five years there has been definite progress, hardly one child in twelve fails.

Some precautions must be observed in this test. We wish to emphasize these three:

1. Some little children do not want to take the trouble to move the pieces of cardboard, or even touch them. In this case, without giving them any precise suggestion, it is necessary to chide them a little to arouse them from their indifference. We consider as having failed those who persist in uniting the pieces at random, or who cover one with the other.

2. In this test, care must be taken not to let the child overturn

one of the pieces of cardboard, for in that case it would be impossible to make a figure like the model. If he overturns the cardboard accidentally and does not notice the difference, the test should be repeated, or else consider the test passed if the two pieces are put together with their longest sides adjacent.

3. During the test the child often stops and looks at us as if to get our opinion. According to what he may read on our faces, he may feel satisfied with his work or he may try something else. One must express nothing, must know how to wait, and must wait in silence.

Counting four single sous. Counting is the last test we make for five year old children. The objection may be raised that this is a test of scholastic training which indicates the instruction rather than the intelligence of the child. This is true; but what being is there so deprived of training that he has not been taught to count? We have studied many imbeciles in institutions and all of those who have intelligence sufficient for counting have learned to count. In spite of the laws for compulsory education there are many illiterates; among soldiers, they say, these amount to more than 5 per cent; but has anyone ever encountered any individual who has never learned to count, if his intelligence permitted it? They must, indeed, be rare.

The study of the act of counting is extremely complicated, and it will be seen from what follows that we have many times in our measuring scale made use of this simple operation realizing that it has great social significance. To be able to count, one must know many things; first one must be able to recite the list of figures correctly, then be able to apply each number to a different object. We have not taken as a test the simple recitation of the figures, because that is merely a matter of memory; we prefer the act of counting which presupposes some judgment. We ask the child to count four sous.

Place side by side four single sous on a table, but not covering one another. Say to the child: "You see these sous, count them; tell me how many there are." Some children, without counting, answer immediately any number whatever; whether this answer is right or wrong, it is not taken into consideration, as the right answer might be given by chance. We insist that the child actually count the sous with his finger. The slightest error suffices for considering that the test is not passed.

A three year old child cannot count four sous; at four years, half of the children succeed; at five years only retarded children fail. This is then a test for five years.

SIX YEAR OLD CHILDREN

Right hand, left ear. Here is another idea that has been learned, one so easy to acquire that when it is lacking this lack is characteristic. Ask the child, "Show me your right hand," and then "Show me your left ear." This is almost a 'catch' question, for by asking the child to show his right hand, he has a tendency to show his right ear.

Sometimes the child shows both hands, or, perhaps with one hand he indicates the other, but the action is so obscure that one does not know which is the hand that points out and which the hand that is shown. To escape this difficulty tell him to hold up his right hand.

According to the manner of replying children may be divided into three classes: (1) There are those who do not know at all which is the right and which the left hand. They may offer the right one, because it is the one they naturally tend to show first; then they will touch the right ear. We entirely disregard those of still less comprehension who do not know at all where the ear is. (2) There are those who have some idea of right and left, but who are not quite sure of it. They present the right hand and touch the right ear, but correct themselves and touch the left ear. (3) Finally, there is a third group of children who without hesitation or error raise the right hand and touch the left ear.

We consider children of the last two groups as having passed the test; those who hesitate and correct themselves as well as those who do not hesitate. But the experimenter must be careful not to give the least suggestion; that would be too naïve. It is evident that if one says to the child, when he touches his right ear, "Are you sure?" or, if one merely seems to disapprove his gesture, the child may be led to touch his left ear; for, if it is not the right it must be the left.

At four years no child shows his left ear; they all show the right ear. At five years half of the children commit errors. At six years there are no mistakes. It is, therefore, a test which is of great value for classification.

Repeating a sentence of sixteen syllables. We have already explained how to conduct this experiment. Half of the five year old, and all of the six year old children succeed in this test.

Esthetic comparison. It cannot be denied that all young children have a sense of the beautiful, and that this sense may be made evident, if a problem is presented in a simple way, for example, by asking the children to compare and make a choice between two figures, one of which is pretty, and the other ugly; but the contrast between the two figures must be very great. This question is very interesting from a philosophic point of view and one can easily demonstrate that there is no faculty found in the adult which does not already exist to some degree in the child.

This is our procedure. We use six drawings (fig. 5) representing heads of women; some are pretty, the others ugly, even deformed: we make the comparison by presenting the faces two at a time, and say to the child each time, "Which is the prettier of these two faces?" It is necessary that the child should reply correctly three times. Care has been taken to place the pretty head sometimes at the right, sometimes at the left, to prevent the subject happening to be right simply because he has acquired the habit of always designating the figure on a given side. One must always be on guard against this automatic tendency to always follow the same direction; it is extremely frequent among children.

At six years children compare correctly the three pairs of faces; at five years they succeed very poorly, only half giving the correct reply.

Definition of familiar objects. Thus far, the verbal replies which we have required of our little ones have been very short; a word or two was sufficient. Now we are going to ask them to make a sentence, because one can not define an object without using a sentence. Definition is not only an exercise and a test of language, it serves also to show us what idea the child has of an object, the manner in which he conceives it, and the point of view which is most important for him.

Ask the subject successively, "What is (1) a fork? (2) A table? (3) A chair? (4) A horse? (5) A mama?" These objects have been chosen from among many because we have discovered that they lend themselves to a useful classification of the replies.

It is not so easy to use this test with very young children. They

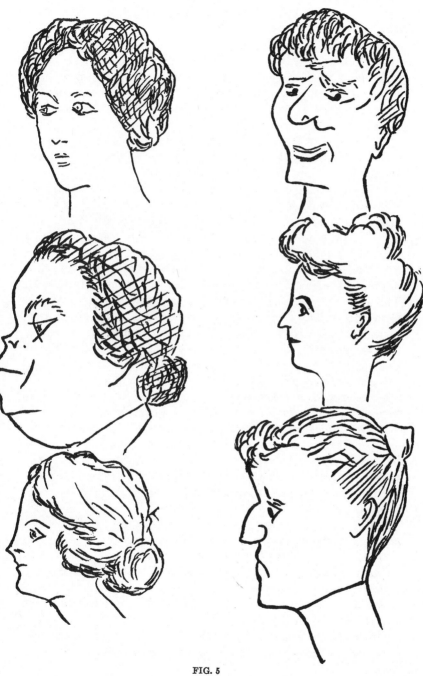

FIG. 5

often reply with an obstinate silence. One may say over and over "You know a table very well, a chair; you have often used a fork," and then conclude a little rashly that, since they know these objects, they must be able to define them. But one does not always succeed in breaking their silence. Some, indicating the table near which they are seated, answer "This."

The replies of the subjects could be classified in a great many ways, if one were making a study of general psychology. For our diagnosis, we establish only three distinctions.

1. Silence, simple repetition, or designation by gesture. We have just given an example of the latter. Repetition is easily understood; it consists in repeating the same word; "What is a fork?" "It is a fork." From the moment that the child has hit upon this manner of avoiding the whole difficulty, one may be sure that he will employ it for the entire series of definitions. He has found the line of least resistance, and he remains faithful to it. This is no spirit of malice. The young child believes that he is answering seriously and honestly what is asked of him and is even greatly satisfied with himself. Do not undeceive him. With a perfect optimism, say to him, "Very good," and mark the result as a complete absence of reply. This result is not extraordinary; it is met with in other psychological experiments, for example, in the association of ideas, some young children and some feeble-minded ones are satisfied to repeat the stimulus word.

2. *Definition by use only.* Example: Horse, *it is to draw wagons, —it is to run;—it is to sit on.* The frequent recourse of the working class and small tradespeople to the horsemeat market explains why a child gave us the following reply: "A horse is to eat." We ask him if he eats horseflesh, and he replies, "Yes."

Fork. *It is to eat with; one eats with it.*

Table. *It is to eat on; a table is for eating,* or, *a table is where one puts the dishes; it is there where one eats.*

Chair. *It is for us to sit on; it is to sit on; it is a place to sit.*

Mama. *She cares for little children; she is to kiss; she is to go on errands; she gets the dinner.*

All these replies are evidently childish, not only for their incorrect form, for the characteristic "it is to," but still more for their conciseness, and finally for the state of mind which they reveal; there is nothing so exclusively utilitarian as a child of seven years.

3. *Definitions superior to use.*   These are so varied in form that we could not cite all the varieties encountered.   But this is unnecessary, for the essential point is not to characterize these definitions but only to distinguish such as are definitions by use.   This distinction is particularly difficult in certain replies where the subject is concerned with the use of the object, but describes it in terms less childish than the preceding.   For example.   Table; *is an object which is used to eat on*; or, *it is an instrument for eating*; *it is a utensil to eat upon*; *it is a piece of furniture to eat upon.*   Horse: *it is an animal which draws carriages.*   Mama: *it is a lady who takes care of the house*; *it is a lady who takes care of the children.*

The use of the expressions: "it is an object, it is an animal, it is an instrument, it is a thing," indicates that the definition is less childish than the preceding.   We have also found definitions learned at school which are interesting for their brevity; a table, *it is a thing;* a horse, *it is an animal; it is a domestic animal;* a mama, *it is a person, it is a lady.*   In other cases the children attempt a description of the object; a fork, *it is a little fork with four points;* a table, *a table is a board with four feet;* a horse *has four legs;* a horse *runs, it bites, etc.*   The following series was given by a nine year old child: *A fork has four feet; a table has four feet; a chair has four feet; a horse has four paws; a mama has two hands and two feet.*   Older children think of the nature and the composition of the object: *a fork is copper, a fork is made of white metal, a table is of wood, a chair is pieces of wood with straw, it is varnished wood, a horse is meat, etc.*   Another point of view is the grammatical: *Table is feminine gender, chair also, horse is masculine gender.*   It is unnecessary to give examples of more learned replies, for this test belongs in our measuring scale to the ages of seven and nine years.   The intellectual development of these two ages is determined according to the type of definition given by the child.

To evaluate these definitions one must take account of the character presented by the majority of them.   We ask five of each child; note the type which is found in three of them.

As early as four years half of the children define by use only.   The number increases a little at five years, and at six we may say that practically all children give definitions of this type.   It is not until nine years as we shall see, that the majority of definitions given are superior to use.

Execution of three simultaneous commissions.   Among the working classes children are very early in life sent on errands to the shops to buy milk, bread, meat, and to bring back a bottle of wine. Physicians who practice at the clinic for backward children know that these children are characterized, not by the lack of ability to perform a single commission, but by inability to perform several commissions at one time. The mothers themselves often give information to the physicians upon this interesting peculiarity. Below is the series of commissions we give with the accompanying instructions. "Do you see this key? You are to put it on the chair over there (pointing to the chair) afterwards shut the door; afterwards you will see near the door a box which is on a chair. You will take that box and bring it to me. Now, first the key on the chair; then shut the door, and then bring me the box. Do you understand? Now go." Very often children do only two out of the three commissions; or, arriving at the door they go out, and close the door behind them. Some are wholly satisfied; others see they have forgotten something and seem to be trying to recall. To pass this test the three commissions must be carried out spontaneously, without the necessity of telling the child, "Well, what next? You have forgotten something," etc. It is evident that one might vary the nature of these commissions according to the surroundings. But one must always take care that they are very simple and easy to execute. The smallest difficulty may intimidate the child. If, for example, we leave our silk hat upon a chair we do not use it as an object to be moved; many a child would not dare to touch it.

At four years scarcely any child can perform 3 commissions; at five years one half do them; at six years all or nearly all do them.

Age. Ask the child "How old are you?" Some remain silent; others give exaggerated ages, which are in general much below the reality; a child of six years will say for example that he is two years old. We have not encountered any who give an age greater than their own; those who are mistaken make themselves younger than they are. It is only at six years that the majority of children know their ages. It is not a question here of the date of birth, of course.

Distinction between morning and afternoon. The perception of time develops late in children; for a long period they confuse yesterday and tomorrow. The distinction in this test is brought out by the following question: "Is this morning or afternoon?" Some children reply at random; others simply say, "Yes;" it is not until the sixth year that children know certainly whether it is morning or afternoon. But it is long before six that the child knows whether or not he has already taken his midday meal.

Apropos of this statement our readers no doubt will remark, as they will more than once in going over the tests that follow, that children are far less advanced, far less intelligent than would have been supposed. To which we reply that a rapid examination such as ours, which puzzles them a little and obliges them to make an immediate display of their knowledge, tends to diminish it. Nevertheless, granting this objection, the previous statement still holds. One would expect and we ourselves were expecting more brilliant results. We should have supposed that much before the age of six, children could distinguish between morning and afternoon. The distinction seems so easy! Recall that children of six are the oldest pupils of the "Maternal School." Recall that the program of the "Maternal School" prescribes the teaching of history and geography, "the principal divisions of the earth, biographies drawn from national history." Such are the regulations for the Maternal Schools in the department of the Seine. Is it not somewhat ridiculous to speak of national history to children who are not yet wise enough to distinguish morning from afternoon?

Seven Year Old Children

Unfinished pictures. Show successively four figures (fig. 6) in which there is lacking the eye, the nose, the mouth, the arms. With each picture ask the child, "What is lacking in this picture?" Often the child does not respond, or makes an incorrect reply. For the first picture, which represents a head, he will say, for example, it is the neck which is lacking, or the body, or the ear, or perhaps the legs, or the feet; and once having made this answer he will not fail to repeat it for all the other pictures (automatic repetition). Strictly speaking this is correct, but it is not what we ask. We desire that he notice the lack which makes the figure incomplete. We consider the test passed when three answers out of four are correct. At five years, the answers are inadequate; at six, two-thirds are incorrect; and at seven, the great majority are correct.

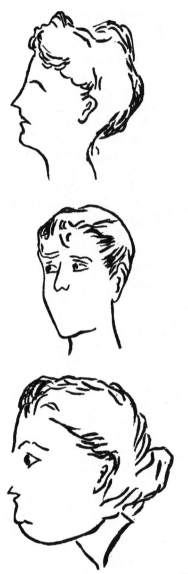

FIG. 6

Number of fingers. "How many fingers have you on your right hand?" "How many on your left hand?" "How many fingers does that make on both hands?" It is necessary that the child reply correctly to all three questions without hesitation. He must reply at once without stopping to think, without counting his fingers, and if he wishes to do so we prevent him. We eliminate therefore those who answer: 4 fingers for the right hand, 5 fingers for the left hand, and 6 fingers for the two hands; 5 fingers for the right, 5 for the left, and 6 in all. Or again those who say 5 fingers for the right, 5 for the left, but for all, "I have not had time to count them." A child knows how to count at an age when he is still ignorant of the number of his fingers.

A priori, we should have thought that a child of six years would have been certain of the number of fingers. This is an error. Half of them do not know it. They do not know it until seven years.

Copy of a written model. The written model is composed of three words, "The little Paul," with capital letters for the first and third words. The copy must be made with pen and ink which increases the difficulty. The model is put before the child. Here again, it may be said, is a test of instruction. Certainly, but on the other hand there may be a degree of defect in the copy which indicates a weakness of intelligence. Thus, some children make only zig-zags, moreover they do not notice that their attempts are unsatisfactory. Others imitate certain letters, which are recognizable in their copy. To pass the test it is necessary that the words, "The little Paul," can be read by a person who is ignorant of the model.

Copying a diamond. We devised this test in an institution. We were surprised to encounter imbeciles who could copy a square, but who could not succeed in copying a diamond. These figures are not very different as to form but the direction of the lines in the diamond is much more difficult to trace. We encountered the same fact among our school children (fig. 7). At five years a child can draw a square, but it is not until seven years that he can draw a diamond; and even at seven years a fifth of them fail. At six years half of the children fail. We give examples of good copies (1, 2, 3) and bad copies (4, 5, 6) so that every one may adopt the same standard as we.

Repetition of five figures. The method has been indicated above. A child four years old repeats three figures; to repeat five figures he must be seven years old; even then only three-fourths of the children succeed.

Description of a picture. At three, four or five years of age, as we have seen, one obtains only enumerations; descriptions are quite unusual. At six years a small number of children, scarcely a sixth, attempt a description. At seven years they have made such progress in language that description has become quite general. There are very few exceptions, and this test shows the enormous

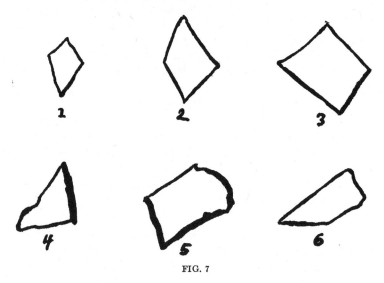

FIG. 7

advance that has been made in regard to language between the sixth and seventh year.

Counting thirteen single sous. The number of objects to be counted increases the difficulty of counting to such a degree, that we must wait until the seventh year to find children able to count thirteen sous.

The thirteen sous are placed near together without covering one another. We insist that the subject count them with his finger and aloud. He must give the right number, thirteen. Sometimes even this is not sufficient, when one is convinced that this answer has been given as the result of chance, or following several errors. There are three essentials to a successful performance: (1) That the subject knows how to count to thirteen, and cannot be deceived in the enumeration; for in this counting every kind of mistake is possible. (2) It is necessary that the subject touch a coin at the same time that he says the number; for this correspondence of the hand and the speech is often what is at fault. There are, for example, children who will repeat one number and touch by two movements two different pieces; as a general rule the hand is swifter than the speech. (3) It is necessary that no piece be skipped and that none be counted twice. This last error, which can be avoided only by using some definite method, is sometimes committed even by adults. We have seen six year old children who take pains to separate each piece from the others as they count. This is the perfection of method—this is a sign of good business heads.

At seven years no one makes a mistake. At six years two-thirds of the children fail.

Giving the name of four common coins. There are nine coins. They may be used in two different tests; the only test with which we are here concerned, consists in determining if the child knows the four following: the 5, 10, and 50 centime pieces and the 5 franc piece. Many young children know only the five centime piece; they call the rest a big sou, a piece, a big piece, or similar expressions. We admit of no error in this test. Hardly any child of six years knows these four coins. At seven years, a large majority know them. It is the most difficult of the tests for seven years.

EIGHT YEAR OLD CHILDREN

Reading with two memories. This test has for us a very special meaning. It serves as the border line between imbecility and moronity. Those defectives who are able to participate in ordinary social life by communicating with their fellows through written language are termed morons. Therefore, it is by a test of reading that we determine whether a defective child is an imbecile or a moron.

Among normal children, this test is of much less importance, for it is the result of school training. When an adult of thirty years does not know how to read, one may, without much fear of being mistaken, question his intelligence. When a child of 8, 9, 10 years does not know how to read, one must suspend judgment, for it may be some prolonged sickness or other cause has prevented him from going to school. Therefore, this test is retained here only under certain conditions. If we use it, and if the child reads fluently, it is a sign of intelligence; if he is unable to read, one must investigate this lack of instruction.

This is what we have the child read:

THREE HOUSES BURN

Chalons-sur-Marne, September 5th. Last night a very large fire in Chalons destroyed three buildings in the center of the city. Seventeen families are without homes. The loss will exceed 150,000 francs. While saving a child in its cradle, a barber's boy had his hands seriously injured.

The test has a three-fold purpose: To make sure that the child knows how to read, to measure his speed in reading, and to ascertain that he understands and remembers something of what he reads. It may be that the subject cannot spell, or cannot read the more difficult words of the text; in this case interrupt the exercise and consider the test as not passed. The speed of the reading may serve as a useful criterion. Let us cite a few figures. To read the above mentioned paragraph, which consists of 53 words [in the French], children of eight years take 45 seconds; at nine years the average time is about 40 seconds; at ten years, 29 seconds; and at eleven years, 25 seconds. There is, therefore, a gain in rapidity up to eleven years; let it be said in passing that these figures permit us to estimate the child's knowledge of reading. We might have included a test of this kind in our measuring scale of intelligence, had we not resolved to measure the intelligence independently of scholastic knowledge. In any case, when we desire to measure the scholastic knowledge of the child, we can employ the following scale:

Average rapidity for reading a selection of 53 words...
- At 8 years; 45 seconds—or about one word a second
- At 9 years; 40 seconds
- At 10 years; 30 seconds
- At 11 years; 25 seconds—or about two words a second.

Several observations are to be made regarding the ability in reading. First, the following distinctions are to be made: spelling out, syllabic reading, hesitating reading, fluent reading, expressive reading. This classification has already been proposed by M. Vaney.[8] Thus, to read the following sentence: "I ate some chocolate this morning," if the child says "I a-t-e, ate, s-o-m-e, some, etc.," it is reading by spelling out. If he says "I (a pause) ate (a pause) some (a pause) cho (a pause) co (a pause) late, etc., it is syllabic reading. If he says "I ate (a pause) some chocolate (a pause) this morning," it is hesitating reading. To be called fluent reading, the reader must stop only at the signs of punctuation; while in expressive reading, one adds the desired tone of the voice to bring out the sense of the selection.

Besides these degrees, notice must be taken of the mispronunciation of words which is frequent among backward and retarded children and may even be encountered in fluent reading.

When the subject has read the selection, allow two or three seconds to elapse, withdraw the paper, and ask the following question, "Tell me what you have just read." Sometimes one must urge the child a little; we urge for ten seconds—not any longer—and then write word for word what the subject says; then count the number of memories which have been expressed, using the following arrangement.

Each word or expression, separated by dashes, constitutes a memory.

Three—houses—burned—Chalons-sur-Marne—September 5th.—A very large fire—destroyed—last night—(Three buildings at Chalons), situated in the center of the city—seventeen families—are without shelter—The loss will exceed 150,000 francs—While saving—a child —in it's cradle—a barber's boy—seriously—injured—his hands.

The maximum number of memories, which however is seldom attained, is nineteen. We have put into parenthesis a portion of the test which is simply repetition.

Let us now apply this calculation.

A child, after the reading, retains the following memories: "A—house—burned—A little boy—burned—his hands." We count this as three correct memories; but *"burned"* his hands is an error. We count only correct memories.

Another example: "Three houses burned—Seventeen families without homes—A barber had his hands seriously injured—He has saved a baby." Eleven correct memories.

As might be supposed there is some relation between the time

[8] We refer the reader to our book on *Enfants Anormaux*, p. 80 and ff., where these definitions of the degree of reading have been developed.

consumed in the reading and the number of memories retained after the reading; that is easily understood. The more difficulty one has in reading, the less attention can be given to the meaning of the words; and consequently those who read slowly, because it is difficult for them, can remember very little of what they have read. Here are the results of our observation. The general rule is that anyone who succeeds in reading the text, however slowly he reads, will retain at least two memories; but in order to be able to retain six memories, he must be able to read it in less than one minute.

Certain errors must be noted, which are quite important for a diagnosis of intelligence. A subject who thinks he can read and who pronounces meaningless words for the space of a minute, while following the lines, gives a poor impression of his intelligence. Such cases are met with. They must be evaluated. Possibly this is to be attributed to the docility of some timid one, who, thinking that he *must* read for us, reads as well as he can. Moreover, we have met a large number of children, who read rapidly, even fluently, but who mutilate the words.   Here then lies an interesting pedagogical question. Those children have not learned well in the beginning; their reading is not inadequate, but faulty.

In conclusion, let us note that certain children, when asked to recount what they have read, give entirely false memories.   One such for instance tells us that the firemen were called; another gave us the following: "*There was a house on fire, and also a child in his cradle, the house was all burnt, the baby has his hands burnt, and his father and mother were dead.*"

Reading with two memories, is rarely accomplished by children of seven years; children of eight years nearly always succeed.

Counting nine sous. (Three single and three double.)[9] On a table prepare in advance a little pile of money, three single and three double sous, side by side, without covering each other. Show them to the subject and say to him "Count this money, and tell me how much there is." Some children do not touch the money. It is then necessary to tell them to handle and count it.

---

[9] *Editor's Note:* The sou or 5-centime piece is in value the same as our cent and is the same familiar coin. Were the old 2-cent piece still in circulation, we could exactly duplicate the test. Since this is not the case, the best than can be done is to use postage stamps. They are stuck to a small card, in a row as follows, 1, 1, 1, 2, 2, 2,

The slight difficulty of the test consists in mixing the double and single sous. No error is tolerated. The slightest error renders the test a failure, and the child must not be allowed to try again. A single necessary precaution is to arrange the money in such a way that all the pieces are visible. The operation lasts from five to ten seconds. If it lasts fifteen seconds, the test should not be considered as passed. Children in this test behave in three different ways: (1) They count correctly, for example, in the following manner, 1-2-3-5-7-9; thus showing that they add two at a time for the double sous; (2) They count correctly, but for the pieces of 2 sous they do not jump two figures, thus, 1, 2, 3, then 4 and 5 (for the first double sous), 6 and 7 (for the second double sou) and 8 and 9 (for the third double sou); (3) they count the double sous, as if they were single sous. The last case is a failure. A great majority of the seven year old children pass this test; all cannot do it until eight years. Therefore, this is a transition test between the two ages.

Naming four colors. Tests of colors might be multiplied. We have chosen the fundamental colors, red, blue, green and yellow, eliminating those whose names are less familiar to children, for example, purple and orange. Our test does not bear on the perception and distinction of the colors, but on their names, which is quite different. The young child distinguishes, recognizes, and easily matches without the least hesitation the most delicate shades of color, and has nothing to envy in the adult so far as his color sense is concerned; it is the verbalization of his color sense, if we may so express it, in which he is defective.

Prepare beforehand a card on which have been pasted four colored papers, red, yellow, blue, green, each measuring 6 by .2 cm. (one must avoid showing too small a surface of color). Point to each color and ask the child, "What is this color?" No error is tolerated. The slightest error causes the test to be a failure. This lasts on the average about six seconds.

To count from 20 to 0. This is partly a test of instruction; one must have learned in order to be able to count backwards. We say to the subject "Will you count backwards from 20 to 0?" If he does not understand, we add "Count like this, 20, 19." Some children cannot count in this way and will not try. Others, in spite of the given instruction, stubbornly insist upon counting forward, either immediately or after having tried to count backwards; they say, 20, 19, 18, 17, 19, 20, 21, 22, 23, etc. Others understand quite well how they are to count, but they succeed only by employing a rather clever trick, consisting in counting forward to find the correct figure, thus, having counted from 20 to 15, they count rapidly, 1, 2, 3, 4, etc., until 15, and find 14 preceding 15. The trick may be discovered either by hearing the child murmuring the numbers, or by the length of time elapsing before each number is pronounced. All these replies are failures. In order for the test to be passed, the operation must not last more than 20 seconds, and there must be not more than one error (one omission or one inversion).

Writing from dictation. We have considered copying in the seven year test. Writing from dictation is far more difficult than copying. Dictate the following words "The pretty little girls." The test is passed when the words are written separately, and if they are legible to one who is ignorant of the dictation. Only a third of the children of seven years can write from dictation; at eight years all succeed.

Comparing two objects from memory. This is a valuable test, for it does not depend at all on instruction, and brings into play the natural good sense. It consists in ascertaining if the child can discover a difference between two objects which he remembers; for this perception of difference in two objects is in reality the habitual and easiest result of a comparison. We say to the child "You have seen butterflies, have you not?"—"Yes," "You have also seen flies?" "Yes." "Are they alike, the butterfly and the fly?" "No."—"How are they not alike?" These expressions are not elegant in style, but have the advantage of being easy to comprehend. We proceed in the same way for the comparison of wood and glass, paper and cardboard. One must always begin by asking the child if he knows the objects in question, and if he thinks they are not alike. Then listen attentively to his reply and weigh it well. We consider as insufficient the replies which consist in simply naming the objects. We have asked in what the paper and the cardboard are not alike; if the subject replies "*cardboard*," it is clear that he has not understood. Another bad reply, although somewhat better, "*A fly, it is a fly.*" Most commonly, the difference noted relates to the size. A butterfly is larger, and a fly is smaller; cardboard is thicker, and the wood is thicker. Again certain details are given. *The butterfly has*

*larger wings—the butterfly has white wings—the butterfly is yellow—
they have not the same color—the fly is black, the butterfly is tri-color
—it is because the butterflies go on the flowers, and the flies go on the
food—paper is soft, cardboard is hard—cardboard cannot be torn—
wood does not break—it is not transparent—glass is used to put in
the windows and the wood is used to make boards for the floor.* To
pass the test we require that two out of three comparisons be correct. In order for the comparison to be correct, the difference
must be a true one. Thus, it often happens that having found a
distinctive characteristic in the first comparison, the subject repeats it for the rest; having said that a butterfly is larger, he will
repeat the same for the cardboard and the wood, which is necessarily an insufficient reply. The time required for this operation
is often rather long, more than one minute for the three comparisons; but if longer than two minutes we consider that the child
has failed. A third of the six-year-old children can make these
comparisons; nearly all seven-year-old children, and all eight-
year-old children succeed in making them.

In conclusion, let us note that it is difficult to distinguish between the intellectual level of seven and of eight years; we succeed
in doing so by using several tests of instruction, which have been
introduced because they are at the same time of value as tests of
intelligence.

NINE YEAR OLD CHILDREN

Complete information regarding the date. The details that we
require under this head are four: the day, the month, the day of
the month, and the year. And here let us remark: we have been
told that in a certain Maternal School (école Maternelle) there is
a language exercise which is given at the beginning of the session,
bearing upon the teaching of the date. Children are taught and
made to repeat, the day, the month, the day of the month, and
the year. However, not a child in this school was able to give the
complete information required, not even the year; concerning the
month, we have had several replies: January, although it was the
8th of February, and that was all. Consulting our scale, one can
see that this complete idea belongs to the age of nine. It is only
at nine years that the great majority of children possess it. This
unexpected discovery leads to an interesting conclusion about precocious teaching. The aim of instruction should be to follow the

natural development of the child, in hastening it a little; but it would be a vain effort to precede it by three or four years, as is ignorantly done, in actual cases where the attempt has been made to teach babies of five or six years, what only nine year old children can retain.

We consider the test passed if the day of the month is within three days of the correct date. Indeed an intelligent person may well believe that it is the 17th of February when really it is the 14th; but one will rarely make a mistake for the day of the week, still less for the month, and never, unless it is a case of sudden amnesia, for the year. Curiously enough, among young children it is the indication of the year, which is most often lacking. They indicate no year at all, they keep silent—they do not know it. For them a year is too great a lapse of time, of which they can form no idea. And moreover, a glance at the calendar will teach them the day, the month, the day of the month—but not the year, which everybody is supposed to know. The calendar for the schoolroom should display very visibly the figures representing the year.

Days of the week. It may be a surprise to some that we place in the ninth year this extra-scholastic acquisition. Nevertheless, it is correct. The knowledge of the days of the week belongs to nine years. We ask the child to recite them, and we insist that he recite them in regular order. To this simple and clear demand, the subject must reply without hesitation, without further explanation, and recite the names of the seven days of the week in their natural order without great effort and consequently with rapidity. If more than 10 seconds are required for this enumeration count the test a failure. We consider those subjects as having failed, who omit one day, who change the order of the days, or who require more than 10 seconds for the repetition.

Making change from twenty sous. This is a test which requires some instruction; nevertheless, it has so great a social value that we make use of it. We think it well to give to this test the appearance of a game; thus it is a recreation and a rest for the mind. On a table there are coins spread about, the nine coins of the national currency (5, 10, 25, and 50 centimes and 1–2–5–10–20 franc pieces), and little further apart a sum of sixty-five centimes, in coins of the following value: three ten-centime pieces, and the rest in five-centime pieces. Now, ask the child, "Will you play store with me? You shall be the merchant." Then, showing him the money, "This is the cash drawer, with the money which you will use in making change for your customers. Now," showing him some little boxes, "this is merchandise which you are to sell; they are boxes. I will buy this box; I shall pay, for example, four sous for it. Is that all right? Do you want to play?" The subject always consents and smiles; our offer pleases him. We give him a one-franc piece, and say "It is agreed, I buy this for four sous, now give me the change," and we extend our hand to receive the money. The only correct reply is the following: the child takes from his change eighty centimes and gives them to us. Sometimes it happens that the subject replies, "I owe you sixteen sous" and yet he does not give us back the correct number, he gives us 15 or 17 for instance. This is a failure. Of course we consider as failures all errors of a still more serious nature such as giving 2 francs or 4 francs, etc. A ten year old school child once gave us back thirty-five francs; this was certainly an exception. In passing let us note how many individual varieties the simple act of making change will bring out.

The quickest and cleverest take at once a ten-sou piece, to which they add six sous. Sometimes, like true merchants, they say, "Four and ten sous are fourteen, and six more are twenty." Sometimes, even, they count in centimes. They are the virtuosos. Others allow themselves to be influenced by the 13 sous that are on the table; they commence by gathering up all the sous and counting them; then they become embarrassed because they could never thus complete the necessary sum; they are obliged to begin the calculation over again and eliminate a certain number of sous which they must replace by a ten- or five-sou piece. It seems that the most ignorant are attracted by the sous, which offer the less difficulty; one must be used to counting money, to take at once one ten-sou piece, then a five-sou piece, and finally add one sou. But these different ways of making change are unimportant for our method. Is the change given equal to 80 centimes? This is the whole matter. At the very most when one analyzes the results, one might consider as slight the mistake of giving one sou too much or too little, and as serious, an error of five sous or more.

Few children of seven years can give the correct change when four sous are to be taken from twenty. At eight years fully a third of them succeed. At nine, they all succeed.

Definitions superior to use. This test is explained above. At seven and at eight years, half the children give definitions of this kind. At nine years all succeed.

Reading with six memories. This test has to do with the reading of the selection already mentioned. All children of eight years are able to read aloud, but scarcely one can retain six memories, which at that age is very difficult; the mechanics of reading absorbs their attention. At nine years nearly all retain six memories.

Arrangement of weights.[10] This test is excellent, for it does not presuppose any scholastic knowledge or any acquired ideas, and expresses the intelligence in its most natural form; but it is a special sort of intelligence, a sensorial intelligence, in no sense verbal; thus a street urchin, who is skillful in the use of words may easily fail with the weights.

For this test we use five little pasteboard boxes, of identical size and color, so that nothing on the outside permits the child to distinguish one from another. They are weighted with filings wrapped in cotton, and weigh respectively 3, 6, 9, 12, 15 grams. Each experimenter should construct his own boxes. For this, it is sufficient to use some letter scales, and five safety-match boxes, the weight of which shall be graded by taking out some matches and replacing them with sous; in this way one can easily make for himself five boxes, weighing respectively 6, 9, 12, 15, 18 grams, which may be substituted for ours.

The five boxes are placed in a group before the subject. Say to him, "These boxes do not all weigh the same. Some are heavy, and some are light. You are going to place here the heaviest, and beside it, the one that is a little less heavy, then here the one a little less heavy, and one a little less heavy, and lastly here the lightest." As we speak, indicate with the finger upon the table the place of each box. We use such simple expressions, because we know that they can be easily understood. The subject is given three trials. When he has placed the boxes in order once, break up the order and ask him to begin again. The weight of each box being inscribed on the side resting on the table, it is easy to know whether the subject has made a mistake or not. Out of three trials, two must be absolutely without error for the test to be passed. Some children do not understand our explana-

---

[10] See p. 62, 1905 scale.

tion and remain motionless; so much the worse for them. Others arrange the boxes at random, without weighing them, and it is easy to see that they do not compare them at all. Others readily understand that the heaviest box must be placed first, and cleverly find it, but are unable to place the remaining boxes in a decreasing order; the idea of a decreasing order is not intelligible to them. What is here lacking, is not the appreciation of weight, but the directing idea. Lastly there are some who grasp the idea of a decreasing order, and who apply it nearly correctly; they make a series like the following: 15, 12, 9, 3, 6, in which only one box is misplaced; they could do better, but they lack attention and care. This is not a very serious error; nevertheless in order that the test be passed we require that two trials must be entirely correct; the entire test must not take more than three minutes.

This test, as has already been said, is one of those which best denote the uncultured intelligence, since it is independent of any instruction. And we also note that the type of intelligence here required is of a very special kind. There are children otherwise very intelligent who do not succeed in placing the boxes in order; while others arrange them correctly and swiftly.

TEN YEAR OLD CHILDREN

The months of the year. We are as exacting for the recitation of the months as we are for that of the days. The subject should recite them without error, without transposing or omitting any, and swiftly enough so that not more than fifteen seconds are required; we permit, nevertheless, the omission or inversion of one month.

Naming the nine pieces of money. They are, as has been said, 1, 5, 10, and 50-centime pieces, 1, 2, 5, 10 and 20-franc pieces.

The main difficulty lies in distinguishing the 1 from the 2-franc piece, also in distinguishing the 10-franc piece from the 20-franc piece. The coins are on the table; we do not handle them, but we point to them, and the subject must name them without touching them. Care must be taken not to allow the coins to be arranged according to value.

This is the order which we propose: 10 centimes, 2 francs, 10 francs, 50 centimes, 20 francs, 1 franc, 5 francs, 25 centimes. The coins must always be shown with the face up.

Children often call the 1-franc a 2-franc piece, and the 10-franc a 20-franc piece, and vice versa. These are only slight errors. The absurdity consists in imagining new pieces of money, as for example, a 3-franc piece, or a piece of 15 sous. A curious error leads sometimes to the confusion of a 10-franc with a 5-franc piece. The time consumed in this test must not exceed forty seconds. Sometimes one can imagine that the error is only a slip of the tongue; in this case we repeat, after an interval of several minutes, the same experiment. We recall that once a twelve year old child correctly named all the coins except the 5-franc piece which he called a 10-franc piece. We said nothing, but several minutes later, we again asked him to name the coins on the table; he made the same error, and consequently we considered that he had failed in the test. We note this fact as a warning against recording the results automatically; there are many cases where a slip of the tongue may be suspected, judging by the sum total of the replies; the test therefore has to be repeated to make sure whether it was really a slip, or not. In other words, in spite of the system of annotation which we have devised, we think it the duty of the experimenter to *judge, weigh* and *examine* the replies. Our method is not an automatic weighing machine like those in railway stations, which register automatically the weight of a person, without his intervention or assistance.

Using three words in one sentence.[11] This is the first time that we require the subject to invent anything. This one is verbal. It supposes that the child knows how to speak and write, and knows the meaning of the words "a sentence."

We write on a sheet of paper, the following words, "*Paris, fortune, stream,*" and read the words aloud to the subject several times and say to him, "Make a sentence in which these three words will be found." Then, hand the pen to the subject. Some will declare that they do not understand. Often it is the expression "*Make a sentence*" which has no meaning for them. No other explanation is to be given, but the instruction already given may be repeated. Others understand, but are not able to invent a sentence of any kind, or at least one that satisfies them. As the latter may be too exacting, therefore we insist that they write some sort of a sentence. The answers given by those who attempt the invention, may be divided into three groups.

[11] See p. 65, 1905 scale.

1. Sentences which contain three distinct ideas. Examples: *"Paris is a city, a person has a fortune, the streams flows," "Paris is a small city; a fortune is a great many sous; a stream is a little river flowing along the sidewalk."*[12]

2. Sentences which contain two ideas. Example: *"In Paris there are gutters and men have great fortunes." "Paris has gutters and a fortune."*

3. Sentences which contain only one idea. Example: *"The Seine is a stream which makes the fortune of Paris." "In Paris I found a fortune in the gutter." "A drunkard without a fortune has been found in the gutter in Paris."*

Beside these three types of unified sentences may be ranged another type, where the sentences are numerous but well coördinated. *"I am in Paris; in our street there is a gutter which empties its water into the sewer; not very far from my father's home I know a man who has a large fortune." "I went to Paris when I was young; I dragged in the gutters for a month; a man took pity on me, took me to his home, and at his death, I inherited his fortune."*

Various stages in the intellectual development of the child are disclosed by these replies. For our purpose we retain only the last two: the three words in two sentences, and the three words in a single sentence. The first test, the three words in two sentences, has never succeeded with children of seven years; at that age they do not write well enough. At eight years almost none pass the test. A third of the children at nine years and half of those at ten years succeed.

We allow a minute for finding a sentence. If after one minute, the sentence, or at least three-quarters of it, is not written, the test is a failure. Note that this test is one of the rare ones in which one child may give help to another; we have met with cases of it.

Another remark. We have said, apropos of the picture test, that a distinction must be made between the intellectual level and the judgment of a child, and we have cited the example of an adult belonging to an advanced mental level, who was able to interpret the picture, but who was guilty of absurdities in his interpreta-

---

[12] The French *"ruisseau"* (stream) is applied both to the river and to the water flowing in the street, *gutter*, and by metonymy to the gutter itself; all the children seem to have understood it in the latter sense, hence their change of the word stream into gutter.—ED.

tion. Perhaps our distinction between the judgment and intellectual level may seem too subtle, but we think not. We find it again in this test. Thus there are children able to use the three words in one sentence, but they form a sentence without sense, and they do not perceive that it is unintelligible. Examples: *"Paris is a city of fortune by the gutters." "In Paris, when there are gutters, she makes a fortune." "Paris is a great fortune, which has a great river."*

These sentences satisfy the requirements of our test, and show that the child has attained the level of the eleventh year, but they prove the weakness of his judgment. Further investigations will undoubtedly teach us the importance that must be attributed to these facts.

Comprehension questions[13] (first series). We give the text of the questions and some examples of replies, good and bad.

1. "When one has missed the train what must one do?" Good replies, *"Wait for another train. Take the next train."* Bad answers, *"Try not to miss it another time. Run after it. Go home. Buy a ticket."*

2. "When one has been struck by a playmate who did not mean to do it what must one do?" Good replies, *"Do nothing to him. Excuse him. Pardon him. Tell him to pay attention another time."* Bad replies, which show that the reservation, "he did not mean to do it" has not been understood, *"Go tell the teacher. Get revenge. Punish him."*

3. "When one breaks something belonging to another what must one do?" Good answers, *"Pay for it. Excuse one's self. Replace it. Acknowledge it."* Bad replies, as a rule unintelligible. *"You must get it paid for. I'd cry. Go to the policeman."*

Our three questions, as may be noticed, are easy to understand and present no difficulty of vocabulary. Therefore, it may happen that even six year old children will answer them satisfactorily, but this is rare. Half of the seven and eight year old children answer acceptably; at nine years three-fourths, and at ten years all children do so. To pass the test we require that two questions out of three be satisfactorily answered.

Comprehension questions (second series). Of the same type as the preceding, but more subtle, and presenting some difficulties of vocabulary.

[13] See p. 65, 1905 scale.

1. "When one is in danger of being late for school, what must one do?" Good answers, *"I must hurry up, I must run."* The bad replies often contain an absurdity. The children have often replied as if they had understood, "What will happen?" they say, *"We are punished, we are stood in a corner,"* *"the teacher would strike me."* Or they look into the future, and try to see how they could avoid a recurrence of the situation. *"We must not do it again. We must start from home earlier."* There is another absurdity still more subtle which is sometimes given. Our question means this: If one is already later than he ought to be, how can the lateness be diminished? That is the real thought. But, instead of this, some children, mistaking the meaning of the question, have understood that they should tell how they can adapt themselves to the consequences of being late. They answered, *"We must ring"* (The school door being closed, those that come late must ring). *"We must bring an excuse from our parents."*

For our purpose, only answers of the first kind are acceptable. "We must hurry up."

2. "Before deciding an important affair, what must one do?" Good replies, *"Study the matter. Reflect. Ask advice."* The bad replies have but little sense, the subject, as a rule, not understanding the idiom, "prendre parti." *"One must care for the sick. One must consult the doctor. One must go away."*

3. "Why does one forgive a wrong action committed in anger more easily than a wrong action committed without anger?" Good answers, *"Because when one is angry, he does not do it purposely. In anger one is not responsible. In anger one does not know what one does."*

Finally the bad answers result from a total lack of comprehension of the question, or because the word "anger" has acted on the child as a suggestion and because the child disapproves the fact of being angry. *"When one is angry, one does not want to listen."* *"One must not get angry."*

This question is the most difficult of all; and it may happen that the child understands it but cannot express his thought. That is a small matter; we must weigh and discover the idea that anger constitutes an excuse.

4. "If someone asks your opinion of a person whom you know but little what must one do?" Good answers, *"One must say nothing. One must not talk without knowledge. One must say nothing for fear of giving wrong information."* The bad answers are mostly unintelligible, *"One must ask. One must answer. We say to him, behave. We say that we do not know his name."*

5. *"Why must we judge a person by his acts rather than by his words?"* Good replies, *"Because words may lie, but acts are true. Because one is surer in seeing the acts than in hearing the words."* Bad replies, often unintelligible, *"One must not lie. Because one does not know."*

In the preceding tests, one sometimes meets with children who remain silent, and the difficulty is to know the cause of this silence. Perhaps the child has no answer, or a poor answer, which does not satisfy him. The experimenter is often at a loss and only from the sum total of the replies can he correctly judge each special case. He must have the patience to allow the child twenty seconds reflection before answering. Two poor answers out of five are allowed.

Children seven or eight years old do not give good answers to the majority of the questions in the second series; only half of the ten year old children answer correctly. This test is therefore transitional between ten and eleven years.

In general, this test is one that best expresses the common notion of intelligence. Sometimes one hesitates about the diagnosis of a child. He fails in one or two tests which scarcely seem conclusive. Not to know the date, not to be able to recite the series of months, might be excusable errors which it is permissible to ascribe either to a lack of attention or of training. But the questions of comprehension dispel all doubt. We recall that several times teachers have asked us to decide if such or such a child was not subnormal; sometimes even they were trying to trap us; but we are not at all adverse to being put to the test ourselves; it is quite fair. Our questions of comprehension enlighten us at once. We remember in particular a child very slow to answer, apparently half asleep, who made a poor impression because of his expressionless face, who did not know the day of the week, nor what day came after Sunday, although he was ten and a half years old; he could read only by syllables. But when we asked the fifth question, *"Why must we judge a person by his acts rather than by his words?"* he gave immediately the following answer, *"Because words are not very sure, and acts are more sure."* That was sufficient. We were enlightened; that child was not so stupid as he looked.

ELEVEN YEAR OLD CHILDREN

Criticism of sentences. This test is not the one we had at first devised. Our aim was to test the judgment of the child; and in order to succeed we followed the method of certain foreign alienists, by giving some absurdities, to see if we could make the child agree with us. Example of absurd questions which we at first employed:

"When two men quarrel, why is there often near them a yellow dog?" "When a man plays marbles, why is he often decorated?" German alienists used to put such questions as this to the insane, "Is snow red or black?"

Experience has shown us that although very dull children accept these absurdities, even looking for and finding a reply to our ridiculous questions, other very intelligent children sometimes fall into the trap.

We have reached the conclusion that the acceptance of an absurd sentence does not depend solely upon the weakness of the child's judgment; timidity, diffidence, confidence, automatism, each plays its part. We recall having dictated our absurd sentences, mixed with others which were not absurd, to a class of backward children in Salpêtrière; imbeciles and morons were not wanting in this class of pupils, but there were about fifteen children who could reply in writing. This constituted a crowd, and a crowd is neither timid nor deferential. Every time that we pronounced one of our absurd "Whys," there was an explosion of ironical laughter from the whole group of pupils. The morons understood therefore the nonsense of our questions, and not feeling obliged to show any deference to us, expressed their feelings noisily. All these reasons induced us to change the form of our test. Now instead of imposing an absurdity, we warn the child that there will be one, and we ask him to discover and refute it; in this way no feeling of reserve, of timidity or of deference, if he has any, paralyses the judgment of the child. The only difficulty for the experimenter is to find out the real meaning of the child when expressed poorly in obscure sentences. Very often the child has the feeling that our affirmation is absurd, but does not succeed in giving the reason for his feeling and cannot translate it into thought. To feel a thing is not the same as expressing it; for in many cases the child contents himself with repeating the same sentence or the part of the sentence which contains the absurdity without other comment than his insistence upon that part of the sentence, or his air of disapprobation.   From this could be deduced interesting analyses of our method of understanding and explaining.   We shall come back to this same subject elsewhere.

For this test we begin with the following explanation: "I am going to read you some sentences in which there is something silly.   Listen attentively and tell me every time what there is that is silly."   Then slowly, very slowly, with a serious tone, we read one sentence, and immediately, changing our tone, we ask, "What is silly in this sentence?"   This experiment usually interests the children by its novelty.

1. "An unfortunate cyclist broke his head and was instantly killed; they have taken him to the hospital, and it is greatly feared that he cannot recover."   Good answers, *"Since he is dead, it is certain that he will not recover."   "If he is dead he cannot recover."   "Since he is dead, he cannot be cared for."   "You say that he is dead, and they take him to the hospital and one is afraid that he will not recover."*   Poor answers, *"It is silly to ride a bicycle."   "It is silly to recover."   "Hospital."   "There is nothing silly."*

2. "I have three brothers, Paul, Ernest and · myself."   Good answers, *"You have only two brothers."   "You are not your own brother."   "If there are three brothers, there must be three brothers, but you, you do not count."   "You ought to say: I have two brothers."*   Poor answers, *"What is silly is that you say 'myself.'"   "You ought to give your name."   "What is silly, it is Ernest."   "What is silly, it is you."   "There is nothing silly."*

3. "Yesterday they found on the fortification the body of an unfortunate girl, cut into eighteen pieces.   It is believed that she killed herself."   Good answers, *"One cannot cut himself into eighteen pieces."   "If she cut an arm, she could not then cut anything else."*   Poor answers, *"What is silly, it is to kill one's self."   "What is silly, it is eighteen pieces."   "It cannot be found out if she killed herself."   "There is nothing silly."   "It is because it is not true."   "If she had nothing at home to cut herself with."*

4. "Yesterday there was a railroad accident, but it was not serious; the number killed is only forty-eight."   Good answers, *"It is very serious when there are forty-eight killed,—it is many."   "It is not serious, and the number of dead is forty-eight!"*   Poor answers,

"Forty-eight dead. There is nothing silly." "It is that there was nobody killed." "One could say many corpses."

5. *"Somebody used to say: If in a moment of despair I should commit suicide, I should not choose Friday, because Friday is an unlucky day and it would bring me ill luck."* Good answers, *"Since he kills himself, it does not matter that it be a Friday or another day." "It does not matter as long as he kills himself, if he kills himself on Friday." "Friday cannot bring him bad luck. He can as well kill himself Friday as Saturday, it does not matter."* Poor answers, *"Friday is like any other day, it does not bring bad luck." "Friday is not a day worse than any other." "What is silly, is to kill one's self." "What is silly, is bad luck." "It is Friday." "There is nothing silly." "One must not be superstitious." "Because we don't know it."*

These five sentences are employed to test the critical sense. To call the test successful we require that at least three of the sentences receive a good reply. This test lasts about 2 minutes. It is one of those which best shows the intelligence of a child. At nine years almost no one succeeds; at ten years scarcely one-fourth, at eleven years, one-half.

Three words in a sentence. The explanation of this test will be found above.[14] Every one succeeds at eleven years; scarcely one-fourth at ten years.

Sixty words in three minutes. The subject is told to cite in 3 minutes the greatest number of words possible, such as *table, beard, shirt, carriage,* etc. Arouse his emulation by telling him that some of his comrades are able to say more than 200 words in 3 minutes, which is true. This test is very interesting, for it furnishes a rich field for observation; besides the number of words, one may note their association. Some subjects say only detached words, each of which demands an effort of invention. Others make series, series of school-room furniture, series of articles of clothing, geological series, etc. Some use only the common nouns, names of objects, others give abstract qualities, or words somewhat unusual. All this gives an idea of the mentality of the subject. To employ a series, to give abstract words, are good signs of intelligence and of culture. But here we consider only the number of words. In 3 minutes one should have time to cite

[14] Page 222.

at least 200 words without hurrying, if he does not have to search for them. However he must search, and everyone has not the same power of evocation. Young children exhaust at once the directing idea; they say, for example, "hat" then they pass to another object without considering that hats have different colors, shapes, parts, uses, connections, and that in mentioning all these one would find a large number of words. There is among them lack of skill in the use of language or in the analysis of ideas, which is very striking. One sees children of ten years who wait sometimes 30 seconds searching for words and finding none. This test allows one to appreciate, in accord with the observations we have made elsewhere, the intellectual activity of a person, as well as his verbal type. Those who have many words at their service, those who think in words, who have acquired the use of abstract ideas or who delight in making puns, seem to us to have an advantage over the others. The test is not passed unless a minimum of 60 words is found. At eleven years, all children succeed; they find sometimes a considerable number of words, 150, 200; one child gave 218.

Abstract definitions. For definitions three abstract words are given, *charity, justice,* and *goodness.* The formula employed is very simple: What is ———?

Charity. A good definition ought to contain two ideas—the idea of unfortunate people and the good that one does them. Good answers, "*It is the act when one helps people in trouble.*" "*It is to give money to old people who are not able to work.*" "*It is to give alms.*" "*Charity is when one sees a poor man, has pity on him, and if one has some sous gives them to him.*" Poor answers, "*It is to be good.*" "*It is to be charitable.*" "*It is to ask.*" "*It is a person who is good.*" "*It is when one is poor.*" "*It is to ask pardon.*"

Justice. A good definition contains the idea of law, that is to say, a rule, of the protection accorded to persons and to interests, or the idea of persons treated according to their merits. Good answers, "*Justice is an act which consists in judging persons who are guilty, and releasing persons who are innocent.*" "*It is a law which commands.*" "*Justice is to punish the wicked even if they are rich.*" Poor answers, "*Justice is the one who judges.*" "*Justice is a judgment.*" "*Justice is to judge.*" "*It is where one judges.*" "*It is to cut the throat.*" "*It is some agents.*"

Goodness. A good definition should express the idea of affectionate feeling, of tenderness, or simply of acts of assistance, without implying the idea of inequality of condition between the one who gives and the one who receives. Good definitions, *"Goodness is to be kind to others." "Goodness is an act which consists in waiting when a person is not able to pay, and in not striking others." "It is to give good for evil." "Goodness is to share with others."* Poor definitions, *"Goodness is to be good." "One must do something good." "To be good, it is to be well dressed." "It is to take off one's hat." "Goodness is diligence." "Goodness is dust." "Goodness is to have cheek or brass."*

To pass the test there must be at least two good definitions. This test is sometimes difficult to interpret. At eight and at nine years, one sometimes finds children who give good definitions, but it is very rare. At ten years, a third succeed; at eleven years, nearly all.

Placing disarranged words in order. This test was inspired by the investigations of Ebbinghaus, who had his pupils fill in blanks left in sentences by the omission of a word. We employ the three following groups which are given to the pupil with the direction: "Put these words in order and find the sentence which they make."

STARTED THE FOR	TO ASKED PAPER	A DEFENDS
AN HOUR EARLY	MY I TEACHER	DOG GOOD HIS
WE COUNTRY AT	CORRECT THE	MASTER BRAVELY

Solutions. *1. We started for the country at an early hour or At an early hour we started for the country.* Poor answer, *"We started country* ———

2. "I asked the teacher to correct my paper."

3. "A good dog bravely defends his master." A variation less exact is *"A dog defends his good master bravely."* Poor variations: *"A master defends his good dog bravely." "A dog defends his master bravely good."*

It is a puzzle which interests many. There are large individual differences in the rapidity with which the solution is found. Some need only five seconds; others need twenty seconds, sometimes even fifty. The time limit is one minute for each sentence. In order to pass the test it is necessary that two out of three sentences be correct.

Many children do not understand the instruction given, and

invent words or make a sentence having no connection with what is written. For instance one child made the following sentence, "*The short dog.*" "*I defend my country.*" "*I have bought some candy.*"

TWELVE YEAR OLD CHILDREN

Repetition of seven figures. This test is made in the same manner as for 5 figures. One warns the subject in advance that he is going to have 7 figures to repeat. Three trials are given; one success is sufficient.

Rhymes.[15] Begin by asking the subject if he knows what the word rhyme means. Whether he knows or not (and very often he thinks he knows when he does not), give him the following explanation. "Two words which rhyme are two words which have the same ending. Thus '*grenouille*' rhymes with '*citrouille*' by the ending in '*ouille.*' In the same way '*mouton*' rhymes with *bâton*, both ending in *ton.* Do you understand? I am going to give you a word and then you must find other words which rhyme with it. It is the word '*obéissance.*' Find me all the words which rhyme with '*obéissance.*' " A minute is allowed for the search and during that period of time the pupil is required to find three rhymes. Stimulate but do not aid him. Generally he begins by reciting the word "*désobéissance.*" Sometimes he gives a series of words which do not rhyme. Others coin words as *fance, niance, servance,* etc., or they give words which do not end in "*ance*" and are unknown; *rirement, miquement.* Finally some children having understood nothing repeat "*grenouille,*" *citrouille.*" While others differently oriented say, *obéir, j'obéis, je désobéis,* or again "*punition, méchanceté.*" Certain ones cite varied examples of disobedience, "To steal things from one's comrades, to give kicks, etc." This test is one of the easiest to measure.

Repetition of a sentence of twenty-six syllables. We have composed a series of 22 sentences each formed of words easy to understand and which are of increasing length; the first of these sentences has 24 syllables; the last has 44. One is able by this process to determine very easily the subject's power of verbal repetition. There are certain effects always to be observed when one proceeds by an increasing order; certain sentences are reproduced exactly; then in proportion as the sentences are lengthened,

---

[15] See p. 63, 1905 scale.

slight, insignificant changes are made in reproducing them; a word is misplaced, a non-essential word is forgotten or even replaced by a synonym. These slight alterations are produced within a limit corresponding to an increase of from 6 to 10 syllables. Then serious omissions are made; an essential part of a sentence is forgotten or changed. We think it more convenient to allow no error.

Let us remark in passing that the memory for verbal repetition does not greatly increase from six to ten years, notwithstanding the immense intellectual difference between these two ages.

Thus a group of six year old children at the Maternal School has given us the following series of maximums of repetition, 22–18–20–18–20–24. A group of nine and ten year old children has given: 16–22–22–22–22–22–22. We had expected a very much greater difference. Decidedly, memory does not make great progress with age.

We require that at 12 years a sentence of 26 syllables should be repeated correctly. Here are the sentences we use.

Twenty-four syllables. *My children, one must work very hard in order to live; one must go to school every morning.*

Twenty-six syllables. *The other day I saw in the street a little yellow dog. Little Maurice has soiled his new apron.*

Twenty-eight syllables. *Ernest is often punished for his naughty conduct. I bought at the store a pretty doll for my little niece.*

Thirty syllables. *That night there was a terrible storm of lightning. My companion has taken cold, he has a high fever and he coughs much.*

Thirty-two syllables. *The tram car is cheaper than the omnibus, it costs but 2 cents. It is droll to see women driving coaches in Paris.*

Problem of various facts. Although a puzzle, this test demands good sense rather than a glance of the eye. We have devised two such tests, each of which contains a problem.

1. A person who was walking in the forest of Fontainebleau stopped suddenly, and then, horrified, ran to the nearest police station to report that he had seen hanging from a branch of a tree a ———— (after a pause). *A what?*

2. My neighbor has just been receiving strange visitors. He has received in turn a doctor, a lawyer, and then a priest. What is taking place at my neighbor's house?

These two questions greatly arouse the curiosity of the pupils. To the first they have answered, "*Someone robbing a bird's nest,*

a snail, a thief, an assassin, a trunk of a tree, a bunch of grass, etc.
The only correct answer as the text indicates is "*a person hanged.*"

For the second question the right answer is, "*He is very ill,
he is dying,* etc." Poor answer: *I do not know.* The wrong
answer often consists in a repetition of the question, *He has
the doctor and priest.*

In order to pass the test it is necessary to answer both questions
correctly.

Thirteen Year Old Children

Paper cutting.[16] A sheet of paper folded in four is presented to
the pupil; in the middle of that edge which shows only one fold,
a small triangle, a centimeter in height, whose base coincides

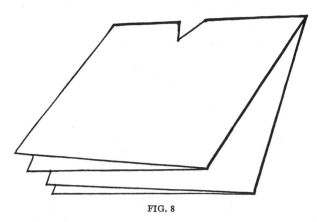

FIG. 8

with the edge of the paper, has been drawn, and the pupil is
told, "Here is a sheet of paper which has been folded in four;
suppose that here (one shows him the triangle) I make a notch
with the scissors, and cut out the little triangle of paper which is
drawn. Now, if I unfold the paper what shall I see? Draw the
paper, and show in what place and how the hole will appear."
It is of course forbidden to touch the paper; it is also forbidden
to try by folding another paper. By the aid of the imagination
alone the subject must be able to represent the effect of the cutting in the unfolded paper. This test is extremely difficult.
Most subjects simplify the problem very much. They imagine
that there is but one hole having the shape of a square, or of a

---

[16] See p. 67, 1905 scale.

rhombus, or sometimes of a five-pointed star, occupying the center of the sheet of paper. They imagine this because the notch was made in the middle of the edge. Some make two rhombuses in a straight line each occupying the center of half the sheet of paper.

When a child succeeds in this test at the first attempt, it is necessary to ask him if he has seen it before.

Reversed triangle. A visiting card is cut in two pieces along its diagonal. It is shown to the subject on a sheet of paper, the two parts in place and touching, and he is told, "Look well at the lower part; suppose it to be turned over and that the edge AC (AC of the figure is indicated by pointing to it) is applied to the edge AB

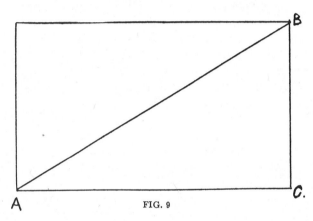

FIG. 9

of the upper part; suppose also that the point C is placed on the point B. Now I remove the piece; replace it in your mind and sketch its contour as if it were in place. Commence by tracing the outline of the first piece." This is a very difficult test. In order to succeed, the pupil must draw a right angle at B, and the edge AC must not be as long as AB. Very often only one of these conditions is satisfied by the pupil's sketch.

Differences.[17] It is asked, What difference is there between

1. Pleasure and happiness?
2. Evolution and revolution?
3. Event and advent?
4. Poverty and misery?
5. Pride and pretension?

---

[17] See p. 68, 1905 scale.

General Conditions of the Examination

First the testing should take place in a quiet isolated room. The examiner should be alone with the child and when possible he should have a secretary whose duty is to record verbatim the child's answers. This secretary may be a child of thirteen or fourteen years, provided he is very intelligent and one can supervise his work a little. The subject to be examined should be kindly received; if he seems timid he should be reassured at once, not only by a kind tone but also by giving him first the tests which seem most like play, for example—giving change for 20 sous. Constantly encourage him during the tests in a gentle voice; one should show satisfaction with his answers whatever they may be. One should never criticise nor lose time by attempting to teach him the test; there is a time for everything. The child is here that his mental capacity may be judged, not that he may be instructed. Never help him by a supplementary explanation which may suggest the answer. Often one is tempted to do so, but it is wrong.

Do not become over anxious nor ask the child if he has understood, a useless scruple since the test is such that he ought to understand. Therefore one should adhere rigorously to the formulas of the experiment, without any addition or omission. Encouragement should be in the tone of voice or in meaningless words, which serve only to arouse him. "Come now! Very good! Hurry a little! Good! Very good! Perfect! Splendid! etc. etc." If witnesses are inevitable impose upon them a rigorous silence. How difficult this is to obtain! Every teacher wishes to interfere in the examination, to supplement the explanation of an embarrassed pupil, especially if he belongs to her class. Have the courage to insist that they keep silent.

Always begin with the tests that fit the child's age. If one gives him too difficult work at first he is discouraged. If, on the contrary, it is too easy it arouses his contempt, and he asks himself if he is not being made fun of, and so makes no effort. We have seen manifestations of this misplaced self-esteem.

On the part of the experimenter, some conditions are necessary. He must not allow himself to be influenced by information regarding the child obtained from other sources. He must say to himself that nothing which he already knows about the child counts at all. He must consider the child as an X to be solved by this means alone. He must be entirely convinced that by using this method, he will be able by it alone to obtain a thorough knowledge of the child without depending on any outside help. But this self-confidence is liable to many fluctuations. In the beginning everything seems easy; it is the period of illusions. After a few trials, if one has at all the critical spirit, errors are seen everywhere, and this leads to discouragement. But if one keeps at it faithfully, patiently, confidence will return little by little; it is no longer the optimism of the beginner, but a confidence grounded upon deliberate reason and proof; one has a consciousness of his own power as well as of his limitations.

This period of initiation should last through at least 5 or 6 sessions of two hours each, and bear upon a total of twenty children. Every experimenter wishing to commence should submit himself to a similar preparation.

Classification of the tests according to age. We here give the series of tests[18] ranged according to the ages at which the majority

[18] These tests are not the first ones of which we had thought; if we keep them it is after long trial; they appear to us all good and practical. But we are far from claiming that they are the best. Those who will take up this work after us will find better; they will certainly succeed in eliminating more strictly than we have been able to do, the tests that are influenced by education. In pursuing the experiments we have ourselves succeeded in making some improvements. But we have made no record of them, in order not to change the economy of the work and the value of our figures as to the result. The main point after all is that on the one hand the principle of the measure of intelligence be stated, and on the other that our method be, in spite of its defects, good enough to be put into practice.

We lack time to establish tests corresponding to ages under 3 years. Our experiment in hospitals showed us which are the tests to be used, but we do not yet know to which exact age of normal development they correspond. In any case we give them here for reference.

Voluntary look (follow a lighted match which the experimenter moves).

Prehension of an object by contact (put the object in contact with the hand.)

Prehension after visual perception. (One hands the object and the child must try to take it.)

Knowledge of food. (One presents a piece of wood, then a biscuit. One notices if the child rejects the piece of wood to take the biscuit.)

Execution of order given by gestures. (For instance, the order to sit down.)

Imitation of simple gestures. (For instance, clap the hands.)

of children succeed in them. This constitutes our measuring
scale of intelligence. Those who adopt our method will very often
need to refer to it.

(For discussion see pages indicated)

Three years

Show eyes, nose, mouth (p. 184).
Name objects in a picture (p. 188).
Repeat 2 figures (p. 187).
Repeat a sentence of 6 syllables (p. 186).
Give last name (p. 194).

Four years

Give sex (p. 195).
Name key, knife, penny (p. 195).
Repeat 3 figures (p. 196).
Compare 2 lines (p. 196).

Five years

Compare 2 boxes of different weights (p. 196).
Copy a square (p. 198).
Repeat a sentence of 10 syllables (p. 186).
Count 4 sous (p. 200).
Put together two pieces in a "game of patience" (p. 198).

Six years

Repeat a sentence of 16 syllables (p. 186).
Compare two figures from an esthetic point of view (p. 202).
Define by use only, some simple objects (p. 202).
Execute 3 simultaneous commissions (p. 205).
Give one's age (p. 206).
Distinguish morning and evening (p. 206).

Seven years

Indicate omissions in drawings (p. 207).

Give the number of fingers (p. 209).
Copy a written sentence (p. 209).
Copy a triangle and a diamond (p. 209).
Repeat 5 figures (p. 210).
Describe a picture (p. 210).
Count 13 single sous (p. 210).
Name 4 pieces of money (p. 211).

Eight years

Read selection and retain two memories (p. 211).
Count 9 sous. (3 single and 3 double) (p. 214).
Name four colors (p. 215).
Count backward from 20–0 (p. 215).
Compare 2 objects from memory (p. 216).
Write from dictation (p. 216).

Nine years

Give the date complete (day, month, day of the month, year) (p. 217).
Name the days of the week (p. 218).
Give definitions superior to use (p. 205).
Retain 6 memories after reading (p. 220).
Make change, 4 sous from 20 sous (p. 218).
Arrange 5 weights in order (p. 220).

Ten years

Name the months (p. 221).
Name 9 pieces of money (p. 221).
Place 3 words in 2 sentences (p. 222).
Answer 3 comprehension questions (p. 224).

Answer 5 comprehension questions
(p. 224).

Eleven years

Criticize sentences containing absurdities (p. 227).

Place 3 words in 1 sentence (p. 229).

Find more than 60 words in 3 minutes (p. 229).

Give abstract definitions (p. 230).

Place disarranged words in order
(p. 231).

Twelve years

Repeat 7 figures (p. 232).

Find 3 rhymes (p. 232).

Repeat a sentence of 26 syllables
(p. 232).

Interpret pictures (p. 193).

Problem of facts (p. 233).

Thirteen years

Paper cutting (p. 234).

Reversed triangle (p. 235).

Give differences of meaning (p. 235).

A few words upon the value of this classification. It is not
exact for the age of three years, because certain tests placed at the
level of that age can be done by much younger children, children
of two years for instance. But this does not trouble us, for the
measuring scale that we present is designed only for children
of school age. Should a child of three years present himself
these tests are sufficient to classify him. The only difficulty that
could arise would be in classifying a child of two years.

At the other extremity of the scale, there is also a little uncertainty. A pupil who passes all the tests for the thirteenth
year may have a mental capacity superior to that age. But how
much? Our tests do not show us.

II. NECESSITY OF MAKING AN ESTIMATE OF RESULTS

In the course of our explanation, we have insisted on the
character of our method of measuring. "Notwithstanding appearances it is not an automatic method comparable to a weighing machine in a railroad station on which one need but stand
in order that the machine throw out the weight printed on a
ticket. It is a method which requires some originality to operate,
and we warn the busy doctor who would apply it by means of
hospital attendants that he will be disappointed. The results
of our examination have no value if deprived of all comment;
they need to be interpreted." We are conscious that in insisting
upon the necessity of this interpretation we seem to open the door
to arbitrary opinions and to deprive our method of all precision.
This is so only in appearance. Our examination of intelligence
will always be superior to the ordinary examinations of instruc-

over

over

tion, because it has many advantages over these. It unfolds according to an invariable plan, it takes the exact age into account; it not only depends upon the replies but compares them with a norm which is at the same time a real average determined by experience.

"If in spite of all this precision we admit that the process must be used with intelligence, we do not think its value lessened by such reservation. The microscope, the graph method, are admirable examples of precision; but how much intelligence, circumspection, erudition and skill are implied in the practice of these methods! And can one imagine any value in the observations made with the microscope by one who was an ignoramus and at the same time an imbecile? We have seen examples of this and it makes us shudder. "

It is necessary then to abandon the idea that a method of investigation can be made precise enough to be entrusted to the first comer. Every scientific process is an instrument which needs to be directed by an intelligent hand. With this new instrument that we have just made we have examined more than 300 subjects. At each new examination our attention has been aroused, surprised, charmed by the observations we have made upon the manner of response, the manner of understanding, the mischievousness of some, the stupidity of others, and the thousand peculiarities which go to make up the attractive spectacle of an intelligence in activity. Some persons to whom, very rarely however, we have accorded the privilege of witnessing our tests, have also understood and have, of their own accord, declared what a deep impression they had received, and how they were able to form a good idea of the intelligence of each child, even those whom they had known for a long time. It is this deep impression that one should know how to gather, interpret and estimate at its true value. The notations that we recommend should serve only as an aid to the memory, and to facilitate the assembling of those elements out of which our mind alone can compose the synthesis.

With these reservations we shall now explain our system of recording.

Recording results. In practice one has before him in a vertical column the names of the tests in the order in which we have here given them. The tests for the different ages are separated by a horizontal line. When one is about to test a child, begin with the tests for his age, and according as the test has been passed or not, mark the answer with the sign + or —. But that record is not sufficiently graded; it is necessary, we think, to adopt the exclamation point for those cases where the failure takes on an evident character of absurdity. Let us cite some examples of absurd replies.

Repetition of sentences. What we have called "bafouillage"— (words that have no sense).

Repetition of five figures. Pronouncing the figures in the natural order. One has said: 2, 8, 7, 3, 9. The child says 8, 2, 3, 4, 5, 6, 7, 9. This is a particularly serious error, if the child who makes it has been able at another time to repeat 5 figures. It is then clear that it is not so much memory that he lacks, as judgment.

Study of a picture. Making lengthy enumerations implies a childish intelligence having had experience which has not developed it. This is often encountered among the subnormal.

To count thirteen sous. To know how to count correctly as far as 30 and then in counting 13 sous to make a serious error— for example of ten units.

Pieces of money. To invent; to discover pieces of 25 sous; 30 sous; 3 francs; 30 francs, etc.

Reading. To mispronounce words when one is able to read fluently.

Counting backwards. To skip regularly 2 figures at the end of a certain time, which indicates that the directing idea is lost; or even after having counted backwards to begin counting forwards.

Defining objects. To repeat the word, as "a chair is a chair." Or to point to the object, "a table." "There it is" (placing his finger on the table).

Date. Inventing extraordinary dates. Saying it is the year 19; it is the month 9, etc.

Memory of what is read. Inventing statements which have not been read.

Comparison from memory. Repeating the word. Saying: "Wood is made of wood. Glass is made of glass."

Making change from twenty sous. Giving change at random, 5 francs, 10 francs, etc; or giving a number much less than 16 sous; using pieces of known value, for example—giving 19 sous with a 10-sou piece and the rest in single sous.

Arranging weights in order. Making mistakes which indicate that the subject has not understood the meaning "decreasing;" or arranging the boxes, hap-hazard, two by two.

Three words in a sentence. To write a sentence without sense as, "Paris is a city of fortune for the streams."

Criticism of sentences. Absurd answers. For instance to answer the second sentence with "It is Ernest who was not kind." To the third, "'Tis like saying, I am not well."

Abstract definitions. Absurdities. Example. "Charity is to raise one's hat."

Arranging words in a sentence. Making a sentence void of sense: "One must finish his exercises." "A good dog his bravely master defends."

Rhymes. Coining words, or sometimes, what is worse, coining words that have not even the merit of rhyming.

Such answers deserve not merely a minus but an exclamation point as well.

Utilization of notes. A series of signs is thus obtained in a vertical column; these signs succeed one another irregularly; here are minus signs, there are plus signs. How shall they be interpreted? First of all it is evident that in whatever order we place the tests, we shall never be able to find any single test of such a nature that when this one has been passed, all the previous ones will also be successful, and all the following ones failures.

This order of tests might be established for one child in particular, but the same order would not be satisfactory for a second or a third. So, let us examine the results of the order of the tests which we have chosen, and let us see how ten children of nine years react. For the five tests at nine years, which furnish 50 replies (since there are 5 tests and ten pupils) there are 6 failures and 44 successes. For the tests at ten years, there are 14 failures and 36 successes. A test limit could never be found which would stop all the children, or which would stop only children of that age, or to which they would all attain. That would be a very convenient criterion, but we have never found it, nor do we believe it exists. The reality is less simple. What we have found is the following: children of nine years pass all the easy tests; in the very difficult tests, children of nine years pass none; in the tests of moderate difficulty some pass one, some another. This varies with each child. This is a fact of which one must take

account. Every child has his individuality; one succeeds best
in test "A" and fails in test "B"; another, of the same age, fails
in "A" and on the other hand succeeds in "B." How shall we
account for these individual differences in the experimental results?
We do not know exactly; it is probable that the mental faculties
involved in the tests are different, and of unequal development
in the children. If a child has a better memory than one of his
companions, it is natural that he should succeed better in a test
of simple repetition. Another who has already a trained hand
will succeed better in the arranging of the weights. Another
reason may be alleged. All our tests suppose an effort of attention; and attention varies constantly in the degree of concentration, especially among the young; now it is intense; a moment
later it is relaxed. Suppose that the subject has a moment of
distraction, of constraint, of ennui during a test; he fails. One
cannot doubt the weight of this last reason. We are so convinced of it that we consider it chimerical and absurd to judge
the intelligence of a child on any single test.

From the preceding considerations we conclude that we can
determine the intellectual level of a child only by the sum total
of the tests. Success in many different tests is alone characteristic. The mark of intelligence is therefore not made nor can it
be made as one measures height. For the height,[19] it suffices
to have a table of average measurements for that age. Being
given a child we take his height and referring it to the table of
average measurements we easily, by a simple reckoning, learn
if the child measures up to the average for his age, or if he is
backward by one year, by two years, etc., or on the contrary
advanced a year or two years, etc. Such a process of estimation is on the whole but slightly artificial.

It is altogether different for the measure of intelligence. "If one
wishes to apply the same system of comparison between the
intelligence of a child and the average intelligence of children
at different ages, one is at once confronted with the difficulty
that we have noted above. A child is backward in certain of the
tests for his age and in advance for others. We think it possible
to overcome this difficulty; but it is on condition that we adopt
some arbitrary rule; and the said rule, however good it may be,

[19] See *Année psychologique*, Vol. XII, p. 9 and ff.

Aimed simitat to M. age concept to here

will always give an artificial character to the procedure, and to such a degree that if, by chance, one had adopted another rule one would arrive at quite different results.

We believe it necessary to insist on this point for we shall later be led to say, for the sake of simplicity of language, that a child of eight years has the intelligence of a child of seven or of nine years. These expressions, because they are arbitrary, might cause some illusions. It is necessary to remember that the expression "retarded" or "advanced intelligence," results partly from the conventional procedure that we have adopted.

This procedure is the following: *A subject has the intellectual development of the highest age at which he passes all the tests, with the allowance of one failure in the tests for that age.* Thus young Ernest has passed all the tests at nine years, except one; he has also passed all the tests at ten years except one; therefore we attribute to him the mental level of ten years.

But this rule is too strict, and an example will serve to make this clear. Suppose that Jean who is nine years old passes all the tests at nine years except two, and all the tests at ten years except two. Would that place him on the level of eight years? That would be to make him lose the advantage of the tests he has passed. We propose the following compensating rule; *When once the intellectual level of a child is fixed, give him the benefit of an advance of one year every time he passes at least five of the tests beyond his level, and the benefit of an advance of two years if he has passed at least ten above his level.* Thus, Jean aged nine is at the level of eight years, which one expresses by saying that he is –1 (that is, in other words, a year behind). But he has passed 3 tests at nine years and 3 tests at ten years; he has been 6 points in advance of his level; he has gained a year; he is then at the level of nine years, he tests at age, and is marked =.

By employing this process, one succeeds in classifying satisfactorily nearly all children. We may even say all, if we ignore two or three exceptions which we found among the pupils of the Maternal School. Thus a little girl of six years lacked two of the tests at four years; she lacked four of those at five years and five of those at six years; unless she was placed at the level of three years one would not know where she belonged. The cause of the

20₁For final rule see p. 278.

difficulty came from the following fact. She had an extremely weak memory and could repeat neither the sentence nor the figures correctly. She had had, we were told, attacks of epilepsy. These are exceptions to the rule, but we have proved that ordinarily these are found in abnormal cases.

Let us cite some examples, giving at the same time the application of our method and the aspect of one of our examinations.

One day we examined in a school two children of seven years. The Director who called them into his office scarcely knew them; they were children who had been in his school only four or five months. We asked for no information about these children, nor did we wish any beyond what was furnished by our psychological tests.

FIRST OBSERVATION

Let us commence with René T ——. We gave to him the seven year tests. He passes all but the last. We reproduce his answers. Tests of seven years: *Unfinished pictures.* + .Answers: The first lacks, the eyes; second, the neck; third, the mouth; fourth, the arms. Except for an error in the second, all are correct.

Ten fingers. + . *Q.* How many fingers have you on your right hand? *A.* Five. *Q.* And on the left hand? *A.* Five. *Q.* And on both? *A.* Ten.

Copying triangle and diamond. + . His copy is very satisfactory, he has even drawn two sides of the diamond with a continuous line.

Copy of sentence. + Excellent.

Repetition of five figures. + . He succeeds. *Q.* 3, 2, 7, 9, 5. *A.* 3, 2, —. *Q.* 6, 1, 8, 3, 9, *A.* 6, 1, 8, 3, 9. *Q.* 3, 0, 2, 8, 5. *A.* 3, 0 —. Notice that he succeeded only once.

Description of pictures. + . He is very slow, but he makes the description. First picture. "A boy and a man who are dragging a wagon in the snow." Second. "I see that the man sleeps with his wife." Third. "A man who is standing on the bench looking out of a window."

Counting thirteen sous. + . He counts correctly.

Four pieces of money. − . He recognizes and names one sou, 2 sous, 10 sous; he does not know the 5-franc piece.

To sum up, he passes all the tests but one; and moreover he almost fails in repeating five figures. Let us now take the tests of eight years.

Tests of eight years. *Reading.* — . He reads with difficulty the various facts and remembers nothing.

Counting nine sous. + . He counts correctly.

Four colors. — . He names all but the green which he does not know, and refrains from naming.

Counting backwards. + . Correct.

Comparisons from memory. + . First question. *A.* The wings are larger. *Q.* The wings of what? *A.* Of the butterfly. Second question. *A.* The wood is thicker than the glass. Third question. *A.* Because the paper is finer. These answers are good.

Writing from dictation. — . Insufficient. He writes three words which he runs together; however, the result nearly attains the required limit.

So he fails on three tests of eight years; two are of instruction and moreover those on which he fails he *almost* passes. Let us go on to nine years.

Tests of nine years. *Complete date.* — . He knows the day, the month, the day of the month, but not the year.

The days of the week. + . He recites these correctly.

Definitions superior to use. + . *Q.* What is a fork? *A.* Silence. *Q.* What is a table? *A.* A table is of wood. *Q.* A chair? *A.* A chair is of wood. *Q.* A fork? *A.* It is of iron. *Q.* A horse? *A.* A horse is of meat. *Q.* And a mama? *A.* A mama is of flesh. These definitions of a chemist are superior to use. Note the naïveté of the last.

Reading with six memories. — . He can recall nothing.

To make change of sixteen sous from twenty sous. + . Very slow. He counts on his fingers to find the differences between 4 and 20. Then he gives a 10-sou piece, a 5-sou piece, and a 1-sou piece.

Arranging weights. + . He makes a mistake but once in three times and this very slight. These are his three arrangements: 3, 6, 9, 15, 12; 3, 6, 9, 12, 15; 3, 6, 9, 12, 15.

If one is not satisfied with recording automatically, but studies each of the tests he still has a favorable impression. René lacked but little of succeeding in the first test, the date; he made change beautifully, using the five and ten-sou pieces. He arranged the weights in a manner almost perfect. Let us pass to the tests of ten years.

Tests of ten years. *Months,* — . He recites only the first four then stops.

Pieces of money. — . We saw that he does not know them all.

Three words in two sentences. — . He fails. Not knowing how to write he does not understand the word sentence.

Questions of comprehension, First series. + . First question. *A.* One must wait. Second question. *A.* To do nothing. Third question. *A.* Pay for it. These answers are good and the test is passed.

Other questions. — . He answers by silence to the five questions.

Thus we see that he is able to answer at least one of the tests of ten years. For the rest he fails chiefly for reasons beyond his intelligence because of the lack of instruction. We were curious to know how many words he would say in three minutes. That is a test that requires no instruction. But he cited five or six words, then stopped, much embarrassed; we waited for him, encouraged him, but he could find no more.

Let us sum up and pass judgment. He succeeded in all but one of the tests of seven years. Then, he is at least of the seven year level. Furthermore, he passed eight tests of the ages following; he is then more than a year in advance of his age.

Let us mark him + 1.

SECOND OBSERVATION.

The preceding pupil was followed by young Mod —— , who was also seven years old. His countenance appeared as intelligent as that of T —— but one should guard against individual diagnoses furnished solely by the examination of a countenance. Or rather one ought to judge the intelligence of a countenance chiefly when the subject is in action, and is making an effort to understand.

From his first answers Mod —— surprised us. Your age? He answered seven years and a half, when he is not yet seven years. Is it morning or evening? He answered, morning; it was afternoon. If we had wished to make only a rapid test, we should give the tests of six years; but as this was a regular demonstration, we continued the tests for seven years as our subject was of that age. Strange to say, he did not pass any; moreover, his failures were complete and serious.

Tests of seven years. *Unfinished pictures.* — . First figure, silence. Second, the neck. Third, the neck. Fourth, silence. No answer correct.

Number of fingers. − . *Q.* How many fingers on your right hand? *A.* Five. *Q.* On the left? *A.* Six. *Q.* On both? *A.* Ten.

Copying diamond. − . His drawing is defective and the diamond unrecognizable.

Copy of a sentence. − . Illegible.

Repetition of five figures. − . Complete failure.

Q. 2, 8, 5, 9, 7. *A.* Silence. *Q.* 3, 7, 2, 5, 9. *A.* 3, 2, 4 —. *Q.* 6, 2, 8, 5, 7, *A.* 8, 9.

Pictures. − . First picture. *A.* A man. *Q.* And then? *A.* A little boy. *Q.* And then? *A.* A wagon. Second picture. *A.* A man and a lady. *Q.* And then? *A.* A hat. Third picture. *A.* I see a man. *Q.* And then? *A.* A table and a chair. It is evident that it is an enumeration such as a three year old child would make. What a level!

Counting thirteen single sous. − . He knew how to count; he did not count the same piece twice, but he lacked method; for having finished, he began to recount a series already counted and so reached 20. It was a great error of intelligence.

Four pieces of money. − . Again enormous errors. He called 3 sous a 5-franc piece. He called 1 sou a 10-sou piece.

Evidently we made a great mistake in applying to him the tests of his own age. Let us go back; in order that the demonstration be complete, let us give him all the tests starting with those of three years.

Tests for three years. *Show your nose, eyes, mouth.* + . He did as commanded.

Enumeration in pictures. + . We have seen that he could do that.

Two figures. + . He repeated them correctly.

Six syllables. + . He repeated them but with a babyish "bafouillage."

Family name. + . He did not give that by which he was registered, but that of his foster father.

Tests of four years. + . He passed all the tests.

Sex. + . He indicated it correctly.

Knife, key, sou. + . He named them.

Three figures. + . He repeated them.

Comparison of lines. + . His designation was correct.

Tests of five years. *Comparison of two weights.* + . He passed this test, but with difficulty. *Q.* Give me the heavier box. In answer he gave a box, but without comparing it with the other. It was necessary to tell him to take both boxes in his hand. At four or five years a child should not need this advice. Moreover in three attempts he made one mistake.

Copy a square. + . Correct.

Repetition of ten words. + . Correct but indistinct.

To count four single sous. + . Correct.

"Game of patience" with 2 pieces. — . He could not do it. He joined the two pieces haphazard and was satisfied with a figure which resembled a triangle.

So the tests of five years were passed, except the last, but they were barely passed; the first needed indulgence.

Tests of six years. *Right hand, left ear.* — . He showed the right ear.

Sentence of sixteen syllables. — . He could not repeat correctly sentences of 12, 14, or 16 syllables. It was indistinct and many words were omitted. For example: *Q.* We are going for a walk; Mary give me your pretty hat. *A.* He does not repeat half the words.

Æsthetic comparison. — . He did not indicate the correct figures.

Definitions. — . He gave them by use only, as at six years. *Q.* A fork? *A.* Silence. *Q.* A table. *A.* It is for eating. *Q.* A chair? *A.* It is to sit on. *Q.* A horse? *A.* It is to work. *Q.* A fork? *A.* It is for eating. *Q.* A mama? *A.* She is to keep house.

Three commissions. + . He executed them quickly.

To recapitulate, he has, with indulgence, the mental level of five years. For if he did not pass all of the tests of five years, he passed those of four years, plus six of the following tests, which gives him five years. If one gives him all the tests of five years, he has only two more, he remains then at five years. Conclusion. He is two years behind his age, that is −2.

Experimental verifications. All of the authors who have devised methods of measuring intelligence, or the various faculties of intelligence, have yielded more or less to a false tendency, which consists in limiting themselves to *a priori* constructions. The methods of diagnosing inferior states which have heretofore been published are certainly not the result of experimentation;

but their authors have made use of experimentation only to give examples and to illustrate the tests. In spite of our aversion to this method, we have shown very often that we naturally were led to treat the present study from a solely theoretical point of view. One must believe that the formulation of rules leads one logically to ignore facts. But one should retrace his steps. We wish to demonstrate the part of experimentation, that is to say, of truth in our work.

First of all, it will be noticed that our tests are well arranged in a real order of increasing difficulty. It is as the result of many trials, that we have established this order; we have by no means imagined that which we present. If we had left the field clear to our conjectures, we should certainly not have admitted that it required the space of time comprised between four and seven years, for a child to learn to repeat 5 figures in place of 3. Likewise we should never have believed that it is only at ten years that the majority of children are able to repeat the names of the months in correct order without forgetting any; or that it is only at ten years that a child recognizes all the pieces of our money.

In order to make perfectly clear the real hierarchy of our tests, we have made a very simple calculation and one easy to explain. We have already said that when a child passed all but one of the tests of a certain age, he has the intellectual level of that age. Let us see if it happens that, according to this rule, a child may lack the level of a given age but at the same time reach that of a higher age. If such a case presented itself, it would be an argument against the hierarchy that we have admitted. Let us suppose that such a case could present itself; the independence of the intellectual faculties is great enough to explain this. But is such a case often presented? Out of 70 children whose replies we have examined from this point of view, the hierarchical depreciation mentioned has not presented itself a single time. Let us conclude that it must therefore be very rare. Let us also conclude that this forms a first experimental confirmation of the order we have established in our tests.

We have a second means of learning if our measuring scale of intelligence is gauged accurately. This means consists in trying out a large number of children of all ages and seeing if on the average they pass the intellectual tests of their age. We have made that experiment at length, in the Primary and Maternal

Slandardy. Jr.   20 3 chil· {103 at age
Based on theory that advanced & ret. should be =.   { 44 adts
                                                        5 6 retarded

schools for boys in Paris, on children of the age of three, four
five—twelve years or within two months of this age. We have
studied 203 children individually, each of whom was examined
during a period lasting a half hour at the least. What result
may we hope to obtain from this study? And what must we
require of this result for it to be a confirmation of our investigation? We ought not to expect that all the children of a given
age should be of the same intellectual level. That is very evident. All are not equally intelligent; and if all were able to reply
in the same manner to any one test it would simply prove that
the test was poorly made, and subject to some error, for example
to suggestion. Let us reckon then that in a group of children of
the same age some are necessarily behind in intelligence, others in
advance, others regular. What we have a right to demand is
that there should be a balance between those who are behind
and those who are in advance; if we have twice as many behind
as we have in advance it would show that our tests are too difficult. But the equalization of those retarded and those in advance
can only be made on large groups. What we ought further to
demand is that in the comparison of two successive ages, the
number retarded from the higher age shall not equal the number
of at age pupils of the lower age. In order to fix our ideas let us
imagine some figures; let us compare nine and ten years. If
the advanced at nine years number 50, and the at age 40, and at
ten years there are 50 at age and 40 retarded, it is evident that the
results obtained by these two different ages are identical, and that
in consequence the children are poorly classified; if they have
faculties of a different level, they have been badly graded. It
is necessary that the advanced of one year shall not equal in
number the at age pupils of the higher year, and that the at age
of one year shall not equal the number of retarded pupils of the
preceding year.

    Glance at our results and see if they satisfy these various con-
ditions. At three and four years, we have a considerable number
of backward pupils. This is explained by particular conditions.
Young children often refuse to answer from ill-will, or from timidity. The latter influence is perhaps the more rare, for timidity is
a feeling of social decorum, a trait of intelligent children, and this
trait usually develops later than three or four years. But ill-
will is frequent. We have seen a child of three years who would

not take the pencil offered him; he would not make any movement even of defense when the pencil was put under his nose. As that child walks and talks, we attribute his action to ill-will, for taking the pencil was a more simple act than speech.

Let us remark also that between nine and ten years the differences are not great. Is it because our tests are insufficient? We do not know.

Nevertheless it is true that the backward pupils of ten years are almost equal in number to the regular pupils of nine years, and that the advanced pupils of nine years equal in number the regular pupils of ten. Aside from these remarks it seems to us that our scale follows in a satisfying manner the progress of age, as the following table, which is the result of many experiments, shows very clearly.

Table showing the number of pupils intellectually at age, advanced, and retarded for the different ages of school life

AGES	3	4	5	6	7	8	9	10	11	12	TOTALS
At age.....................	3	9	13	5	7	16	11	14	13	2	103
Advanced by 1 year........	3	2	6	8	7	5	9	2			42 ⎫ 44
Advanced by 2 years.......		1				1					2 ⎭
Retarded by 1 year.........	4	4	4	6	3	1	2	9	5	5	44 ⎫ 56
Retarded by 2 years........		1		1	1			3	2	4	12 ⎭

So 103 pupils are at age, have exactly the mental level that we attribute to their age; 44 are advanced; 56 are retarded. We have here a confirmation, which is greater even than we had supposed *a priori*. In fact we should not have thought that so large a proportion of children of normal intelligence could exist, that is to say, having the intelligence of their age, and that those advanced or retarded should form such a small minority.

Let us add a detail; we speak of advanced and retarded pupils. But how many are there? There are 86 who are irregular by one year; only a very limited number, 14, who are irregular by two years; now this is really very interesting. The insignificance of these deviations proves to us that the degree of the intelligence, estimated according to our procedure, varies less from one subject to another than the volume of the head or even the height.

If it were necessary we could cite other verifications of our scale, which though partial seem no less significant. Often we have asked that the brightest pupil be sent to us and that subject has always brilliantly passed our test. On the contrary almost all the subnormals, that is, pupils having a scholastic retardation of three years, show a serious defect in intelligence. Thus, having recently had to examine 14 subnormal pupils who were three years backward, we found the following intellectual retardation: −2.5, −1, −4, −3.5, −1, −3, −3, −2, −1, −1 −3.5, −5, −3.5, −2.

One notices here a retardation of intelligence which is extremely great, and to which we found nothing analogous among normal pupils. All these facts confirm the preceding; they appear to us less convincing than those which show the correspondence between the age and our tests; but they add to the demonstration, the force of individual observations.

III. Apropos of the Definition of Intelligence

We have not attempted to treat, in all its scope, this problem of fearful complexity, the definition of intelligence; if we wished to take it in its entirety we should be obliged to present some *a priori* views, the least danger of which would be to lead to certain distinctions and certain subdivisions which might seem important to us, and which perhaps would not be so at all. Our intention is altogether different; we wish to confine ourselves to an examination of the facts that we have collected; this examination compels us to give first a brief definition of what we mean by intelligence, and further leads us to distinguish several forms of intelligence which hitherto have been confounded, and whose distinction offers a practical interest. Thus we shall give no general theory of intelligence, but a detailed examination of some special facts hitherto misunderstood.

Distinction between intelligence and scholastic aptitude. Let us commence with the easiest distinctions. We have often said that in our study we have sought to find the natural intelligence of the child, and not his degree of culture, his amount of instruction.

A very intelligent child may be deprived of instruction by circumstances foreign to his intelligence. He may have lived far from school; he may have had a long illness; or he may, for example, have been sent to Berck; or may be some parents have preferred to keep their children at home, to have them rinse bottles, serve the customers of a shop, care for a sick relative or herd the sheep. In such cases our scale teaches us the degree of intelligence that can be found among illiterates; for them it suffices to pass lightly the results of tests which are of a notably scholastic character, and to attach the greatest importance to those which express the natural intelligence.

Furthermore, the intellectual faculty appears to us to be independent not only of instruction but of that which may be called the scholastic faculty, that is to say, the faculty of learning at school, the faculty of assimilating the instruction given in school with the methods used in school.

We have shown in our previous investigation for the recruiting of subnormal classes[21] that it was only by weakness of the scholastic faculty that we defined the subnormal at school. We said: "Any pupil is subnormal who is three years behind in his studies, when that retardation is not the result of lack of sufficient instruction." Now it appears to us wise and prudent to admit, until further investigations be made, that this aptitude is not necessarily confounded in every case with the intellectual faculty that we measure by our method. In the first place theoretical reasons require us to avoid this confusion. "It seems to us that the scholastic aptitude admits of other things than intelligence; to succeed in his studies, one must have qualities which depend especially on attention, will, and character; for example a certain docility, a regularity of habits, and especially continuity of effort." A child, even if intelligent, will learn little in class if he never listens, if he spends his time in playing tricks, in giggling, in playing truant. The lack of attention, of character, of will, do not appear or scarcely so, in our tests of intelligence, the test is too short; the pupil is not left to himself sufficiently. In fact, in our examinations we have not found an inattentive child except among those of three or four years. All make a good effort; they are near us and our presence alone is sufficient to prevent a weakening of attention. It is not under such conditions that one can measure the ordinary power of attention of a child; it is when he is left to himself. A little incident will serve to show this.

See also
p 256

[21] *Les Anormaux*, one volume in 18 vo., Paris, Colin, 1907.

Experimenters have long recommended a test of attention which consists in having the pupil cross out certain letters in a printed text. The number of letters crossed out correctly, without error or omissions, in a given time, is taken as a convenient measure of attention. Some want to see in this a dynamometer of attention. We agree to it with this reservation—that the pupil be not left alone with the experimenter. Call to you an inattentive child and make the experiment, you will not see much difference in the numerical result between his work and that of a more attentive child. Do not be surprised. Your presence, either intimidating or encouraging, explains everything. You have prevented the inattentive child from losing his time; he has not dared to lift his eyes or watch the flies on the ceiling. In reality, you have coöperated in his work, and the letters he has crossed off represent your action combined with his. It is thus that we explain the entirely negative results of an investigation made eighteen months ago on some subnormal pupils in a special class. We were assured in advance that these pupils had a very slight power of attention, and that in consequence they would show a pronounced weakness in the test of crossing out letters. Now it happened that these subnormal children crossed out as many letters as the normal.

Let us take the same test, but under entirely different conditions; let us have five children sit at a table and give them the same text to cross out; command silence and leave them to themselves. Five minutes later when the copies are taken up it will be seen that there is a curious difference, if one compares the work done by each child working without supervision among his comrades, with that which he did at first when he was alone. The attentive child has resisted the temptation to distraction; and he has been able to furnish the same quantity and quality of work in the two sessions, if they were of equal length. The inattentive child shows a decided loss in the second effort.[22] Here are the results in number of letters crossed:

[22] Here are the exact results of the tests made by one of us (Binet) with M. Vaney. There were 17 pupils composed of two groups; in one, the attentive, the studious, the disciplined; in the other, the inattentive, the unstable, the unruly. We had them cross out the letters a, e, d, r, s, in three sittings each one lasting 5 minutes.

NAMES OF PUPILS	JUDGED BY TEACHER	JUDGED BY US	NUMBER OF LETTERS CROSSED IN FIVE MINUTES		
			In our presence	In our presence	Alone with their comrades
Dou.........	attentive	attentive	200	166	164
Gr..........	attentive	attentive	126	125	118
War........	attentive	inattentive	84	91	60
Anth........	attentive	inattentive	172	143	67
Bertr........	attentive	inattentive	154	180	56
Bau.........	attentive	attentive	144	137	140
Dutir.......	attentive	attentive	152	162	173
Dur.........	attentive	attentive	119	114	128
March......	inattentive	inattentive	87	102	69
Gay........	inattentive	inattentive	129	157	94
Dast........	inattentive	inattentive	76	77	33
Pasq........	inattentive	inattentive	95	97	38
Coha........	inattentive	inattentive	116	142	102
Laug........	inattentive	inattentive	80	90	48
Plai.........	inattentive	inattentive	71	108	56
Barr........	inattentive	inattentive	95	132	55
Blia.........	inattentive	inattentive	47	73	57
Ete.........	inattentive	inattentive	177		61

According as the figure of the third column, expressing the amount of work, is equal to or less than the second figure, we conclude that the child is attentive or distracted; but, one sees that out of 17 cases, we were 14 times of the same opinion as the teacher.

"This explains to us that our examination of intelligence can not take account of all these qualities, attention, will, regularity, continuity, docility, and courage which play so important a part in school work, and also in after-life; for life is not so much a conflict of intelligences as a combat of characters." And we must expect in fact that the children whom we judge the most intelligent, will not always be those who are the most advanced in their studies. An intelligent pupil may be very lazy. We must also notice that the lack of intelligence of certain subnormal pupils does not account for their great retardation. We recall what we saw when we followed the lesson for many hours in a subnormal class. It was surprising to see how restless they were, always ready to change their places, to laugh, to whisper, to pay no attention to the teacher. With such instability it would require double the intelligence of a normal pupil to profit from their lessons. And now as a pedagogical conclusion, let us say that what they should learn first is not the subjects ordinarily taught, however important they may be; they should be given lessons of will, of attention, of discipline; before exercises in grammar, they need to be exercised in mental orthopedy; in a word they must learn how to learn.[23]

In summarizing we arrive at the conception that if there is a general parallelism between the scholastic faculty and the intellectual faculty, nevertheless some striking cases of divergence occur.

Do our tests permit of this distinction between the scholastic faculty and the intelligence? All the tests have been empirically arranged, according to the difficulties they present and from the best of our experiments, in order to obtain a good classification of children. Many interesting remarks may be made on this subject.

Some of these remarks are forced on us by observations. Thus there are some tests which may easily be performed in a premature way by children much younger than those to whom the test normally belongs. For example, the naming of four colors belongs to eight years; it is only at that age that the majority of children learn the names of the colors; however one sometimes finds six year old children who know them. The same is true of the days of the week and the months of the year. Usually it is only at nine years that pupils know the names of the days of the week, and at ten that they are able to repeat the names of the months without error. However we have found at the Maternal School many children of six years who knew the days of the week. This shows that there are a certain number of extra-scholastic attainments, which may precede the ordinary age of acquisition; this is due to the fact that the parents or the teacher have had the idea of teaching the child the names of the days and the months. Moreover this acquisition does not demand a notable effort of intelligence. One must take into account the extra-scholastic attainments which depend solely on memory.

Another group of tests which may be passed precociously are those which, by their form or by their essence, depend on the intelligence alone and do not demand the use nor the compre-

[23] We take pleasure in recording here that one of us with the devoted collaboration of the primary school inspector, M. Belot, has succeeded in introducing these exercises of mental orthopedy in the classes for sub-normals in Paris, and even as an experiment in a class of normals.

hension of a special vocabulary, nor the concurrence of scholastic attainments. Thus the arrangement of weights, the definitions superior to use, abstract definitions, and the interpretation of pictures are among the tests which are most frequently passed before age. It is a very interesting group; it is less influenced than the preceding by the child's surroundings and is therefore a more adequate expression of spontaneous intelligence.

A third group represents tests which are generally correct for their age, neither in advance nor behind; these are the obviously scholastic tests, expressing a knowledge that one acquires at a fixed date, or even the mixed tests in which natural intelligence is combined with knowledge. Thus counting backward from 20 to 0 is an operation for which children show no signs of precocity; likewise the number of facts remembered after a single reading of a selection depends more on the facility of reading than on the extent of the memory; and this test is not often passed by children under eight years. To place words in a sentence pre-supposes a knowledge of the language and a handling of syntax which prevents a child's passing this test much before his age. There is a final exercise which is never passed before the age of its level, and that is the answers to the second series of comprehension questions, because they are not merely questions of intelligence since being intelligent alone does not suffice to pass them; it is also necessary to know certain words of the vocabulary; there are certain expressions such as "prendre parti" which not being understood checks the most active intelligence. Now the vocabulary of a language is slowly assimilated; it demands a long experience which cannot be improvised.

In a last group we should place the tests which are remarkable for the frequency of failures even when the pupil is older than the age to which these questions normally belong. We have found only one test to place in this category; it is the arrangement of weights; now as the arrangement of weights is also one of the tests performed precociously, one must conclude that the slight amount of cleverness of judgment and ability to weigh, which this test implies, constitutes a faculty independent of the whole.

wgts

All these diverse verifications permit us to judge intelligently what we measure with our measuring scale of intelligence. We do not measure the intelligence considered separately from a number of concrete circumstances—the intelligence which is needed for understanding, for being attentive, for judging. It is something far more complex that we measure. The result depends: first, on the intelligence pure and simple; second, on extra-scholastic acquisition capable of being gained precociously; third, on scholastic acquisitions made at a fixed date; fourth, on acquisitions relative to language and vocabulary, which are at once scholastic and extra-scholastic, depending partly on the school and partly on the family circumstances.

Does our measuring scale fail to do justice to a child of uncommon intelligence without culture, or with a scholastic culture much inferior to his intelligence? We do not think so. Such a child will show his superiority in the repetition of figures, in the repetition of sentences, paper cutting, the arrangement of weights, the interpretation of pictures, etc. And it is a specially interesting feature of these tests that they permit us, when necessary, to free a beautiful native intelligence from the trammels of the school.

not true to original means to form desugate the nature? form it scholar moved tests

DISTINCTION BETWEEN TWO KINDS OF INTELLIGENCES

It remains for us to make a distinction between the two kinds of intelligences which hitherto, we believe, have been confounded. We may call them the *maturity of intelligence* and the *rectitude of intelligence*. The maturity of intelligence is the growth of the intelligence with age. An intelligence which is not mature is childish; an intelligence which is mature before the age of maturity is precocious. These phenomena of retardation or advancement are especially noticeable when produced in the character. Every one has seen intelligent persons whose characters remain childish; old ladies who simper, who show affection, who shed torrents of tears on the death of a canary; men of fifty who have the humor for practical jokes, and who enjoy playing the clown. One knows less of the maturity of the intelligence and it is this which appears in our work. In fact, it is this maturity mingled with many other elements that we have especially studied. In what does it really consist? It consists in part, in the increase of the faculty of comprehending and of judging, at least this is probable; a child understands less and judges with less penetration than an adult; it consists also in the increase of acquisitions of every sort. But these are perhaps secondary characteristics which one may lack without compromising his maturity. We believe that this is brought

over
over

out in 3 or 4 tests which certainly were not designed for that purpose. These tests are definitions, the work on pictures, the construction of sentences containing 3 words and perhaps also the
arranging of weights. Let us return to the analysis we have made
of these tests; in the results which have been recorded, it is easy
to see in what the range of a child's thought consists. For the
definition, it is the strictly utilitarian point of view; he does not
go outside of himself and he views objects in their relation to himself. For the pictures, it is the act of enumeration to which he
limits himself. For the construction of sentences, it is the pro-
duction of three different ideas, without power of synthesis. For
the comparison of two weights, it is the contrast between the difficulty of understanding that one ought to compare, and the rapidity
with which one estimates the difference of two weights. For the
arranging of weights it is something analogous, the difficulty of
understanding and keeping in mind the fact that the weights
should be arranged in decreasing order, and the facility of comparing them two by two. Those are some of the traits of child intelligence. Let us add that the child is equal to the adult in simple,
but not in reasoned, memory, and in fine perception, but not in
reflective perceptions. But it would require a study much more
vast than ours, and above all more specialized, to set forth all
the traits of a child's intellectual physiognomy.

The maturity of intelligence is very distinct from the rectitude
of intelligence, and the proof is that there exist very plain examples, already cited by us, where the intelligence has maturity
without rectitude. Thus a pupil of twelve years succeeds in
uniting in one sentence the three words given him, but the sentence is meaningless; he has maturity, not rectitude. Another,
a true adult, a man of twenty-four, a veritable block-head—to
quote his companions—gives us the interpretation of a picture,
but his interpretation is remarkably false. To interpret is to
have maturity; to make gross errors is to lack rectitude.

The same distinction is also observable when one compares the
answers to the tests of intelligence given by the subnormal with
those of normal pupils. Let us take for example, without choosing, 13 subnormals of nine to twelve years, whose intellectual retardation varies from one to four years. The absurdities committed by these in their answers reach the following numbers per
child: 9, 3, 5, 3, 2, 2, 2, 7, 4, 4, 0, 1, 1. With this series, let us com-

pare those of normal pupils aged nine years; their absurdities are far less in number; 0, 2, 1, 0, 0, 0, 0, 1, 0, 0. The average of absurd mistakes for the subnormal would be 3, for the normal scarcely 0.5. A very sensible difference which shows us, be it said in passing, that what is lacking in the subnormal is not only the *maturity* of intelligence (which is doubtless also lacking, for they are constantly retarded) but also the *rectitude* of intelligence. We limit ourselves for the present to formulating these remarks; they are stepping-stones.

Other traits of childish intelligence must also be studied so as to discover if in certain cases, the lack of rectitude does not also result from lack of maturity.

IV. The Use of the Measuring Scale of Intelligence

Our principal conclusion is that we actually possess an instrument which allows us to measure the intellectual development of young children whose age is included between three and twelve years. This method appears to us practical, convenient and rapid. If one wishes to know summarily whether a child has the intelligence of his age, or if he is advanced or retarded, it suffices to have him take the tests of his age; and the performance of these tests certainly does not require more than thirty minutes which should be interrupted by ten minutes rest if one thinks this necessary for the child.

Furthermore when one wishes to be more precise, or to make a closer approximation, one may make many more tests; if the child is seven years old, he may attempt the tests of eight, nine and ten years for example. One would also be able after an interval of several days to substitute analogous tests.

One question remains to be examined. To what purpose are these studies? In reading the reflections which we have interspersed in the course of our treatise, it will be seen that a profound knowledge of the normal intellectual development of the child would not only be of great interest but useful in formulating a course of instruction really adapted to their aptitudes. We fear that those who have drawn up the programs actually in force, are educated men who in their work have been led more by the fancies of their imaginations than by well-grounded principles. The pedagogical principle which ought to inspire the authors of programs seems to us to be the following: the instruction should always be according to the natural evolution of the child, and not precede it by a year or two.   In other words the child should be taught only what he is sufficiently mature to understand; all precocious instruction is lost time, for it is not assimilated.   We have cited an example of it in regard to the date, which is taught in the Maternal School, but which is not known and assimilated before the age of nine years.   This is only one example, but it is eloquent; it shows the error of what has hitherto been done; it suggests a method which will enable us to improve upon the past,—a method less literary, less rapid, and even extremely laborious, for it demands that one establish by careful investigations the normal evolution of a child's intelligence, in order to make all our programs and methods of instruction conform to that evolution, when it is once known.   If by this labor we have succeeded in showing the necessity for a thorough investigation conducted after this plan, our time has not been lost.   But we are far from flattering ourselves that we have inaugurated a reform.   Reforms in France do not succeed except through politics, and we cannot readily imagine a secretary of state busying himself with a question of this kind.   What is taught to children at school!   As though legislators could become interested in that!

It now remains to explain the use of our measuring scale which we consider a standard of the child's intelligence.   Of what use is a measure of intelligence?   Without doubt one could conceive many possible applications of the process, in dreaming of a future where the social sphere would be better organized than ours; where every one would work according to his known aptitudes in such a way that no particle of psychic force should be lost for society.   That would be the ideal city.   It is indeed far from us. But we have to remain among the sterner and the matter-of-fact realities of life, since we here deal with practical experiments which are the most commonplace realities.

We shall not speak of parents; although a father and mother who raise a child themselves, who watch over him and study him fondly, would have great satisfaction in knowing that the intelligence of a child can be measured, and would willingly make the necessary effort to find out if their own child is intelligent.   We think especially of teachers who love their profession, who interest themselves in their pupils, and who understand that the first condition of instructing them well, is to know them. All such teachers seek, more or less successfully, to make an estimate of the intelligence of their pupils; but they have no method, and in the normal schools the courses in psychology are generally so antiquated, that one cannot learn there how to observe mental phenomena. Primary School inspectors have often told us of zealous teachers who have had the ingenious idea of composing psychological portraits of their pupils, and we have looked over these collections of portraits with interest. We have congratulated and encouraged the authors without telling them frankly what we thought, which was that they were working without method, like a very intelligent but unscientific man who would try experiments in bacteriology with unclean tools.

It seems that the simplest process that comes to the mind of an instructor, when he wishes to elucidate intellectual characteristics, would be to interest himself in every one of his pupils and to apply to each one separately all the information he has gleaned here and there. Seeking to make a study, of which he expects an individual application, he confines himself to the individual. That appears very logical, very simple. One proposes to himself a goal and runs thither directly. But in the sciences the straight line is not always the shortest road. Even when one seeks only the individual application, it would be better to make a detour, and go from the individual to the general in order to come back to the individual. This is the precise point that our instructors have not understood, the route that they have not found, or which, after entering, they have not followed, deeming it too long. In consequence their investigations profit them alone; they remain empirical and arbitrary. In any case, we offer them our method which has been built on particular facts generalized, and which in consequence might and should render service to everyone. We are certain in advance that many instructors will desire to make use of it. Some having witnessed our experiments, and being charmed by what they saw, have already commenced its use.

But we are of the opinion that the most valuable use of our scale will not be its application to the normal pupils, but rather to those of inferior grades of intelligence.

It is well known, as we have often affirmed, that the alienists are not agreed on the definitions of the words *idiot, imbecile* and *moron*. There are as many definitions as writers. Moreover the formulae employed and the processes of diagnosis in use, are so vague that the most conscientious author is not sure of remaining constantly consistent with himself. How, for instance, can one make use of formulae of diagnosis, founded on difference of degree, when these differences are not measured?[24] Finally, the most serious criticisms that one can make of the actual medical practice is that if by chance, a child of normal intelligence were presented at a clinic, the alienist would not be able to know that he is dealing with a normal child. He will be unable for a very simple reason; he does not know what is necessary in order for a child to be normal; let us add that everyone is equally ignorant of how an individual intelligence can be studied and measured. This is then a consequence of much weight. The doctor suspects every child who is brought to a mental clinic of being backward, and if, by chance, he is not at all backward, the alienist will not know it; he will not even have the means of finding out.

But one will say: You are making objections built on purely theoretical cases, cases possible, but invented at pleasure to sustain a thesis, cases which in reality have never been presented. You do not know an example of an error so great. It is true, we answer, that a certain number of children who are brought to the asylum either by parents or by officers, are so noticeably deficient that there is no need to be a doctor to recognize that they are not normal. When a boy of seven years does not know how to dress

---

[24] We should never cease to criticize these absurd formulas, which are to be met with in the best authors. In the idiot, we are told, *the intelligence is but little developed, it is a little more so in the imbecile.* Conscientious physicians have lately published statistics of slightly feeble-minded and profoundly feeble-minded, which were made in primary schools; they seriously give figures of percentages. There are so many slightly feeble-minded, they tell us, so many profoundly feeble-minded. But by what controllable and precise sign, can we distinguish such a slightness from such a depth? Not a word! It is about as if we said that there are in Paris 43 per cent of tall men and 42 per cent of short men, without defining what we were to consider tall or what short. It is as if the military law decided that to be passed, the recruit must have a *reasonable height.* How arbitrary! And how comical when these vague notions are accompanied with figures! We cannot be blamed if in the presence of these grave medical statistics, we irresistibly think of Molière.

Editor's Note: The famous comedies of Molière are here alluded to in which the ridiculous pretensions of the doctors are made the occasions of mirth "Le medicin malgré lui," "Le malade imaginaire," etc.

himself, when he does not understand a sentence, when he drivels, he would be recognized as feeble-minded by the first attendant who passed him.

But besides these cases so evidently feeble-minded, one meets others whose deficiency is much less noticeable, and whose diagnosis must be much more delicate.

During the past year one of us examined 25 children who for various reasons had been admitted to Sainte-Anne and later confined at the Bicêtre, at Salpêtrière, or at other places. We applied the procedure of our measuring scale to all these children, and thus proved that *three of them were at age in intelligence, and two others were a year advanced beyond the average.*

On reflection, these cases should not surprise us; and it is not necessary to be in touch with questions of mental medicine to inveigh against arbitrary segregation. One ought to confine a child of normal intelligence, or even of super-normal, if he has epilepsy, or irresistible impulses which constitute a danger to his neighbors or to himself. But it is none the less true that the doctors who were obliged to diagnose these cases, have had to judge the degree of intelligence of these children; it is very interesting to show the errors of diagnosis which have been committed in this regard. To two of these children who showed normal intelligence we regret to say that the term *mental debility* had been applied without consideration. The third had received the term, truly extraordinary of its kind, of "*enfant idiot.*" The child was named T——, aged seven years. A doctor had written concerning him, "Idiotic, with attacks of furious anger. Wishes to bite. Does not know how to read or write." This last is a little too naïve. Since the normal child does not know how to read and write at seven years, to be astonished that T—— who is just seven is still illiterate, is like reproaching a three year old baby for not knowing how to play the piano. Finally, one of these children who was a year in advance, was classed as a moron; and as to the other nothing was said concerning his mentality. Nothing could show more clearly, that with the means which it has at its command, the mental clinic is not in a position to diagnose correctly a child's intelligence.[25]

[25] We cite this fact for the benefit of M. Royer, interne of M. Bourneville, who took upon himself to inveigh against our last book, *Les Enfants Anormaux.*

He means the medico-psychological clinic

Let us show in what practical manner one ought to utilize our scale. Two cases are to be distinguished: the backward adult and the backward child. Let us begin with the simpler of these cases which is the first.

We shall use the customary words idiot, imbecile, and moron, giving to them a precise definition and a possible application by means of the tests of our scale. An idiot is a person who cannot communicate with his fellows by means of language; he does not speak and does not understand; he corresponds to the level of normal intelligence between birth and the age of two years. To establish a differential diagnosis between the idiot and the imbecile it suffices to employ the following tests: first, to give verbal orders like touching the nose, mouth, eyes; second, to have him name some easy familiar objects that he can find and point out in a picture. These are our tests for the age of three years; in reality they belong as much to two years as to three.

The border line between imbecility and moronity is not more difficult to establish. An imbecile is a person who is incapable of communicating with his fellows by means of written language; he can neither read, nor understand what he reads, nor write from dictation nor write spontaneously in an intelligible manner. To him may be applied the tests for eight years. As it is possible that one may sometimes have to deal with a person who is illiterate through lack of schooling, one would need to employ many other tests of seven and eight years; the description of pictures, the counting of mixed coins, the comparison of two objects from memory; these supplementary tests define the boundary which separates imbecility and moronity.

There remains a third limit to establish—that which separates moronity from the normal state. This is more complicated; we do not consider it fixed but variable according to circumstances. The most general formula that one can adopt is this: an individual is normal when he is able to conduct himself in life without need of the guardianship of another, and is able to perform work sufficiently remunerative to supply his personal needs, and finally when his intelligence does not exclude him from the social rank of his parents. As a result of this, an attorney's son who is reduced by his intelligence to the condition of a menial employee is a moron; likewise the son of a master mason, who remains a servant at thirty years is a moron; likewise a peasant, normal in ordinary surroundings of the fields, may be considered a moron in the city. In a word, retardation is a term relative to a number of circumstances which must be taken into account in order to judge each particular case. We can make the boundary between moronity and the normal state more definite by considering a special category of subjects. We wish to speak of defective adults whom we have had occasion to observe in the Parisian hospitals who were subjects for custodial care. This forms a special category for many reasons: first on account of nationality and race, it is a question as to whether they are Parisians or persons living in the region of Paris; second, on account of social condition; all belong to the laboring class. The limit that we place for them would not be correct for any others; we express complete reserve for the application of it which one would wish to make for subjects of different environments.

In making a detailed study of the intellectual faculties of 20 of these inmates, we found that the best endowed did not surpass the normal level of nine or ten years, and in consequence our measuring scale furnished us something by which to raise before them a barrier that they could never pass. There is always a reservation to be made in applying our scale to them, which was prepared exclusively from observations upon young persons. Some of our tests consist of the usual knowledge that children acquire somewhat late. Thus the names of the days, of the months, of colors, of the principal pieces of money, are notions that an ordinary child does not possess before the age of eight, nine or ten. A defective adult even of inferior degree, for example an imbecile of forty, who is in general of the mental level of five years, may often recite without a mistake the names of the days, months, colors, pieces of money, and even the playing cards. From this point of view he is certainly much superior to the child of five years, and the reason is that he has profited by an experience very much longer. Let us then lay aside these practical notions which have no bearing here. There remain six or seven fundamental tests uniquely expressive of the intelligence; these are the tests that may be considered as forming for the laboring class of Paris and its environs the border line between moronity and the normal state. These tests are: first, arrangement of weights; second, answers to questions difficult of comprehension; third, the construction of a sentence containing three given words; fourth, the definition of abstract terms; fifth, the interpretation of pictures;

sixth, the making of rhymes. Our subjects in the hospital were able to pass some of these tests but not one could pass all, nor even three of them. Now this is not a special localized success which is important for diagnosing a level of intelligence. All our work has shown that intelligence is measured by a synthesis of results. We hope then that we are not dangerously precise in admitting that the six preceding tests will apprehend all feeble-minded adults; and that one who can pass the majority of them, or at least four, is normal. For us every subject from the laboring class of the region of Paris is normal if he has satisfied the condition of this examination of intelligence; however, the examination shows only that he has intelligence enough to live outside of an institution, and that intelligence may coexist with accentuated instability, or with irresistible impulses, or even with other pathological symptoms grave enough to necessitate his segregation.

The mental level of a backward person having been determined, one may conjecture what advantages can be drawn from the medico-pedagogical treatment of the person, and what progress can be attributed to that treatment. It has sometimes been proposed to treat the drowsy class of subnormals with thyroidine, and those who have recommended this new medication have pronounced its results marvelous. Instead however of allowing one's self to be too optimistic, or of relying upon the statements of hypnotized relatives, it would be much simpler to take a measure of the intelligence before and after treatment. That would be a means for ascertaining once for all what is the value of the famous medico-pedagogical treatment of defectives, so lyrically chanted by certain alienists, and in which the pedagogue sees only certain procedures which are themselves very defective.[26]

Other investigations which are a little different, will be equally aided by the measure of intelligence; thus the cephalometric study of the relation of the mental functions with the cranium development, will gain in value when one knows how to make an accurate measure of intelligence. Autopsies will become more eloquent

[26] It is interesting to note that according to Sollier, who published a special study on the medico-pedagogical treatment of idiocy, there does not exist any medical treatment of the idiot, and the pedagogical processes of Bicêtre are "very little different from the education of normal children." (Sollier, in *Traite de Thérapeutique appliquée*: Treatment of Mental Diseases, p. 258).

To eval. intell. y child must consider age 2 yrs ret., 7 in 100. This more or less serious 3 yrs, usually unknow. But may change with age. Refuses prognosis.

THE USE OF THE SCALE   269

when the anatomo-pathologic study of the brain will be made clear by a study of the quantitative psychology which will have been made on the living subject. Let us content ourselves with these allusions. We shall elsewhere return to the consequence of the diagnosis of inferior states of intelligence among adults; and we shall show how the diagnosis may be perfected by the establishment of many sub-degrees of idiocy, imbecility and moronity.

Let us pass to cases where the backward subject is young and in the course of mental development; the subject to be studied is eight years old.

The problem is complex; one is unwilling to class the child, as if he were an adult, in a special group of defectives, without taking account of his age, and of all which that age permits him to attain. If he is eight years old we have not the right to consider him an imbecile simply because he does not know how to read; a normal child of eight years does not read very well, and one would never have the temptation to class him as an imbecile. To establish the diagnosis of the subnormal child we must take into account two elements; his age and his intellectual level.

But how combine these two elements? We shall not know with certainty until an extensive experience will have taught us what we do not yet know; how do idiots, imbeciles and morons develop; and what prognosis can be made from a certain retarded condition at a certain age? These are investigations of prime importance though hitherto impracticable, since empiricism was the only method, and consequently there was no way of measuring the mental development of the feeble-minded.

The process that we now recommend may be only provisional. We have sought to render it as simple as possible. In examining the table of our experiments upon normal pupils, one will notice that an intellectual retardation of one year is so frequent that it becomes insignificant; one need attach no particular value to it. On the contrary a retardation of two years is rare enough; it is found only in the proportion of 7 to 100. Let us admit that this retardation has in itself a prejudicial significance; let us admit that every time it occurs, the question may be raised as to whether the child is subnormal, and in what category he should be placed. The first determination being made, and its extreme facility is evident, the child is placed in the category to which he belongs by actual development. Thus idiocy corresponds to a development of from 0 to 2 years; imbecility from 2 to 7 years; moronity begins at 8 years.

Whenever one deducts the retardation of a child from his real age he falls into one of these categories. For example the child B ——, who is seven years old, and five years behind the normal grade, presenting in consequence the development of a two year old child, is found at the limit between idiocy and imbecility; Br ——, who is thirteen years of age and seven years behind has in consequence a development of six years, and is an imbecile who approaches the limit of moronity. Lay ——, who is nine years old, is four years behind, and has a five year development; she is plainly in the class of imbecility.

It is understood that these diagnoses apply only to the present moment. One who is imbecile today, may by the progress of age become a moron, or on the contrary remain an imbecile all his life. One knows nothing of that; the prognosis is reserved.

There is a third class of subnormals of which it remains for us to speak; these are the subnormals in the school. They differ from the subnormals in institutions only by a less accentuated state of backwardness or of instability. We could then limit ourselves to saying that the same methods of diagnosis are applicable to them as to the subnormals in institutions, if the necessity of entrusting the selecting of them to persons who are not professional alienists did not oblige us to simplify the procedure they are to make use of in order to recognize them in the crowd of normal school children among whom they are placed. In a recent work we have given a very practical definition of a subnormal, in stating that it is one who is three years behind in his studies without the excuse of having been frequently absent from school.

That formula is usually sufficient to guide the pedagogic diagnosis; but it sometimes happens that one lacks information on the scholarship of a child, especially if he comes from a parochial school, or if he has passed successively through different public schools where he remained only a short time. In this case the examiner must establish the value of his retardation; but one hesitates at the interpretation of this retardation, and questions if it is by fault of scholarship or by fault of intelligence that he has been retarded. The intellectual test allows us to avoid all doubt, and we habitually resort to it when it is the question of a candidate for a special class.

Evidently, let us say it in the most emphatic manner, our test of intelligence will not suffice to know absolutely that a child is subnormal; we have shown above, with an example for the support of the theory, that one may be among the less brilliant in the test of intelligence and yet follow the course of study for his age at school; when one is able to follow the course of study for his age, he is saved from a suspicion of backwardness. We consider only a situation where there are doubts on the causes of scholastic backwardness; and in such a case, if to a serious retardation of scholarship is added a serious intellectual retardation, there is sufficient reason for sending the pupil to a special class. Thus in a recent study, we have examined some twenty children who had been proposed by their teachers for that class; the information in regard to their scholarship seemed to us vague for the majority of them. Three of the candidates were but one year behind; we sent those to an ordinary school, and sent to the special class only those who were two or more years retarded.

One of these cases, to us a very striking one, was that of little Germaine, a child of eleven years who came from a Paris school. Her parents, having carried their Penates to Levallois-Perret, had sent their child to one of the schools for girls in that city. But the directress refused little Germaine under the pretext that her school was full; in reality because the child was extremely backward. In fact the retardation was at least three years; her reading was hesitating, almost syllabic; faults of orthography spoiled her dictation exercise. She wrote the following phrase under our eyes: The pertly litl grils stude the flwr that the gathrd yesty (which signifies: The pretty little girls studied the flowers that they gathered yesterday). Her number work was equally poor. She was asked, "If I have 19 apples, and eat 6 of them, how many have I left?" The child, reckoning mentally, said "12" which is inexact but reasonable. Trying it on paper, she was lost; she made an addition instead of subtraction and found 25. In other calculations she showed that she had the power to reckon mentally, but not on paper; in the last case she made the addition correctly when she should have subtracted. It is however a frequent, not to say constant rule that those backward in arithmetic do the operations better than the problems, and do more easily operations of addition and multiplication than those of subtraction and division. In short, this child had a retardation of three years; but knowledge of her scholarship was lacking. On the other hand her wide awake and mischievous air, and the vivacity of her speech made a favorable impression upon us. We made the test of intelligence and that showed us that her intelligence was normal; she was backward scarcely a year. This is a characteristic example which shows the use of our measuring scale.

In terminating this account, it will suffice to make a very brief allusion to the appreciation of penal responsibility; there also our scale will render service. The problems of penal responsibility such as are actually placed before the tribunals, are most complex and recently have caused discussions that are highly curious on account of the attention which has been paid to words rather than to things. We have scarcely the space here to make the multiple distinctions which would be necessary in making clear the real situation. It will suffice to remark that in certain cases experts have to give their opinion on the degree of intelligence of an accused person; and that according to their customary point of view which consists in distinguishing health from illness they are preoccupied in learning if the accused should or should not enter the group of feeble-minded. It is strange that so far, no other criterion than a subjective impression can guide them; they weigh each case with their good sense, which presupposes in the first place that this is a possession common to all men, and in the second place that everybody's good sense is equal to every other person's.

We suggest to them that they should use the six differentiating tests that we have described above. By the methodical employment of these tests, they will arrive at precise and controllable conclusions, which at the same time cannot help but enhance in the mind of the judges the value of the medico-legal appraisement of the alienists.

These examples to which we could add many others[27] show that

[27] Let us point out the very great utility to humanity that would result from giving the intellectual test to young recruits before enlisting them. Many morons, that is to say, young men who on account of their weak minds are unable to learn and understand the theory and drill of arms and to submit to a regular discipline, come to the medical examination, and are pronounced "good for the military service," because one does not know how to examine them from the intellectual point of view. We have learned that in Germany they pay attention to the mental debility of the recruits who are measured before enlistment by means of examination questions, writ-

the methods of measuring the individual intelligence have not a speculative interest alone; by the direction, by the organization of all the investigations, psychology has furnished the proof (we do not say for the first time but in a more positive manner than ever before), that it is in a fair way to become a science of great social utility.

ALFRED BINET AND TH. SIMON.

ten by Dr. Schultze, professor of psychiatry, on the Faculty of Medicine at Greifswald. These examination questions are made so that a twelve year old child of average intelligence and without any training can answer them. One of us referred these questions to the Minister of War, who answered that he would ask for a report on the matter. We have reason to believe that this answer is not the polite refusal which is customary with the State Administration, when they are importuned with propositions from the outside. And we shall most probably soon have the pleasure of telling the readers of *L'Année* the result of our experiments on defectiveness among the recruits, and the means of detecting it and avoiding the simulation.

NEW INVESTIGATION UPON THE MEASURE OF THE INTELLECTUAL LEVEL AMONG SCHOOL CHILDREN

L'Année Psychologique, 1911, 145–201

The method which we worked out with Dr. Simon for the measuring of the intellectual level of children has not passed unnoticed; it has received eulogies and has raised criticisms;[1] we have thought it worth while to revise and perfect it; many devoted collaborators, among whom we are happy to cite MM. Bichon, Levistre, Morlé, and Vaney, school directors at Paris, Mlle. Giroud, M. Jeanjean, students at our laboratory, and numerous other persons, have collected new facts which have permitted us to bring important modifications to our first plan. The points which we shall specially study are the following:

1. What modifications ought to be introduced into the series of tests?

2. What are the existing relations between the intellectual level and the scholastic level?

3. What modifications are presented by testing the intellectual level of a given child at intervals of fifteen days?

---

[1] Besides the references that we shall cite in the text, we would especially mention among the authors who have discussed, practiced, or criticized this method: H. H. Goddard, *The Binet-Simon Tests of Intellectual Capacity, in the Training School*, December 5, 1908 (the author has applied the method to a large number of subnormal children); Guy Montrose Whipple, *Manual of Mental and Physical Tests*, Baltimore, 1910; at the end of the book our method is set forth at length, with a reproduction of our pictures. Whipple has transformed certain ones of our tests in order to make them adaptable to English children; for example, the tests with the money have received the necessary modifications. But what is curious is that the author has believed it useful to substitute for our sentences to be criticised, new sentences, under the pretext that our sentences are too gruesome. We refer particularly to the woman cut into pieces, of an accident on the train which produced 48 deaths, and the man who committed suicide; it appears that these stories seem frightful to the American youth. Our Parisian youths laugh at them. However that may be, we believe that the new sentences of Whipple's should not be accepted without being tried out experimentally. No other tests will present the same difficulty of comprehension as ours.

274

Changes.

4. How can teachers, by their own means, estimate the intelligence of a child?

5. What differences exist in the intelligence of children belonging to different social conditions?

6. What are the differences between our method and the methods with tests not arranged in a hierarchy?

7. Review of several recent works which have criticized our method.

Proposed Corrections to the Measuring Scale of Intelligence

Some objections to our scale have been made which seem to us just; we ourselves, in employing it, have discovered its defects and have sought to repair them. Here are the points which demand improvement.

1. Certain tests have been repeated. For example at five years, there is a test of repetition of ten syllables and at six years one of sixteen syllables. We suppress the second repetition because it too closely resembles the first.

2. There are tests which require a knowledge outside the intelligence of the child. To know his age, count his fingers, recite the days of the week indicate that he has learned these little facts from his parents or friends; we have thought well to suppress these three tests.

3. There are tests too exclusively scholastic, as that of reading and retaining a given number of memories of what has been read, or copying a written model, or writing from dictation. We suppress these, believing that the tests of instruction devised by M. Vaney, will suffice to establish the scholastic knowledge of a child. We advise recourse to his method when the need is felt.

4. It results from the preceding investigations that the tests for twelve years are too difficult, also those for eleven years. We have therefore carried over to twelve years the tests first classed under eleven years.

.5. Lastly, to fill the blanks produced by our suppressions, we have devised some new tests and have tried them upon new subjects.

In taking count of all these modifications we have obtained the following series (the tests under six years have undergone no change. We have not considered it worth while to reproduce them. They will be found in *L'Année Psychologique*, 1908, p. 59).[2]

Six years

Distinguish morning and evening (p. 206).
Define by use (p. 204).
Copy diamond (p. 209).
Count 13 pennies (p. 210).
Compare 2 pictures esthetically (p. 202).

Seven years

Right hand, left ear (p. 201).
Describe a picture (p. 210).
Execute 3 commissions (p. 205).
Count 3 single and 3 double sous (p. 214).
Name 4 colors (p. 215).

Eight years

Compare 2 objects from memory (p. 216).
Count from 20 to 0 (p. 215).
Indicate omission in pictures (p. 207).
Give the date (p. 217).
Repeat 5 digits (p. 210).

Nine years

Give change out of 20 sous (p. 218).
Definitions superior to use (p. 205).
Recognize the value of 9 pieces of money (p. 221).
Name the months (p. 221).
Comprehend easy questions (p. 224).

Ten years

Place 5 weights in order (p. 220).

Copy a design from memory (p. 60, 282).
Criticize absurd statements (p. 227).
Comprehend difficult questions (p. 225).
Place 3 words in 2 sentences (p. 222).

Twelve years

Resist the suggestion of lines (p. 284).
Place 3 words in 1 sentence (p. 229).
Give more than 60 words in 3 minutes (p. 229).
Define 3 abstract words (p. 230).
Comprehend a disarranged sentence (p. 231).

Fifteen years

Repeat 7 figures (p. 232).
Find 3 rhymes (p. 232).
Repeat a sentence of 26 syllables (p. 232).
Interpret a picture (p. 193).
Solve a problem composed of several facts (p. 233).

Adults

Comprehend a cut in a folded paper (p. 234).
Reversed triangle (p. 235).
Answer the question about the President (p. 287).
Distinguish abstract words (p. 286).
Give the sense of the quotation from Hervieu (p. 287).

We have satisfied ourselves that the application of these new tests produces no important change in the results; and on the other hand, as the number of tests has been lessened, the examination

---

[2] Page 238, in this volume.

gains in rapidity which is an advantage. In employing our modified plan, MM. Levistre and Morlé, school directors, measured the intelligence of many school children; we indicate in Table I the distribution of the pupils according to these investigations, how many are of average intelligence, how many superior, and how many inferior to the average.[3] Other trained persons have been willing to experiment for us; we have utilized them; but for reasons which are too long and uninteresting to explain here, we do not describe their results at present.

TABLE I

Table showing the number of intellectually regular, advanced, or retarded children, for the different school ages

	7 YEARS	8 YEARS	9 YEARS	10 YEARS	12 YEARS
Regular..............................	5	9	17	9	8
Advanced 1 year........................	1	4	6	1	1
Advanced 2 years......................		1	1	4	2
Advanced 3 years and more............					4
Retarded 1 year........................	3	6	1	7	1
Retarded 2 years......................	1				4
Retarded 3 years and more............					3

10   20   25   21   23   *99 cases*

It will be seen that there are children who are advanced or retarded in intelligence by more than two years. In our first study we did not encounter any such; the reason is easy to understand; because in our first study we operated only upon children chosen among those who were regular in their studies. We thus limited our field of experiment because we were in haste to secure a knowledge of average children and the individual deviations did not then interest us. Sufficient unto the day is the task thereof. Since then we have thought best not to select our pupils, but take them as they come. MM. Levistre and Morlé made a special point of choosing only such pupils as were within at least two months of their birthday at the time of the examination; and it is within this contingent that they found the scholas-

[3] In the table, the figures are not percentages, but indicate the number of children for each test. Thus, for the age of seven years, there were only ten children studied; for the age of eight years, there were twenty, etc. The schools of MM. Morlé and Levistre are situated in the poor quarters of Paris, rue des Récollets and rue de Sambre-et-Meuse, in the XII ward. Experience has shown us that these are important circumstances to note.

tically retarded and advanced; as a result of this we find that individual deviations have become greater. Another director, whose school is situated in the richest quarter of Paris, measured the intellectual level of seven or eight children; he found those who were four, and even five years in advance. It must not therefore be considered as an anomaly to find an advance or a retardation of three years.

It will further be noticed that in our new scale there are exactly five tests for each age. We have thus introduced more regularity into our tests. The preceding scale published in 1908 contained sometimes five, sometimes six, sometimes seven. The modifications which we have adopted present, among other advantages, that of permitting a more rapid application and one arriving nearer the intellectual level. Here is the rule to follow: take for point of departure, the age at which all the tests are passed; and beyond this age, count as many fifths of a year as there are tests passed. Example: a child of eight years passes all the tests of six years, 2 of seven years, 3 of eight years, 2 of nine years, 1 of ten years; he has therefore the level of six years plus the benefit of eight tests or eight-fifths years, or a year and three-fifths, equaling a level of seven years and three-fifths, or more simply 7.6. This calculation permits the appreciation of the intellectual level by means of a fraction. But it must be well understood that this fraction is so delicate an appreciation, that it does not merit absolute confidence, because it varies appreciably from one examination to another.

It has seemed to me worth while to publish, at least once, the figures expressing how many times a given test has been passed and how many times missed by pupils of the different ages. I have therefore made a calculation, based upon a great number of experiments old and new, which is given in Table II having, I hasten to say, especially an empirical value. It is interesting to consult because it shows the number of children upon whom we have operated; but like all gross results, it needs to be liberally interpreted, and perhaps even rectified, because the gross result may lead to error. Note, in effect, what course we followed in our experiments. We felt the need of economizing effort in the investigation. It requires indeed, a great deal of courage to continue through long afternoons, a work, from which very slight conclusions can be drawn relative to the effort put forth. This

TABLE II

Empirical table of the results obtained in the experiments relative to the intellectual level of Primary School children of Paris, belonging to a mediocre social level. The figures of the table indicate the number of children who for each test have furnished positive, negative, or doubtful results. Example: For the problem of several facts, which is a test of 15 years, 2 children of 10 replied correctly and 19 failed. These crude results need to be interpreted: see text.

DIFFERENT TESTS	7 years			8 years			9 years			10 years			12 years		
	+	−	?	+	−	?	+	−	?	+	−	?	+	−	?
Six years															
Right hand, left ear	12	4													
Compare 2 faces	13	6													
Define by use	24	2													
Execute 3 commissions	20	6													
Distinguish morning and evening	16	3													
Seven years															
Indicate omission in picture	10	10		7	2										
Copy a diamond	22	7		10	0										
Repeat 5 digits	15	15		5	5										
Describe a picture	23	7		13		2									
Count 13 single sous	23	5		9	1										
Eight years															
Count 3 single and 3 double sous	17	7		37	6		18	0							
Name 4 colors	15	10		38	4	1	19	1							
Count from 20 to 0	12	13		36	7		27	2							
Compare 2 objects from memory	18	6	1	34	9		17	1	1						
Suggestion of lines															
Nine years															
Give the date	20	0		13	5		35	0		17	0				
Define better than by use	10	10		18	21	1	37	12		23	12				
Give change from 20 sous	3	16		17	23		46	4		29	10				
Place 5 weights in order	5	11		11	29		27	24		22	20				
Copy a design from memory															
Ten years															
Name the months							38	11		44	3		24	2	
9 pieces of money							40	6		41	6		23	3	
Put 3 words into 2 sentences							12	33	5	20	25	2	21	5	
Comprehend 3 easy questions							40	9	1	41	6		30	0	
Comprehend 5 difficult questions							10	37	3	14	32	2	22	7	2

AGE OF THE CHILDREN

TABLE II—Continued

DIFFERENT TESTS	AGE OF THE CHILDREN														
	7 years			8 years			9 years			10 years			12 years		
	+	−	?	+	−	?	+	−	?	+	−	?	+	−	?
Twelve years															
Criticize sentences................							14	25	3	15	25	2	23	10	
Put 3 words into one sentence.....							8	32	4	10	22		27	7	
60 words in 3 minutes.............							5	17		12	17		21	12	
Abstract definitions...............							4	36	5	12	28	3	12	19	2
Words to be put in order..........							3	20		10	12		22	11	
Fifteen years															
Repeat 7 digits...................										5	14		12	17	
Rhymes...........................										10	29	2	16	12	2
Repeat 26 syllables...............										4	18		7	16	1
Interpret pictures................										3	36		9	17	1
Problem of several facts..........										2	19		10	18	

explains why, after finding the level of his intelligence, we have not put the entire series to each child. Being given a child of eight, for example, we have given the tests of eight, nine and ten years; and we have used the tests of seven and six years only when the child has failed on the succeeding years. As a whole we have economized our work, doing only what was necessary to establish the intellectual level of each child, and not concerning ourselves deeply with the manner in which each test is comprehended by children of all ages. A double consequence results from this, which makes itself plainly felt now that we attempt the tabulation of our results. In order to explain, let us continue the example of children of eight years. Here where we have 30 or more who have been given the tests of eight years, there are only 10 or 15 of them who have been given those of seven years; in the same way there are only 5 or 6 who were given those of ten years. How are we therefore going to represent these results? Out of the 42 to whom a certain test of eight years has been given, for example naming the colors, there are 38 who named them exactly and 4 who miscalled at least one. We take these two numbers, the relation between which is especially interesting, and place them in our table. But for the tests of seven years which were given to fewer subjects than those of eight years, can we proceed in the same way? Only 10 were asked to repeat a series of five digits; 5 succeeded and 5 failed. Is it correct to record this number without comment and consider them as of the same value as 38 and 4? Evidently not; because if that test had been given to only 10 children taken from the group of 42 pupils of eight years, one would conclude, *a priori*, from the table of results, that it was only those 10 pupils whose results were doubtful, and one would presume in advance that for the 32 others, good replies were certain. We must therefore say that 5 pupils failed, not out of 10, but out of the contingent of 42, which completely changes the proportion. An analogous reasoning can be made relative to the tests of ten and twelve years which were given to some children of eight years; all those to whom the test was not given might be considered as unable to pass it, because if it was not attempted in their case, it is clear that the poor results obtained from the earlier tests permitted no chance of securing better results from the more difficult ones; thus again in the case where 5 subjects succeed in a certain test of ten years, and 5 fail, it will not do to count 5 successes among 10 subjects, nor 5 successes against 5 failures but rather 5 successes against 42 failures.

I do not disguise the fact that there is something arbitrary in this manner of presenting the figures; but I believe that the absence of interpretation is far more dangerous. In any case after having calculated this table from the empirical results, I thought necessary to calculate another where the figures are interpreted in the way I have just indicated; that is to say in calculating the good and the bad replies according to the rule of probability, whose justice I have attempted to make apparent. It is to Table III that one must refer in order to judge of the value of the tests.

This Table III was constructed from experiments tried upon an average of 20 children for each age; I owe these experiments, which have been made in the most attentive and serious manner, to M. Levistre and to M. Morlé. These two directors have their schools situated in the tenth ward of Paris; the population which frequents these schools is of average social standing. In order to appreciate the value of our figures it will be understood that these indications are very important; because the intellectual level of the children is modified according to the wealth of the population.

Finally it will be seen, that the new order of tests which we propose is justified by the figures of the table; we have arranged the tests according to their difficulty, so that the easier ones are placed before the more difficult . The degree of difficulty is indicated by the figures. These figures are always reckoned in their relation to 10. Thus 8 signifies that 8 children out of 10 have passed the test.

It sometimes happens, that for a given test, certain astonishing irregularities occur. It is passed by the 10 children of nine years, that is to say by all, and only by 9 children of ten years; this is altogether inexplicable in theory, because it is certain that children of ten years in general are more intelligent than those a year younger; without doubt there slipped into the group of ten years several children with but little intelligence or those who were distracted, which produced this failure. One can here appreciate the difference between a theoretical and an experimental

 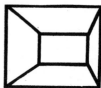

DESIGN TO BE DRAWN FROM MEMORY AFTER BEING STUDIED 10 SECONDS

curve; the latter almost always presents slight imperfections. These must not be ignored; they are proofs of the sincerity of the experiments; when an experimental curve is of a too regular beauty, it is often proof that it has been tampered with.

Our Table III should be kept, to judge of the results which other observers will hereafter obtain; it is a norm. If other results are obtained in quarters widely different from ours, the reasons must be sought for, either in the incapacity of the experimenter, or perhaps in the differences of social conditions; we shall return soon to these differences of social conditions, and we shall show their importance.

Some additional explanations are necessary for the new tests which we propose.

Copy a design from memory (test of ten years). We show during ten seconds a card upon which are drawn the designs here given and we ask the subject to reproduce them from memory.

TABLE III

Table-type of the results obtained in experiments upon the measure of the intellectual level, among children of the primary schools belonging to the average sections of Paris. The figures of the table are the proportion of successes obtained with 10 as a standard; for example, the figure 5 signifies that 5 out of 10, that is one-half, have passed the test.

DIFFERENT TESTS	SCHOOLS OF M. L. AND OF M. M. SITUATED IN PARIS RUE DES RÉCOLLETS AND RUE SAMBRE-ET-MEUSE				
	7 years	8 years	9 years	10 years	12 years
Six years					
Distinguish evening and morning.......	10	10			
Define by use..........................	10	10			
Copy a diamond.......................	9	10			
Count 13 single sous...................	9	10			
Compare 2 faces.......................	9	10			
Seven years					
Right hand, left ear...................	8	10			
Describe a picture.....................	7	10			
Execute 3 commissions.................	7	10			
Count 3 single and 3 double sous........	4	9	10		
Name 4 colors.........................	4	9	10		
Eight years					
Compare 2 objects from memory........	4	8	10	10	
Count from 20 to 0....................	3	9	10	9	
Indicate lack in pictures...............	3	8			
Give the date..........................	4	8	10	10	
Repeat 5 digits.......................	2	5			
Nine years					
Give the change from 20 sous..........		4	10	9	10
Define better than by use..............		3	6	7	7
Pieces of money.......................		2	10	9	9
Months...............................		2	8	10	9
Comprehend easy questions.............		2	9	9	10
Ten years					
Arrange weights.......................		1	5	6	
Copy design from memory..............		2	4	5	
Criticize absurd questions.............			4	5	8
Place 3 words in 2 sentences...........			3	5	8
Comprehend difficult questions.........			3	3	7
Twelve years					
Suggestion of lines....................			2	3	
3 words in 1 sentence..................			2	4	8
60 words in 3 minutes.................			2	4	5
Abstract definitions...................			1	2	4
Disarranged sentences.................			1	4	7

Before showing them, one prepares the attention of the subject by saying that the drawings are going to be shown, and that they must be reproduced from memory, and that the exposure before his eyes will last only ten seconds, which is very little. It is quite difficult to appreciate the exactitude of the reproduction, without taking a host of measurements which are here unnecessary. We have adopted the following rule whose practice is easy; the test is counted passed when one design is exactly, and the other design is half reproduced. The section of the prism is always represented to the left, as it is the one upon which the pupil ordinarily first fixes his attention, and without doubt this is the reason why this figure is better reproduced than the Greek design.[4]

Suggestion of lines. This test belongs to twelve years. A booklet containing six white pages is first prepared. On the first page are traced in ink two lines, a and b, of which the first, the one to the left, measures 4 cm., and the second 5; they are on the same level separated by an interval of 1 cm.; on the second page, two lines are similarly placed; but the first on the left measures 5 cm., that to the right 6; on the third page the line to the left is 6 cm., that to the right 7. On each of the three pages which follow, there are two lines placed in the same way only they are equal, each measuring 7 cm. If we designate the lines by the letters of the alphabet, we have then the following order:

$$a > b \qquad g = h$$
$$c > d \qquad i = j$$
$$e > f \qquad k = l$$

In showing the first three pairs of lines, the experimenter simply says to the child, "Which is the longer of these lines?" When he reaches the last three pairs, he changes slightly the form of the interrogation and simply says "And here?" We consider the child as having passed when at least twice out of the three times he has seen that the lines are equal. Experience proves that very young children, even children of seven years are capable of distinguishing the difference between the lines a and b, c and d, e and f. When he comes to the equal lines, the child finds himself the object of two influences; he has first the influence of suggestion; thus far, for three times, he has seen that the line on the

---

[4] In spite of this statement, the design is printed in *l'Année Psychologique* as we here reproduce it. Possibly a printer's error.—Editor.

right is the longer; he is therefore led to suppose that this will continue; it is a supposition, a generalization, in case we should admit the operation to be conscious and due to reflection; but we think that more often there is no conscious operation, but a blind tendency, a natural automatism, a habit or rather the first outline of a habit; and though it certainly is not strong, yet the tendency exists, and it may be the determining factor in the replies, if no conflicting cause interferes with its action. The second influence is precisely the reflection occasioned by the perception of the lines. A single glance suffices to show that the line at the right ceases to be longer than the one at the left. If the child realizes this, he will resist the automatism and cease saying that the line at the right is longer, and will reply on the contrary, that they are equal. Thus theoretically analyzed, this test seems to reveal the suggestibility of a child; the most suggestible is the one who is guided by automatism for the last three pairs of lines; the least suggestible is the one who declares them equal; finally we admit, according to the rule which we have thus far applied, for passing the test it suffices to have two correct replies out of three.

As the term suggestibility has more than one sense, it is important to remark that here is a question of suggestibility not through lack in the quality of judgment but from heedlessness, lack of attention. The child falls into the trap because he allows himself to follow the lead of habit, and does not pay attention to the real length of the new lines which are presented to him. But I am not sure that the analysis of this particular form of suggestibility is exactly correct. Rarely does suggestibility depend wholly upon the intelligence; character and feeling add their influence. There are children who, having successively replied under the eye of the master that the longer line is to the right, are, as it were, incited emotionally to persist in this designation to the right; they believe themselves forced to it; if they perceive that they have committed an error, they are at times ashamed, blush and feel themselves ill at ease; they do not dare correct themselves, but continue the error. There is here a slight emotional trouble which is very curious and which we have insufficiently analyzed.

The test is difficult enough for a child of seven years to succumb; from the very careful studies of M. Morlé, out of 10 children of eight years, a single one escaped; out of 13 children of ten years, 5 avoided the error.

A final word upon the experiment.   One might think that the
automatism would be especially great for the pair g-h, which follows the pair where a difference of length really exists.   It does not
seem that this is the case.   In lumping the replies given by all the
children, we find an equal number of erroneous replies for the
couples g-h, i-j, and k-l.

I at first thought of a little different disposition of the lines, in
order to avoid what seemed to me a cause of error.   I said to myself it is as easy to perceive a slight difference of length between
two lines, as it is difficult to judge if they are of the same length;
there might result from this a certain difficulty for the children to
pronounce upon; I thought that perhaps it might be better to
change the nature of the test, by reversing the inequality of the
lines in the following manner:

$$a < b \qquad g > h$$
$$c < d \qquad i > j$$
$$e < f \qquad k > l$$

It will be seen, in this new arrangement that the lines have ceased
to be equal, which forms the innovation; g has grown larger than
h by 5 mm.; same difference for other pairs.   But we found that
with this modification the experiment became much too easy.
The child who had formed the habit of designating the line to the
right, was not able to persevere in it when the new pairs were presented to him, because the greater length of the line to the left
stares him in the face.   From the investigations of M. Morlé all
the children of seven, of eight, of nine and of ten years, upon
whom he tried the test, succeeded; it was too easy for what we
desired to do and hence we rejected it.   We have preserved the
first form, with three pairs of equal lines; and we have made a
twelve year test of it.

Abstract differences (test for adults).   *What is the difference
between idleness and laziness?   Between event and advent?   Between evolution and revolution?*   Such are the questions asked.
Two good replies suffice.   It is necessary in distinguishing between *idleness* and *laziness*, to clearly indicate that idleness comes
from exterior circumstances, while laziness comes from character.
For the distinction between *event* and *advent*, it is scarcely necessary to recall that *event* is a completed fact of any kind, while the
advent is a coming.   *Evolution* is a slow progressive change;

revolution is a sudden change; some persons take the word evolution in the sense of the manoeuvers of a troop, and revolution in the sense of a serious popular insurrection; in this case the distinction is not so good, because here the two words are different without being opposite, and it must be understood that we are here searching for opposites, and not simply differences. Nevertheless, we admit that these replies are passable.

Reproduction of the thought of Hervieu (test for adults). Read aloud, slowly and with correct intonation, the following selection which we usually call the thought of Hervieu; it is only his thought developed; he wrote three lines that did not adapt themselves to our needs; we have therefore amplified his thought to prevent its being retained by the memory alone, something which might have occurred if the selection were too short.

One hears very different judgments on the value of life. Some say it is good, others say it is bad. It would be more correct to say that it is mediocre; because on the one hand it always brings us less happiness than we desire, while on the other hand the misfortunes it brings are always less than others desire for us. It is the mediocrity of life which makes it just; or, rather, that keeps it from being positively unjust.

Before beginning the reading, the listener must be warned to give close attention, for he will be asked when the reading is finished, to repeat the sense of the selection. In this way the test is carried into the domain of memory, and whoever has failed to understand the somewhat subtle sense of the thought of Hervieu, will not have the slightest wounding of his pride such as would occur if he had to admit not understanding it; he will blame his memory or failure of attention, which is infinitely less painful. The central thought, the one necessary to reproduce is the following:

Life is neither good nor bad, but mediocre, because it is inferior to what we desire and better than what others desire for us.

It is of slight importance what words are used. The essential is that the thought be well understood; and one will grasp this in proportion as he abstains from reflecting upon it word for word.

Question of president (test for adult). Question: there are three principal differences between a king and the president of a republic. What are they? The three differences are the following: the power of the king is hereditary; it lasts through the life of the monarch; and it has extensive power; the president of a republic is elected; he has a limited term, and his powers are less extensive than those of a king.

What are the Relations Between the Intellectual Level and the Scholastic Standing?

At the time of our first investigations in 1908, we begged the directors to send us only the children who were regular in their instruction; this time we have taken all of the children who were within two months of their birthday and we have designated the children as advanced, regular, or retarded in their studies. The group upon which we have operated has not therefore been a selected one. We have measured the intelligence of about 100 children; out of this number, there have been

```
Regular.....................................................  64
In advance..........................  12 { advance of 1 year  12
                                         { advance of 2 years  0
                                       { retarded 1 year  17
Retarded...........................  21 { retarded 2 year   3
                                       { retarded 3 year   1
```

It is therefore natural to search for the deviations to be noted between the intellectual level and the scholastic standing.

Thus far we have been unable to study these divergences; we have simply noted this fact, that the scholastic divergence is greater than the intellectual divergence, and that for instance, subnormal children who are sometimes retarded in instruction six or seven years, are not equally retarded in intelligence. But these are only partial views. Out of our hundred little children who are all normal, let us see how the intelligence distributes itself according to the scholastic situation. Let us draw an average of the differences which can be seen between the two figures expressing the two levels; a child for instance, retarded two years scholastically, has an intellectual retardation of one year; the difference is one year. What is the average difference? It is very low, exactly 0.7 years; in other words half a year. That is to say; in general, children have an intelligence in accord with their degree of instruction. Thus the rule that we have proposed for some time past, by which we can quickly select the most intelligent children of a school, is confirmed, take the youngest in each class, because the youngest are the most advanced in their studies; we have just seen, that the intelligence generally goes hand in hand with the degree of instruction, hence the most advanced in their studies have the chance of taking rank among the most intelligent.

This rule is not absolute; it is an empirical rule, a result produced by a certain number of factors; and if the factors are lacking the rule ceases to be applicable. One can, with great probability, imagine country children who have been kept at home too long herding the cows; when they come to school they are very much behind, but this backwardness is no sign of a lack of intelligence. One of our subjects is in this condition, a child of twelve years, he is therefore regular as to intelligence. But as to instruction, what retardation? He is in the elementary class second year. His master, of whom we asked information regarding the children measured, writes of young Dufour: "Illiterate surroundings, unfavorable for intellectual progress; the child remained long in the country; irregular in school because of illness. Has been in school the last six months." This information, although brief, clearly indicates that Dufour's retardation in instruction is not the result of intellectual retardation. We have since learned that he is progressing rapidly, and making up for lost time. This confirms our demonstration of the measure of his intellectual level.

If the case of Dufour can be explained by an insufficiency of scholastic training, other cases can be explained by indolence, or by other special reasons. With M. Levistre, school director, I have made an analysis of the circumstances which might explain the difference of two years between the scholastic level and the intellectual level of the children of his school; this analysis was made for six pupils, and note the result. For two children no explanation has been found; for one who is regular scholastically but retarded intellectually, the Director informed me that that child had been placed in a class in advance of his powers in order to fill a vacancy; consequently the figure showing his scholastic situation is not correct, and should not be taken into consideration; as to the three others who have more intelligence than instruction, they are all indolent. Thus, I believe, that a minute and impartial examination of the facts will generally result in an explanation of the apparent anomalies.

However it be, the comparison of the figures of the intellectual and the scholastic levels gives rise to a very interesting consideration; it is, that never, or almost never, does a pupil present two contrary signs for his intellectual and his scholastic level. Thus, a scholar retarded one year, may be retarded in intelligence, or he may be regular in intelligence; he will never be advanced in intelligence; having the sign + for one level he will not have the sign − for the other level. A single exception has presented itself in one hundred examinations of level;[5] this is altogether insignificant. That is to say putting it in less abstract terms, that when a child has a decidedly brilliant intelligence he is never behind in his studies; that when he has an intelligence decidedly below medium, he cannot be advanced in his studies. It is equally true that when a child is behind in his studies he cannot be a bril-

TABLE IV

This table shows the relation between the intellectual level and the scholastic level

	CHILDREN BEHIND IN SCHOOL INSTRUCTION	CHILDREN REGULAR IN SCHOOL INSTRUCTION	CHILDREN ADVANCED IN SCHOOL INSTRUCTION
Intelligence above the average.....	1	16	7
Average intelligence...............	9	33	5
Intelligence below the average.....	14	16	0

liant subject; and when he is in advance, he cannot have a mediocre intelligence.

As this assertion is not without importance, I think it well to support it with new combinations of figures. These will be found in Table IV.

Thus one sees a remarkable correlation between the two levels; and we can express it in the following manner: When children are backward in their studies, they have one chance of having an average intelligence as against two for having an intelligence inferior to the average, and no chance whatever for being brilliant; if they are regular in their studies, they have one chance of being brilliant, one chance of being dull, and two chances for being of medium intelligence; if they are in advance of their studies, their

[5] Later investigations made on thirty children have again shown the justice of this rule, without any exception whatever.

chances are nearly the same for being brilliant or for being of medium intelligence. Certainly this is not a demonstration of parallelism between the faculty of intelligence and the scholastic faculty; one recognizes that the two faculties are independent; but they are not contradictory; they develop in the same general way; it is a new proof of that truth, to be held in opposition to so many paradoxically-minded persons, that the first in school are likely to be the first in life. Before leaving this point, I wish to call attention to a special question which perhaps is of interest only for professional experimenters. After having proved how far the scholastic situation of a child informs us of his intelligence, I asked myself if one could not obtain a more exact determination, by replacing the exact scholastic situation by what might be called *an appreciated scholastic situation.* Here is what must be understood by this term. In certain schools a class may have a very low level; or a pupil who belongs to a certain grade might, supposing he was always one of the first, be considered as belonging to a higher grade; or again, if he is always one of the last it would be just to consider him as belonging to a lower grade. I have therefore begged the directors of the school to rectify the school grading of their pupils, by taking into consideration these given differences. Later I made some calculations to find if the revised school grading, when compared with the figure denoting intellectual level, presented less deviation than that of the actual situation; I was very much astonished to find that the deviation was greater in the first case. In a series of 45 pupils, who have been carefully studied from this point of view, the mean deviation is 0.66 between the intellectual level and the scholastic level (that is to say a little more than half a year) when the school level is taken as it stands; and it is about 0.83 (that is to say a little less than a whole year) when the school grading has been corrected. The difference is slight, but quite constant. How explain it? It would seem that from the moment that one makes a serious and penetrating estimate of the degree of instruction of a child, the resulting figure should be more significant than the one which results from a grading which is somewhat arbitrary; one might therefore expect that the scholastic level when revised would more nearly approach that of the intellectual level. After having sought for an explanation of this enigma, I believe that I have found it. As a matter of fact when a director classifies his pupils

Corrected grade location

292   DEVELOPMENT OF INTELLIGENCE

in school, many things are taken into consideration and among them, a very important one, is that of the age of the child. On the contrary, when a professor attempts to estimate exactly the amount of instruction of a child, he does not take the age into consideration; as a result the figure representing the estimated school standing is farther removed from the age of the children than the school grade. I have noticed this. It is, however, very evident that the age is a very important factor in the formation of the intelligence; and this is also the reason why the estimated school standing, taking less account of age accords less nearly with the intellectual level; and this factor of age is very important.

On the Effect of Repetition upon the Taking of the Level

A Belgian pedagogue, who tried our psychological tests upon the pupils of his school, wrote me one day that it would be desirable to have a fresh supply of tests, in order to be able to follow from year to year the progress of a given pupil. (This desire is quite legitimate. We think that it will be easy to find such tests; it will suffice to have a little patience, and above all, a little collaboration. The method is so simple!) While waiting to have this lack supplied, I thought well to find out if the same experimenter, after a two weeks interval in taking the level of a certain child, arrived at practically the same conclusions. Upon this point, I had only vague conjectures; I knew from earlier investigations upon attention and adaptation, that children make quite rapid progress in the experiments, especially when they are taken individually, which removes the occasion of distraction and of ennui. I could therefore suppose that if the measure of the level were taken individually, every pupil would gain more or less from one sitting to another.

M. Jeanjean willingly devoted two afternoons to this question. He knew the method sufficiently to practice it correctly. He examined 5 children first on the 26th of April, 1910; he noted the results, then sent the children back to their class without, of course, telling them his intentions; and he examined them again the 10th of May of the same year. The examinations were made in the presence of M. Vaney, director of the school, rue Grange-aux-Belles, and upon children of his school. The five children serving as subjects were all about nine years old.

There was an appreciable progress for all at the time of the second examination, and this progress naturally should be credited to their having become accustomed to the situation. We mean a better adaptation, a better comprehension of what was required; perhaps the pupils had talked together about the experiment and had asked their comrades for information. That is not impossible. One among them, the young Allain, had already been examined by us two years previously as it turned out, and he informed M. Jeanjean that he remembered that in the test of making change it was necessary to give 16 sous to be correct.

Here is the result. From 22 to 23 tests were given to each pupil. Out of this number, there was a variation of two or three or even four tests, the others remaining the same. In the series of figures which follow, we have indicated, under the title "number of new failures," the number of tests which the subject had passed the first time and failed on at the second trial; under the title "number of new successes," we indicate the number of tests not passed at the first trial that were passed at the second.

NAMES OF PUPILS	NUMBER OF NEW FAILURES	NUMBER OF NEW SUCCESSES	TOTAL OF THE VARIATIONS
Allain...........................	1	3	4
Bouchard........................	0	3	3
Danel...........................	1	2	3
Guillemin.......................	0	2	2
Defremont.......................	0	4	4
	2	14	16

These changes were made from time to time, apparently by chance, upon the following tests: months of the year, arranging of weights, definitions, pieces of money, disarranged sentences, placing 3 words in one sentence. But the most frequent variations centered upon two tests in particular; one of these was the number of memories retained after a reading of diverse facts; its variation was almost constant; it passed from 5 to 6, from 2 to 5, and even from 7 to 10. That is easily understood. These children read twice the same selection; they should the second time remember more than the first time. The second of the tests upon which the most progress was made, was the number of words spoken in 3 minutes; here improvement was the law; one pupil passed from 54 to 79, another from 57 to 87. I repeat that they had learned the way. Perhaps they had practiced in the interval, and surely they had the right since no one forbade them.

In our new series of tests, that of reading is eliminated, because it belongs to the degree of instruction; but that of finding words still remains. On an average—if it is possible to find an average from so few experiments—a child in an interval of fifteen days gains two tests or a little more. According to our new method of counting, two tests represent about five months (5 tests in reality form one year). It is a material gain. But notice on the other hand that in repeating the tests two weeks apart, we have favored the effects of repetition; if one had waited a year, it is very possible that these effects would have been lessened, and that the subject would have recalled almost nothing of what he had done at the former trial. From all this let us conclude that it would be useful—but not indispensable—to have a new set of tests for successive trials.

Here are a few, which we have eliminated from our new scale, but which nevertheless are worthy to be retained under the head of a reserve supply.

Tests of 6 years
: Tell the age.
: Distinguish evening and morning.

Tests of 7 years
: The fingers of the hand.
: Copy a written sentence.
: Name 4 pieces of money.

Tests of 8 years
: Read and remember two facts.
: Write from dictation.

Tests of 9 years
: Days of the week.
: Read and retain 6 facts.

PRACTICAL SUGGESTIONS UPON THE TAKING OF THE LEVEL

We have noticed that it is useful to make certain recommendations to every experimenter. Note first if one is alone with the pupil, or, if other persons are present, who those persons are. In any case, impose absolute silence upon the witness. Before many witnesses a child becomes timid, which tends to lower his level. Avoid this cause of error as far as possible. The presence of relatives is the cause of still more serious trouble. It is useless to add that when the witness or the relative interferes to scold the child or to whisper the reply to him, a good experimenter has but one thing to do, either close the experiment or dismiss the witness.

The attitude to be taken in regard to the child is delicate; first of all there must be good will; one must try to remain in touch with him; excite his attention, his self respect; show satisfaction with all of his replies, whatever they may be, encourage without aiding, without suggesting; the questions being of standardized difficulty, change nothing. Avoid disturbing the child by fixedly regarding him. Naturally, one will not fall into the ridiculous error of teaching him; it is a question here of ascertaining the state of his mentality not of teaching.

The tests should be prepared in advance; one must have at hand without being obliged to search for it, the slight amount of material needed; in a special purse, have all the coins that will be needed. One must have besides, two registers; in the first, one will inscribe in a column the sign representing the result of the experiment; in the second, which is a note book, will be reproduced the replies in detail; one might, for the second, have the aid of a secretary, so as to save time; but this is not indispensable. The first register consists of a series of large pages of square paper upon which is written in advance, in a column to the left, the names of the tests, grouped by age, in some such form as is represented in our Table III. After these names, rule as many vertical columns as there are children to be tested. Above each column write the name of the pupil. When the pupil answers the test write the result in the column opposite the test; this result will be expressed in the following symbols: + indicates that the test is passed; − indicates failure; 0 indicates silence; ? indicates that the result is doubtful; if the doubtful result is nearer failure than success, write − ?; if on the contrary it is nearer success, with + ?; we also use the sign + ! when the result is excellent, and the sign − ! when it is altogether bad. We advise putting the desired sign as soon as each test is completed, and not after the sitting while re-reading the notes taken. It will be easily understood why we give this advice. Note that a sign is not merely to record automatically that which has just transpired, it is truly to pass a judgment; but the judgment stands the chance of being exact just in proportion as the facts are recent. However detailed the notes may be, they never give, except in a very incomplete manner, all the features of an experiment; they contain an immense number of things understood; one would therefore be wrong in placing confidence in them.

As soon as the results of the test are marked by a sign, take the note book, and commence a more detailed account. This must contain the name of the pupil, his age, date of birth, the actual date, the place, the number of witnesses, and every exceptional circumstance that could influence the examination. Very often this information is neglected; later when one takes up the pages, one no longer remembers what they express. I advise noting also the school standing of the child, the number of pupils in his class, the attitude of the pupil during the examination (natural, giddy, timid, dull, undisciplined, etc.) and lastly, the social condition of his parents (misery, poverty, moderate circumstances, ease, wealth). If by chance, some important fact has transpired in the history of the child, be sure to note it. A certain little pupil of nine years has arrived from the country, and has never been to school; mention of this is necessary.

The notes to be taken relative to each child are variable; it is, above all, experience which teaches what is useful to record. One must remember first of all that a mere symbol is insufficient, and that one must have sufficient notes in order that another experimenter may be able to judge results for himself. Thus, the replies to the *questions of intelligence,* the manner in which a certain pupil has explained or criticized the absurdity of certain phrases, should be written in full; when digits are to be repeated, it is well to have an invariable series; then one should write the digits given by the pupil himself; in taking this precaution, one avoids letting interesting facts escape. Example: one has given the digits 1, 3, 9, 2, 7. The pupil, believing he is repeating, says 1, 3, 4, 5, 6; the error is serious, very much more serious than if he had said, 1, 3, 8, 5, 0; because in the first repetition, he followed the natural order of figures, he has therefore implicitly admitted the absurdity that he was asked to repeat figures in their natural order. Make note of this fact in order to fix it in the memory. The definition of words and things, the résumé of the sentiment of Hervieu, are also to be written in full. In the test of 60 words, it is often difficult to write all the words given by a pupil, because he goes more rapidly than one can write; one can often make in passing interesting indications; for instance, one notes each word by a vertical mark and commences a new group every half minute (the total experiment lasts three minutes); one knows thus how many words were said in the first half minute, how many in the second, how

How teachers judge intel., of child. Forcing open door

many in the third, etc. One can thus see if the subject has progressively increased or diminished the series of words, and that gives an indication upon his *faculty of work*; I have also the habit of indicating the marks corresponding to the names of objects to be seen in the room, and I underscore whenever the subject employs a superior word which does not belong to current speech. I also advise writing the rhymes found, or the sentence given containing the three words. In requiring all these notes from my collaborator, I make myself capable of judging with what care the experiment has been made. A measurement of the intelligence of a child, which presents no data but symbols, seems to me not to be trusted; this must not be tolerated; it encourages negligence and even fraud.

How Do Teachers Judge the Intelligence of Their Pupils?

One of my colleagues, of a very superior mind, but whose high administrative functions have not perhaps prepared him for the scrupulous observation of small facts—because where one observes from an elevated situation one observes not only from above, but from afar—reproached me amicably, one day, for having taken too great precautions to organize a measuring scale for the intellectual level. According to him, I had broken down an unlocked door. After having cited certain of my conclusions which seemed to him obvious even to triteness, he finished by declaring that all teachers know how to judge the intelligence of their pupils without difficulty.

Is he correct? I remember that an intelligent teacher, who for a certain time was a pupil of mine, gave as his opinion a very different idea. "We believe," he said, "that we can judge of the intelligence of a child; and two months after having begun the class, we imagine that we can give to each child a mark expressing the degree of his intelligence; but the paradoxical fact remains, that the more we study him, the less we are sure of our own judgment. The increase in the number of these embarrassing cases," he added, "comes especially from the contradictory observations to which a prolonged study gives rise." This opinion seemed to me altogether just, and in perfect accord with my personal experience. I have always observed that when one knows a person but little, one has a well defined opinion of his grade of intelligence, and one believes him either very intelligent or the reverse.

forced an open door

As one knows him better, the opinion that one forms is less extreme, because the more intelligent appear less so, and in the less intelligent one almost always discovers slight manifestations of intelligence which make one judge him less stupid.

I wished to know what teachers think of their ability to judge the intelligence of children. At my request, M. Belot, primary instructor of Paris, agreed to send to his teachers a small questionnaire in which he requested information upon the two following points: 1st. What do you think is the proportion of errors that you have committed in estimates you have made of the intelligence of your pupils? 2nd. What are the methods which you employ for arriving at an exact estimate?

The replies elicited by these questions have been numerous, in the neighborhood of forty, very verbose, some forming a veritable memorial of 8 or 10 pages; on an average, however, they were content with 3 or 4 pages. The primary inspector in delivering them to me, remarked that I had here found an excellent means of classifying the intelligence of certain teachers. Among the number were certain very confused studies; and also pages where a devout optimism was curiously displayed; the teachers believed that they were never deceived!

In analyzing all these missives, I occupied myself first in establishing an average expressing the number of errors of which the teacher accused himself. But this is a calculation which seemed to me, on reflection, thoroughly useless. What advantage would there be in knowing, for example, that this average number of errors is 1 out of 8 or 10 pupils? It is only a figure, and one does not know exactly what it represents; because we completely ignore its origin. It is a question of recognized errors; and how many unrecognized errors may have been committed? One correspondent related for example that a young pupil had the most limited intelligence; she was found several years later in a notion store, in the rue Rivoli, where she was very much appreciated. "Her amiable and gracious air, her lively and intelligent conversation," said her teacher, "convinced me anew that it is rash to say in school that certain children are devoid of intelligence." Would our correspondent have known of her error, if chance had not taken her to rue Rivoli? And then, one would like to know how far the estimate of the teacher must deviate from the truth before he perceives that he has deceived himself.

If I say of a plank that it is 3 m. 45, and it is afterwards measured
before me, I put myself under such conditions that my error will
be easily detected. But if I content myself with saying that
this plank is very long how can the amount of my error be known?
How would it be possible even to establish the fact that I am in
error? It is practically impossible. In order that a statement
be subject to error, it is necessary that it be precise; precision is
as necessary a condition of truth as of error, and consequently is
a necessary condition of verification. But I ask myself, did these
teachers when they judged of the intelligence of their children
submit themselves to this precision? I have read many judgments given and I find them of a vagueness that is most dis-
couraging. They say of a child that he is very intelligent, or
"intelligent enough,"—and this last term is so very vague that
it changes in value according to the inflection of the voice—
or very little intelligent (still another expression of the same kind)
or again, below the average, and that is all. Very many teachers,
asked to divide their classes from the point of view of the intelligence, make only 3 groups. With such estimates one seldom runs
the risk of being found lacking.

All this leads me to attach only a moderate importance to the
mean error of $\frac{1}{8}$ which I have here indicated. That which appears to me more significant is the disagreement of the teachers;
it reduces itself here to what one calls the mean variation.
While certain ones affirm that in a career of from ten to twenty
years, they have been deceived only once or twice, which makes
the admirable percentage of 1 error out of 1000, others recognize
that one is apt to be deceived once out of every three times, which
gives 300 for every 1000! Such divergences of opinion, are much
more striking than any average; and they are the best argument
for finding a precise and exact method upon which everyone may
agree.

Let us continue then the analysis of our documents; having
seen the replies made to the first question, let us see what is said
of the second. We asked the teachers to indicate to us how they
went about establishing the intelligence of a child.

The question is vast enough and vague enough for each one to
be able to develop at his ease his manner of viewing the subject
and especially of recording what he has learned during his career
as teacher; the career, often long, has given him the opportunity

of studying the children under the admirable conditions of variety and of precision. I have often thought that in the brain of every intelligent teacher there is a treasure consisting of observations which have been deposited there from day to day; but it is difficult to get possession of this treasure; and he who possesses it, often knows neither its value nor its use. By extremely skillful questions one might perhaps obtain from each teacher something of his knowledge.

I have read and re-read all the replies to our questionnaire, classifying them, passing judgment upon them, discarding those that were pointless, simply verbose, or too clearly inspired by manuals of psychology, keeping only those which indicated personal observations, acuteness of insight and actual effort. It seemed to me after reading them and trying to make a synthesis of all they contained, that these diverse replies gave information upon two different points. On the one hand were scattered observations, half conscious, upon the signs of intelligence of children, which one perceives without hunting for them; and on the other hand certain precise methodical operations, more nearly resembling tests.

Our question related to the intelligence but it did not demand a definition. Seldom did the teachers recognize this point of distinction. One school mistress, somewhat naïve, has carelessly written that intelligence consists in the faculty of acquiring instruction. This is to confound intelligence and memory, that is to say the whole with the part, it is to see in the child nothing but the pupil. Others have reduced the intelligence to the faculty of knowing and understanding; still another definition of the whole by the part, and this definition is worse than the other because it fails to recognize the purpose of the intelligence, that which forms its utility. Another definition worth repeating is that which sees the intelligence in the faculty of making use of acquired matter in a way to produce new ideas. The one who expressed this thought, wished to react against the tendency, so common among masters of routine, to confound the intelligence with memory; but this point of view is too restricted. To produce new ideas is not the only function of the intelligence; there are very original minds which lack balance; and fantastic dreamers, who certainly find what is new, cannot be taken as models of intelligence. It would be better to say that the intelligence

Physiognomy misleading

serves in the discovery of truth. But the conception is still too
narrow; and we return to our favorite theory; the intelligence
marks itself by the best possible adaptation of the individual
to his environment; this is what one school mistress has very
cleverly understood. She recounts how she made an error in the
case of a young girl, who learned badly in the class, and who had
passed for stupid but who afterwards proved her intelligence by
her practical sense of life. And the teacher adds, "The intelligence not only serves to learn, above all it serves to live (a faire
sa vie)." What a beautiful expression, how picturesque and
true! In speaking of one's adaptation to one's surroundings we
mean just that.

get on in life

Our teachers therefore passed in review all the signs of intelligence which they knew, and in making a synthesis of the replies
one obtains a very exhaustive table of these signs. Only, we
shall continually show that these signs are indeed subject to
caution. One teacher says the intelligence of a child can be
judged indirectly by heredity. Intelligent parents have intelligent children, "especially" she adds, "when they are young."
Here we perhaps have to make reservations; these questions of
heredity are still but little known; and we could object that one
encounters backward children in families where the brothers and
sisters are normal; with still stronger reason one may expect to
find families where the intelligence varies; if the observation of
teachers corresponds to a general rule, which is possible, how
many exceptions! It seems that in reality, teachers are attached
to the idea of the influence of heredity. If they hesitate upon the
intelligence of a child, they draw an argument from the fact that
a brother is not very intelligent or is backward, or on the contrary
brilliant in his studies. But let us come to the child himself.
Occasionally, teachers take into consideration the form of his
head; ordinarily they take no notice of this, and the reason is
that malformed heads are quite rare. The attention attaches
itself more to the manner of conducting themselves; embarrassment is an unfavorable sign. The physiognomy above all is
considered important.
This is a point to which they constantly return. The intelligent child has an open, awakened, mobile countenance; another
expression is that the countenance is sympathetic. But how take
account of this? How define it? How be certain of not de-

ceiving oneself either in judging it intelligent or otherwise, or in drawing from it a conclusion? With equal frequency the eyes and expression are spoken of. The glance of the intelligent is quick, that of the unintelligent is dull. "There are eyes awakened and deep!" One teacher writes that the first have an *active* look, and the other a *passive* look. One can understand about what she wishes to express; she means to speak of the activity of the intelligent type which causes them not only to follow the lesson, but to go in advance of the questions; and this activity can be read in the expression. We do not contradict; but how shall we replace this intuition by a clear description? We do not see the means. Furthermore, one would be wrong to place confidence in these impressions, because certain teachers see a world in the countenance of a child and we at once become suspicious. One mistress writes, "While recounting to children an interesting or touching fact, it is extremely important to observe their expressions which seem to me a sure revelation of the state of their intelligence. All are interested and upon all faces one reads a keen attention; but while the eyes of most of them express simply naïvete, curiosity or a slight emotion, a few show an acuteness or a depth of penetration which reveals a superior nature." That is well said and well felt. But by what precise detail can one recognize the depth of the expression, and distinguish it from simple curiosity? Besides more than one teacher puts us on our guard against such interpretations, as being superficial. "Open, animated, expressive countenances rarely belong to unintelligent pupils. Nevertheless one is sometimes deceived; these lively, penetrating subjects lack depth and solidity, while a passive countenance, sometimes almost without expression, may hide reflection, and judgment, that are discovered little by little." One teacher writes, "I have found myself deceived by children with dainty, agreeable faces and bright eyes who gave the impression of being intelligent, but who are not so. Nevertheless this impression which a casual visitor might experience cannot hold sway long over the every day teacher." Still more precise is the following observation: "There are countenances which are expressionless and gloomy; one never obtains from these children an intelligent answer; the lessons are badly learned; they are nevertheless strong in composition and arithmetic. On the contrary one may be deceived by open, frank, wide awake countenances; one obtains good oral replies; their choice of words is good; but they are children incapable of sustained attention, and characterized by an absolute lack of ability in arithmetic." These affirmations, these correctives, and these vague impressions compose something very difficult to define. The master is influenced by an open face, a quick glance, and above all by a sympathetic manner. He says that, without doubt, that child is intelligent. All the same he is obliged to add under his breath one or even many "buts;" and then one does not know exactly what remains of the first statement.

We are also told that one must observe children during play. In class they are immobile and unnatural because of discipline. In the school yard, they are free, and become more natural, and the recreation period with its play, its movement, its comradeship and its combats, brings them nearer to real life. It is at this moment that one gets an insight into their personality, their character. One of the best teachers writes me that two principal elements serve him in discovering whether a child is intelligent or not; his replies in class, and the way he plays. There are a hundred ways of playing. Some children do not know how to play. This is a sign of low intelligence. It is true that some intelligent children isolate themselves in the yards and never play; but that does not prove an incapacity. One may note the aptitudes of the children in their manner of playing; there is an unintelligent way; it is where imitation predominates; true intelligence manifests itself by initiative and creation. We do not contradict; a school yard, like the street, is a marvelous field for observation; and we can understand that one might remain there hours and hours observing; but nothing of that is described, especially is nothing tabulated; it is not sufficient to observe, one must interpret what one sees, and the manner of obtaining a just interpretation has not been indicated.

All these are only incidents at the threshold. According to the majority of our correspondents, it is especially in the class room that one judges of the intelligence of each child. The master is there to dispense instruction; it is therefore quite natural that his attention should be fixed upon that instruction; and following the manner in which this instruction is received by the child, the judgment of good or bad is passed upon him. In principle he is not wrong. The school child is there to learn;

if he does not learn, or if he learns poorly, he fails in his task, he is at fault, and his intellectual insufficiency may be the cause of that failure. Let us imagine a master who is in charge of an elementary class; the benches are filled with little tots of six or eight years; his principal task is to teach them to read; this will be the great work of his scholastic year; and according to the manner in which each pupil acquits himself in this regard, he will be judged. If he encounters a child who, in spite of two years of assiduous training, is still unable to pronounce syllables correctly, he will pass an unfavorable judgment upon that pupil; and thus for all; the sum of their knowledge, compared with their age and attendance at school, furnishes the principal criterion for the appreciation. The instruction therefore answers for the intelligence, but we very well understand that this idea is only approximately correct; there are minds which rebel at reading; there are intellectual aptitudes which cannot develop in class, and which will never take a scholastic form.

And to speak of older pupils, it is incontestable that their knowledge is not a measure of their intelligence. In reality, knowledge represents only the intelligence of others; there is some merit in having assimilated it; this proves first, memory, then attention, comprehension, work, method; but many intellectual qualities are not comprised in the list. Many of the correspondents have realized this, and they have endeavored to distinguish instruction from intelligence. In the examples which they give, in the methods which they advise, they especially strive to eliminate memory. Memory is the grand simulator of intelligence. When a child makes an ingenious reply, finds a witty word, or gives a just appreciation, one must ask what is original in the reply, and what is taken from the book he has read. We must credit him only with what belongs to him personally.

It is curious to see how teachers have sought to apply this principle. It is not easy. In the execution, difficulties of every sort show themselves.

Without doubt, one must take account of the activity which a child shows in class. Those who have the taste for study, those who love to be questioned, those who reply well, those who go in advance of the question will be marked favorably. The rapidity of comprehension is also a good sign; but one must not allow himself to be deceived. There are children who seem to

No g questions asked not safe criterion

understand and scarcely ask any questions, because they content themselves with nearly understanding. "This year I have a little girl who makes me repeat my explanations twice, and she is nevertheless the first in the class; but she asks me to repeat because she wishes thoroughly to understand while the others think they have understood. Unintelligent children are not able to recognize at what point in the explanation they no longer understand, so that often it is the most intelligent who say 'I do not understand.'" One with justice attributes intelligence to those who make sensible progress. Only, let us remark that the absence of progress may result from the lack of a special aptitude.

Certain children, to whom the ordinary work of the class is distasteful, make compensation in manual work, sewing, designing, writing; little girls weak in orthography, are strong in sewing and capable in the instruction concerning housekeeping; and, all things considered, this is more important for their future. In certain matters of instruction, it has seemed that one could easily distinguish between the part played by memory and by reasoning. Arithmetic has often been cited. Mental arithmetic furnishes a means of judging. By the way in which the child handles it, by the ingenuity of his methods, judge of his intelligence. In the discussion of problems, one easily sees who understands and who knows how to connect ideas. Teachers zealous for mathematics, think that every intelligent child ought to excel in arithmetic, and that the converse is equally true; that is to say that any one strong in arithmetic is intelligent; he may lack memory, but not the power of reasoning. We think this is an error. In the first place, no account is made of the diversity of aptitudes. A certain writer, and also a certain politician whom we know, comprehend nothing in mathematics; they are not, however, blockheads. In the school one sees certain pupils who are strong in arithmetic but who seize a grammatical application or get the sense from a history lesson with difficulty; there is a lack then of intelligence on certain sides, but one cannot say absolutely that he is not intelligent. Another difficulty. How can we distinguish between mathematical knowledge and mathematical intelligence? One who knows a great deal, helps himself by means of the memory of problems analogous to those proposed to him; while he who is very ignorant, would be stopped by the undeveloped state of his faculties, and through the want of certain indispensable ideas.

Can one judge of the intelligence of a child by his success in history? No, the difficulties are analogous; granted that the dates are banished, and that one avoids even the recitations which can be learned by heart and which make use chiefly of the memory. One questions the child, not upon what he knows but upon what he thinks. This is the ideal: lead him to judge, oblige him to express some personal opinion. But, besides its being ridiculous to make such demands of little children, how difficult it is to know if the child, who gives us his ideas of a war, or of a great man or an historical act, is not simply the faithful echo of the teaching of the master! After having sent me reflections analogous to the preceding, a school mistress wrote me: "In reality, very few children understand history." Another teacher seemed to find in the lessons of history much information regarding the mentality of her pupils; I asked her to send me some documents to support her opinion. She asked her pupils of from ten to twelve years to express in writing their opinion on Napoleon I. One of these wrote, "Napoleon I was the greatest warrior that ever existed; but his pride has made the name of France long detested by foreigners. His ambition cost the lives of half a million Frenchmen." This is very well. But let us read what another pupil wrote, "Napoleon I was a great warrior, but his pride attracted the anger of the people of Europe against France. He left France smaller than he found it. One must admire his military genius, but one must blame his indomitable pride." These two opinions resemble each other too closely not to be the reproduction of the opinion of the teacher. What vanity to suppose that such young children could be capable of judging Napoleon! I have also been the recipient of short essays, where the children of twelve or fourteen years had been asked what they thought of the Revocation of the Edict of Nantes, or the Partition of Poland. Naturally, as to writing, orthography, punctuation, style, these attempts differed a little one from the other and it would be possible to draw from these slight differences some arguments; but the foundation, that is to say the opinion emitted, seemed to me to be the same for all, and consequently very suspicious. All the children agree in seeing a fault in the Revocation of the Edict of Nantes, and a theft in the Partition of Poland. These are not personal historical judgments.

Again a certain singular aptitude has been pointed out, which a few pupils present, of correctly following the orthography in use; it is what is called natural orthography. So much the better for those who possess it; it spares them a great deal of troublesome effort. But one cannot make from it a general sign of intelligence. The aptitude for orthography is a special gift, very limited, like an accurate ear or voice. A correspondent makes the following reasonable remark: "Certain children seem to have natural orthography, which is in reality the memory for written words, and make but few mistakes although they scarcely reflect while writing; they are incapable of comprehending the results of reasoning in a problem and even in the grammar grades there are those who cannot distinguish when to subtract and when to add."

Certain correspondents attach great importance to expression or rather, if I understand them rightly, to expressive reading, which is not altogether the same thing; one can have expression badly governed, breathe badly, have a rude voice, pronounce badly, mutilate the words and possess, nevertheless, an expressive reading. Therefore, in order to judge of the intelligence of a child, one must give him a selection that is within his reach, and watch his reading with care. The intelligent child, says a teacher, makes one feel the punctuation. The intelligent child, it is said again, reads with the sense of the text; he understands not only the general sense but the shades of meaning; and he not only understands what he reads but he feels it. This is all very true; and every one is favorably impressed by expressive reading and pleased with the little reader. It is only necessary to listen to children as they talk to judge of their intelligence; certain among them have fine intonations of voice which indicate even at this early age, different shades of meaning. But in what embarrassment one would be placed if one attempted, out of these fugitive and vague impressions, to pass a precise judgment! In the first place one would be obliged to eliminate those who cannot read or who read poorly, because they have defective habits, faulty pronunciation, and cannot yet read fluently; in a primary school, one would be obliged for this reason, to abstain from judging more than half of the children.

As for those who have the good fortune to possess an expressive reading, they are often the intelligent ones; but take care; often they are only artists, future actors; one knows by illustrious examples that an actor may be very talented, without possessing a great intelligence; in the school, I have sometimes had pointed out to me children of a noticeable lack of intelligence who put a charming expression into their oral reading.

I will terminate this review, by noting that for many teachers, the surest and the most direct means for judging the intelligence of a child is to put questions to him, to make him talk. In the class one questions him in such a way as to solicit a personal reply, a reply which does not come from the book. There is an excellent exercise, so it seems, that of *explained reading*. When the child has read a passage stop him to sum up the essential idea of the selection, or to criticise it; still better, lead him by questions to reveal what he has seen, observed, felt, noted, reflected outside school. Appeal to his judgment, to his imagination or again, leaving the reading book, question the child during recreation; gain his confidence, make him talk; show an interest in his response, and question him upon his future projects, upon his friendships, his duties, his life at home. Freed from the constraint of the class, certain minds open, and thus one makes unexpected discoveries. This is the charm of confidences; a silent child begins talking; one finds that he is full of imagination, and often of mischief. One sees that another, strong in composition, has never used his powers of observation. Again it is the spontaneous reflections of the child which indicate his intelligence. Here is one who asks his master "Why do people of warm countries in summer wear clothing made of wool," or "Since the earth turns, why are not the houses upset?" Another makes the following remark. He had been told "The oleomargerine is good and is less costly than butter." He replied, "The bakers must use it then in their cakes." Another, to whom it had been explained that Bonaparte left the army in Egypt to return to France, replied, "He had no right to do it, they ought to have shot him." Certainly these words, these reflections denote a keen intelligence, especially if the child is young and the saying is authentic, but the inconvenience of these remarks is, that they are spontaneous, that one has not been able to foresee them, nor to judge them beforehand, and consequently one does not know

Change g estimates. Test does not change its verdict

TEACHERS' JUDGMENT OF PUPILS 309

exactly what quality of intelligence they .contain. To appreciate them, one experiences the same embarrassment as in the
clinic, when a lunatic of a low intellectual level, utters a speech
whose form seems intelligent; yet one does not exactly know if
this speech reveals a former state of intelligence of which it is a
relic, or if it might come from an imbecile. In the same way,
when one undertakes to appreciate the value of a childish saying
which has come spontaneously, one lacks a measure, a point of
comparison by which to judge.

A teacher, whom I know, who is methodical and considerate,
has given an account of the habits he has formed for studying
his pupils; he has analysed his methods, and sent them to me.
They have nothing original, which makes them all the more
important. He instructs children from five and a half to seven
and a half years old; they are 35 in number; they come to his
class after having passed a preparatory course, where they have
commenced to learn to read. For judging each child, the teacher
takes account of his age, his previous schooling (the child may
have been one year, two years in the preparatory class, or else
never passed through that division at all), of his expression of
countenance, his state of health, his knowledge, his attitude in
class, and his replies. From these diverse elements he forms an
opinion. I have transcribed some of these notes on the following page.

These judgments were passed by the teacher in the beginning;
out of 35 pupils he judged 31, having reserved 4 upon whom he
could not pronounce. At the end of the year his indecisions and re-
serves had increased; they now rested upon 9 children; and besides,
he had changed his opinion about 8. In reading these judgments
one can see how his opinion was formed, and of how many elements it took account; it seems to us that this detail is interesting;
perhaps if one attempted to make it precise by giving coefficients
to all these remarks, one would realize still greater exactitude.
But is it possible to define precisely an attitude, a physiognomy,
interesting replies, animated eyes? It seems that in all this the
best element of diagnosis is furnished by the degree of reading
which the child has attained, after a given number of months,
and that the rest remains constantly vague.

Is this equivalent to saying that the empirical method of knowledge, which we have here brought to trial, presents no advantage?

NAME OF THE CHILD	AGE	PREVIOUS AMOUNT OF SCHOOLING IN YEARS	FACTS NOTED	CONCLUSION
Dess	7½	2	Does not know how to read in spite of 2 years of schooling.	Below the average
Mont.....	7	0	Ignorant, timid, does not reply.	Below the average
Par.......	7	0	Ignorant, embarrassed manner. Comes from the country.	Below the average
Mene.....	6½	0'	Ignorant, expressionless face. Does not reply.	Below the average
Lal........	6½	0	Unintelligent face. Does not reply to questions. A brother remained until he was 13 in an elementary class.	Below the average
Devo......	7	1	Child stupid, sleepy. Does not reply. Some of the elements of reading.	Below the average
Dopf......	6½	0	Unintelligent face, expressionless, small, weakly, brutal.	Below the average
Duval.....	6½	1	Elements of reading. Child difficult to interest.	Average
Drou......	7	2	Elements of reading. Heedless. Lack of care probable cause of retardation.	Average
Subi.......	6	1	Fluent reading. Awkward replies. Face wide awake and animated.	Average
Bonnet....	6	0	Ignorant. Interesting replies.	Average
Berma....	6	1	Cannot read, but young, open countenance keen look, easy to interest.	Average
Besse.....	6½	1	Reads by syllables. Easy to interest. Air alert.	Superior
Heissle....	7½	1	Reads by syllables. Replies often. Heedless.	Superior
May......	6½	1	Fluent reading. Quick glance. Interest easy to excite. Replies well.	Superior
Dub.......	6½	1	Expressive reading. Face animated.	Superior
Belile.....	6	0	Ignorant, but child quick and animated.	Superior

Oh yes, it presents one very great advantage. It is based upon long observation, continued during weeks and months; if the facts observed have not each a great value, on the other hand they are numerous, diverse, and when needful they correct one another. Herein lies the incontestable superiority of observation over the test; the latter is an experiment; moreover a short experiment, which, therefore, contains a certain element of chance. If it is a question of judging the ability of a child in composition, I prefer ten tests to one; I prefer ten tests distributed over an entire year rather than grouped together, if the thing were possible, in one afternoon.

But on the other hand what indecision in the observation! What errors! One rarely arrives at certainty and never at a measure.

So much for observations; let us now speak of experiments. The teachers have made several; and we are going to examine them closely. In the first place, to reply to our question, certain of our correspondents have sent in fragments of questions to put to the child. Here are some of them: "Why do you love your parents? Why is the department of the Seine-Inférieure so called? Three persons take seven hours to do a piece of work; would five persons require more or less time? If any one asked you to choose between a quarter of a pie, or the half of a pie, which would you choose? In a square, which is the longer side? Which is the heavier, a kilogram of lead or of feathers? What could you buy with a 1 franc piece? Which would you prefer, two pieces of 5-francs or one gold 10-franc piece?" A teacher tells me that every year, in order to know his new pupils better, he makes use of some simple test questions; he has them give an opinion upon some fact of current life, describe an object placed before their eyes; he has them learn by heart a text of a dozen lines in as short a time as possible; he has them make a map allowing them all the time necessary.

There would be indeed some criticisms to make upon these tests; the principal of these is the following: These tests unfortunately presuppose that in order to make a satisfactory reply, the child has had a certain amount of instruction; one must know a little geography, a little arithmetic, to comprehend most of them; and a child who has never been made familiar with fractions, nor with the rule of three, neither with a definition of a square, would find himself embarrassed without his intelligence

The trial. Cf below

being at fault. But these are slight, very slight defects, that
could easily be effaced. We have here the true method; and the
teachers who sent us these questions and tests were no doubt
unconscious of this. It is the true method for the following
reasons: (1) the problems are experimentally put; it is no longer
a question of observation when one waits for a time when some
happy expression may escape the child; one provokes his reply
at the necessary moment, which is the indispensable condition
for an examination of the intellectual level; (2) the questions
have nothing personal to the child; consequently one could give
them indiscriminately to all. What is now necessary, is that
by a prolonged investigation one determines how children of
different ages reply to these questions, in order that the difficulty
be classified and that one may have a point from which to measure.

At my request, three teachers came and spent the afternoon
in our laboratory rue Grange-aux-Belles, and we asked them each
to examine the intelligence of five children whom they did not
know. They had full liberty to conduct the examination as they
thought best. They put to the children different interesting
questions. I was present, and noted several of these. Thus,
since in the neighborhood of the school there is a canal with
locks, one mistress wished to know if the children understood
what a lock was, what purpose it served, and what was its mechanism. The question thus put, seemed to me curious, and the
interrogation laborious; the teacher did not put exactly the same
question to all, she aided some more than others; and besides,
this was a purely local question, it could not have been asked in
another school, and this is wrong for it makes comparison impossible. Another teacher had brought pretty pictures, which
he showed the children, then he asked them diverse questions
about the objects there represented, for instance, why a certain
roof was a mansard and not an ordinary roof, and how one distinguished a mansard. Excellent idea, but it was badly carried
out. In the first place, the questions seemed to me too easy;
then they changed from one child to another; lastly, the teacher
wasted time in teaching those who answered badly. During one
of the examinations, blows of a hammer were heard; they came
from a factory that was in process of construction. One teacher
profited from it by asking if it were better when building a factory,
to have thick or thin walls; too local a question in the first place,

and not given in the same terms to all; and above all the form requiring yes or no for answer was used, which is dangerous; because the correct reply to such a question may be due to chance. Ask a pupil if blood is acid or alkaline, and there is one chance out of two that he will reply correctly even though he be perfectly ignorant. Then they asked questions about the streets of the neighborhood, about the way to go from one place to another, in order to find out if the children knew their surroundings and observed, noticed. Notes were made during their recital. As King Edward of England had recently died, they asked details upon this event, in order to discover if the children read the paper or if they listened to what others might have read to them. These again are too special questions, which make all comparison impossible; besides they were badly put, certain children who were judged intelligent in advance were aided too much. I noted, apropos of this, a surprising fact; to one of these questions, two children gave identical replies; nevertheless, one received a better mark than the other, simply because the teacher had the idea—he admitted it to me—that this pupil was brighter than the other. Lastly, like every good examination, this one terminated in scholastic exercises; there were questions of history, of literature, recitations of fables, and problems of the metric system, after assuring themselves that the children knew its elements; and for this too, explanations were given when the children did not know, and one wished to discover the rapidity with which they could comprehend. I have no need to say how much I disapprove of this mixture, of indefinite proportions, of questions of instruction and questions of intelligence; it is the means of establishing nothing at all, neither the degree of instruction nor the degree of intelligence. In conclusion, I will remark that our three examiners were not altogether agreed in the classification of the children from the intellectual point of view; but that is of no importance.

I asked them at the end, how they had proceeded in order to evaluate the replies; because they had surely been obliged to rate them since they had all given marks to the candidates. One of them frankly told me that he had taken the first child as the point of departure, and it was to him that he had compared the others, judging them intelligent or not according as they were above or below their little comrade. Think of the inconvenience of such a practice, which leaves so much place to what is arbitrary, to sympathy, or antipathy. The first pupil suffered greatly from it because he was not judged comparatively with the others, and he was the recipient of an excessive and unreasonable severity. Another teacher provided himself with a more ingenious method; he imagined as model, a child of the same age as those who were brought to him, a child who seemed to him of average intelligence; and it was with this ideal model that he compared the successive candidates. It is a method that requires a great familiarity with children, and much intelligence; and I do not hesitate to pronounce it wrong. When one can say, "The method depends upon the man who uses it," one is not praising the method. The best is the one that requires the minimum of dexterity and of knowledge. And then, does one not realize that these comparisons with an ideal average, are perilous? In reality one has not made previous experiments, one has not put to this average being the same questions, one does not know exactly how he would reply, one only makes conjectures; and the most expert may be mistaken.

Thus, our three teachers, whom we were designing enough to put for a moment in our place and whom we had charged to make only once that measure of the intellectual level that we take nearly every day, had been lead almost naturally to employ the same method as ours, the method of tests; and they were forced to it, because under the conditions in which they operated, there is no other. I remember an alienist, a doctor, who bitterly criticised our method for the examination of subnormal children; very well, let us see how this severe critic handles the matter, and what methods he employs; he says simply that he prefers to show them postal cards and make them talk about them. But what is this exercise, if it is not a test? Our critic of tests employs tests; only he employs them badly; it is the only credit that can be given him.

To sum up, our teachers had recourse instinctively to the method which we extol. We shall simply state without the slightest intention in the world of reproaching them with it—because this is not said in criticism—that they committed numerous errors; that their questions were often of a needless length, that they were frequently put in the dangerous alternative form just noted, that they often supposed scholastic knowledge which had nothing to do with the question, that they were of a nature too special (they could only have been given that particular day, or to the children of that school), that they were put in terms that differed from pupil to pupil according to the chance of the conversation; when a child replied badly or incompletely, something which often happens with young children, they whispered to him without taking exact account of that aid; and the definite ·reply was not judged in the same manner for all even when given in identical terms. One can see that our teachers *practiced very badly, a very good method.*

And this example demonstrates the exactitude of an excellent remark (*un bien joli mot*) which was said to me by an English lady, a teacher who had wished to know the method used in my laboratory for the study of children. "Science" she said to me, "invents no more than practice; but science does better. (*Science n'invente rien de plus que pratique; mais science fait mieu.*)" It is the exact truth, at least in what concerns psychology and pedagogy.

There are sciences which invent; chemistry for example has recipes of which one has no idea in ordinary life; but the moral sciences do not invent, properly speaking, they only bring to a point and perfect empirical means; and this is why they give to those curious enough to initiate themselves, a first impression of triviality. When one speaks to another about measuring the intelligence of a child, he thinks that one is going to disclose to him some surprising and mysterious method; and when one says that this method is going to consist in putting before him little problems, which vaguely resemble social games, he will likely exclaim with an undisguised disappointment, "Is that all!" Evidently he could do the same, anybody could do the same. But "Science fait mieux."

Must we conclude from this that a teacher must always have recourse to our method in order to obtain a knowledge of the intelligence of his pupils? This would be a great exaggeration. Let us not increase indiscreetly the work of teachers who have from 60 to 80 pupils in the class. Our method, which is slow, particular, and which requires some training, is an exceptional one, a *de luxe* method. The vernier is also an instrument *de luxe;* one does not employ it unless one wishes to measure to the tenth of a millimeter; it is not to be used for ordinary purposes. The microscope is also an instrument *de luxe;* one does not employ it to analyse the fabric of the costume one buys. These instruments are only employed when there is a real interest in a careful study. And the same is true for taking the intellectual level.

WHAT DIFFERENCE EXISTS IN THE INTELLIGENCE OF CHILDREN BELONGING TO DIFFERENT SOCIAL CONDITIONS?

M. Decroly and Mlle. Degand have published in the *Archives de Psychologie*[6] a study upon our method. They applied it to 43 children (boys and girls) of a private school which they conduct at Brussels, and they were careful to publish very detailed results of their experiment. In reading their work, in scrutinizing their tables, and weighing their conclusions, we have been somewhat undecided; we have asked ourselves if it were a confirmation, or a criticism of our investigation. Without doubt there was some wavering in the thought of the authors; and that is easily understood; the method is delicate, the facts which they have collected are so varied and so numerous, that there results in the mind a sort of obstruction; one cannot clearly see the conclusions to be drawn therefrom. Apropos of this, a very significant fact has been produced; authors who have analysed a little severely the work of Decroly and Degand, have thought they must present it as unfavorable to our investigations; they say the tests are too easy, they do not exactly apply to the ages for which Binet and Simon organized them; on the other hand, some of the tests are defective because they involve too much instruction, and not enough of the natural intelligence. A superficial mind, in holding to this analysis, might think that the two Belgian savants had made a complete refutation of the whole of our method. Granted that Decroly and Degand have made a great effort, granted that their whole study breathes honesty and good faith, conscientiousness and care, still we have thought that it would be regrettable to leave the matter there. We have asked them for their tables and their notes; and we have submitted these documents to an analysis which we here sum up. In this manner we have been able to account for the very interesting corrections and additions which the Belgian study has contributed to our work.

[6] January, 1910, No. 34, Vol. IX, p. 81–108.

One fact has struck us forcibly; it is that the children studied by Decroly and Degand give very much better replies to the tests than our subjects. In calculating their level of intelligence, according to the method which we have before indicated, we do not find one who is backward, not one, and this is a very significant fact, because our subjects present an equal amount of advance and backwardness. The only little Belgian who would present a very slight degree of backwardness is a child of twelve years, eight months, who has a level of twelve years; this is very little. The amount of the advance is on the other hand quite marked; there are twelve children who are advanced more than a year, their advance being equal to two years or less; there are eleven children who are advanced more than two years; the greatest advance is two years and a half. *The average is a year and a half.*

This is a considerable difference. To what can it be ascribed? To three possible causes—outside material errors, which truly we could not suspect. First. The Belgian authors may have made their estimates with an excessive indulgence; without being conscious of it, they may have aided their subjects, diminishing the difficulty of the questions. We regret that M. Decroly and Mlle. Degand have not been able to come to Paris, and see us operate; they know our technique only through reading; they are not, strictly speaking, our pupils. In reading their work, we have had the feeling that they really are more indulgent than we. But the difference has seemed to us very slight, quite insignificant; in our opinion it could not create among the children an advance of a year and a half. Second. The children studied are not of the same social condition as ours. Our subjects belong to the primary schools of Paris situated in the 10th ward (rue Grange-aux-Belles, rue Récollets, rue Écluses Saint-Martin) the district is poor without being indigent. It is to be supposed that the school conducted by M. Decroly and Mlle. Degand is differently recruited. At our request, M. Decroly and Mlle. Degand informed us that their pupils belong to a social class in easy circumstances; they have parents who are particularly gifted and understand education in a broad sense; they are renowned physicians, university professors, well known lawyers, etc. They also wrote us, "We know perfectly well the mentality of our pupils, since there are only 8 or 9 or 10 at most in each class; we see them a great

deal between whiles, they are free, joyous, open, their countenances cannot deceive us, we can therefore know them well!"
To sum up, here are two causes which, it seems to us, explain the difference of results, a superior social condition, and an education which tends toward individualism (and which is directed to a small number at a time). Already M. Rouma has told us that he had applied the method to children of the upper classes in Belgium, and he had been surprised to find how far the children were advanced, compared to children of the primary school. Is this a matter of heredity? Is it a matter of education? It would be difficult to establish a difference between the two factors which are here operating in conjunction. On the other hand individual education has superior advantages; a professor succeeds better in developing the intelligence of his pupils when he has only 8 or 10 than when he has 60; when he has 60 he cannot even know them all. What occurs in our subnormal classes proves this clearly, and we believe that the principal advantage of these classes lies in the very simple fact that there are fewer pupils there than in the ordinary classes. Thus is definitely explained the disagreement which seems to exist between the work of M. Decroly and Mlle. Degand and our own.

I feel that M. Decroly and Mlle. Degand have had the privilege of studying a very interesting question, the difference of intelligence between the children of the poorer classes and those of the rich. This I have already written them. That this difference exists one might suspect; because our personal investigations, as well as those of many others, have demonstrated that children of the poorer class are shorter, weigh less, have smaller heads and slighter muscular force, than a child of the upper class; they less often reach the high school; they are more often behind in their studies. Here is a collection of inferiorities which are slight, because they are only appreciated when large numbers are considered, but they are undeniable. Some probably are acquired and result from unavoidable and accessory circumstances; others are probably congenital. The investigations of Decroly and Degand naturally belong to this group, they confirm what we already knew; and in a subject so new as this, a confirmation is not useless. In addition, there is here something more, there is a measure of this difference.

A second remark should be made upon the documents sent us by Decroly and Degand; for their pupils who are a year and a half in advance of those of the primary schools of Paris, there is a whole series of tests in which the advance is more marked than in the others; and consequently it is perhaps possible to deduce something interesting upon which aptitudes are most favored in the education of a rich child. *A priori* one would suppose that these children, little used to serving themselves, constantly surrounded by willing servants, would be more awkward with their hands than future workmen. But without making suppositions let us see what the facts reveal, or rather let us see how we can draw some conclusion from the tables which have been submitted to us.

With those children having an average advance of a year and a half, we have noted the tests for which they have on an average an advance of more than a year and a half, and tests for which they have on an average an advance of less than a year and a half. They show no special weakness for any test and are not specially backward for any aptitude; but their advance is very unequal. Here is the list of tests for which their advance is particularly strong.

TESTS FOR WHICH THE PUPILS OF DECROLY AND DEGAND HAVE AN ADVANCE OF MORE THAN A YEAR AND A HALF	APTITUDES WHICH ARE PROBABLY CORRELATED WITH THESE TESTS
Description of pictures Interpretation of pictures	Intelligence and language
Count 13 sous.	Home training.
Repeat 5 figures.	Attention.
Name 4 colors.	Home training.
Comparisons from memory.	Faculty of language and observation.
Lack in pictures.	Habit of looking at pictures, and language.
Arrangement of weights.	Attention.
Naming the days of the week.	Home training.
Abstract definitions.	Language.
Knowledge of pieces of money.	Practical life.
Naming the months.	Home training.
Finding 60 words.	Language.
Criticize sentences.	Comprehension and language.
Repeat long sentence.	Attention.

Opposite each test we have placed the aptitude which it seems to require. But we are far from presenting our interpretation as final; it is only assumed. It has seemed to us that, when one makes experiments upon minds as young as these, one is especially struck by the difficulty which the child experiences in handling the language, and in expressing in words what he thinks. For example, in the test of criticising certain sentences, the children often show that they have understood the absurdity of the sentence only by the play of the countenance, the intonation of the voice, or by the simple fact that they repeat the sentence. Thus when asked, "Yesterday there was an accident on the railroad, but it was not serious, the number of deaths was only 48," they say simply, "The number of deaths was only 48 and it was not serious!" There is in this manner of expression, or rather of non-expression, a simplicity which recalls primitive poetry where the facts are announced but not judged. Consequently we have felt justified in supposing that language played a part in a good many of the tests contained in the above list. It is the same with the 60 words, the abstract definitions, and the criticism of sentences. Many others seem to us to depend upon home training. It is not in school that the children are taught the days of the week, the months, or colors; it is at home, or at least, it seems so to us. Taking all into account it would seem that these little rich children are advanced for: Attention, in 3 tests; Home training, in 4 tests; Language, in 6 tests.

This last point seems the most characteristic; the little children of the upper classes understand better and speak better the language of others. We have also noted that when they begin to compose, their compositions contain expressions and words better chosen than those of poor children. This verbal superiority must certainly come from the family life; the children of the rich are in a superior environment from the point of view of language; they hear a more correct language and one that is more expressive.

Now note the tests for which the children show an advance of less than a year and a half.

TESTS FOR WHICH THE PUPILS OF DECROLY AND DEGAND ARE ADVANCED LESS THAN A YEAR AND A HALF	APTITUDES WHICH ARE PROBABLY CORRELATED WITH THESE TESTS
Copy a sentence.	Scholastic exercise.
Reading.	Scholastic exercise.
Counting 9 sous.	Practical life or home training.
Counting backwards.	Scholastic exercise.
Writing from dictation.	Scholastic exercise.
Copying a diamond.	Scholastic exercise.
Giving change from 20 sous.	Scholastic exercise.
Putting 3 words into one sentence	Language.
Finding rhymes.	Language.
Problem of different facts.	Judgment.

Here again, we make the most emphatic reservations upon the aptitudes which we have felt to be correlated with the different tests. Nevertheless our list shows that the tests of language are fewer than in the first list; on the other hand scholastic exercises abound. As Decroly and Degand have already remarked, it is especially in the degree of instruction that the children of the rich approach those of the poor. They are not backward in instruction but they do not show the same marked advance that they showed in other tests. This may be the result of accidental circumstances which have no importance; for example, the habit of the parents of not pushing their children and of not sending them to school too early.

To sum up, the experiments of Decroly and Degand when thoroughly examined cannot lead us to change the tests; because if most of the tests have seemed too easy for their children, it is due simply to the fact that the intellectual level of their children is that of the rich. On the other hand the work that the two Belgian savants have done is interesting and has shown us with equal precision two new facts: First. That the intellectual superiority of children of the higher classes over that of children of the lower amounts to an average advance of a year and a half. Second. The intellectual superiority manifests itself especially in the tests where language plays a part.

I have sought to find a confirmation of the preceding investigations by making a fresh study of documents gathered a long time ago. Among the pupils of the schools of the 10th ward whose intelligence we measured three years ago, there are those who come from indigent conditions; there are others who are in easy circumstances. All this was noted at the time of the examination. But in comparing the average of the intellectual level of children from wretched surroundings with the average of children in easy circumstances, I have found no appreciable difference. What causes the negative result? Perhaps because the social condition was not noted with sufficient care, or perhaps also because the difference of the conditions was too slight.

I therefore asked the school director, M. Morlé, who measured the intellectual level of 50 children from his own school, to note with great care the social standing of each of them; and to give in his report of each child one of the four following qualifications: *indigence, poverty, mediocrity, ease*, from definitions devised in a previous work with my habitual collaborator, M. Vaney. Strange to say, the results which have been obtained by M. Morlé and which I calculated from the pages which he sent me, are entirely negative. Here is the exact statement.

Intellectual Level of Primary School Children in Relation to their Social Condition

INTELLECTUAL LEVEL	INDIGENCE	POVERTY	MEDIOCRITY	EASE
Average..........................	2	1	12	9
Inferior.........................	4	1	9	5
Superior.........................	4	1	2	4

By attentively reading this table, one can see that the children of an intelligence superior to the average are just as numerous in the group of indigence as in that of ease; and it is the same in regard to children inferior to the average. How shall we interpret these results? It is clear that we cannot accuse the experimenter of negligence. How does it happen then that the social condition, which exercises such an influence over the pupils of Mlle. Degand, is not of the least importance in a primary class here in Paris? Perhaps it is because the social differences among children of our primary school are not distinct enough to produce a difference of intellectual development; for even when the children come of parents in easy circumstances, they do not see their parents as often as do the children of the rich; they are left more to themselves; the parents make a good living, but they live away from home, enter late at night, and do not bother much with the children; with others the environment is unfavorable to their education because the parents are wine merchants or alcoholics. And it must be added that what equalizes the children of different social conditions in the primary school is that they all receive the same kind of instruction in class. To sum up, there is persumably here a question of very slight social differences which cannot exercise a noticeable influence upon the intellectual level.

Very different have been the results obtained by Madame Thévenot, directress of a primary school for boys, rue Cadet. Mme. Thévenot measured the intelligence of 18 children, of whom 15 were between eight and nine years of age and three were between seven and eight. These children belonged to her class because the school is small and Madame Thévenot teaches at the same time that she is directress. Mme. Thévenot has worked with M. Vaney and me and she uses the measuring scale very well. Immediately one is struck with the figures which she obtained. Not one of her pupils is behind in intelligence, and many are in advance. Some are three years ahead, 6 are two years and over; as an average the advance is 1.7 (that is a little more than one year and a half); it is an advance analogous to that of the pupils of Mlle. Degand; it is considerable since this is a mean value.

Mme. Thévenot considers that these children are of a higher intelligence than those of other schools where she has taught; we think that the social condition of the parents (the rue Cadet is located in a commercial quarter in the center of Paris and is quite rich) must have an influence. It is also worthy of note that several of these little pupils are of foreign birth. The instruction is more individual than in most schools as Mme. Thévenot has only 15 pupils in her class. Ordinarily classes number from 30 to 40 pupils. Finally Mme. Thévenot felt it worthy of note that these children were started the preceding year by a very superior teacher who taught the preparatory class. Thus one sees many slight causes operating to produce the results, and it would be rash to try to explain each one of them; good social conditions and individualized education agree in producing the same result.

Miss Katherine Johnston, of the University of Sheffield, during the year 1910 came to visit my laboratory, rue Grange-aux-

Belles; she was especially interested in the measure of the intellectual level, and, returning to England, repeated the experiments upon 200 school children of Sheffield. The results were made public by her, at a meeting of the British Association at Sheffield in 1910; she courteously communicated these results to me and replied to my questions. It appears from the documents which I have seen that she worked with children of very unequal social standing. The schools which opened their doors to her presented very different conditions; here the population represented the liberal professions, there the trained mechanics, again the extremely poor mechanics. It is a pity that these heterogeneous elements have been confused in the averages, which thus lose some of their significance. I strongly urge the author to calculate new averages, taking account of the state of poverty or wealth represented by the parents of the children. A detail in passing. I suppose that in the rich schools, there are fewer children in a class than in the poor schools; and that is, I believe, an important condition to note in order to correctly estimate the intellectual development of the child; I believe that, everything else being equal, a child's intellect will develop better in a class composed of 15 or 20 pupils, than in a class composed of a great number. The information furnished by Miss Johnston confirms this idea to a certain extent, because in the schools of the rich, it is said that the number does not exceed 15 or 20, while in the schools of the poor it varies from 40 to 60. But this rule is not without exception.

From the accounts of the experiments which have appeared in the journals I have not understood the results of Miss Johnston's experiments because she has sometimes employed a method of calculation which is personal to her and which I consider open to criticism. But in putting the results in a form which I have myself calculated here is the table which one obtains.

Distribution of Intellectual Levels of the Pupils in Miss Johnston's Experiments at Sheffield

INTELLECTUAL LEVEL	AGES OF CHILDREN					
	6 years	7 years	8 years	9 years	10 years	11 years
Superior to the average..........	4	24	8	12	6	1
Average.......................		8	10	10	12	2
Inferior to the average..........		5	2	8	17	17

It results from the above table (and this commentary will explain it) that 55 children are superior to their level, 42 are equal to it, and 49 are inferior. If one notes besides, that starting with 11 years the number of children below the normal level has distinctly increased, which results as we have shown from the fact that the tests of 11 and 12 years were much too severe, one might conclude that Miss Johnston's results were in perfect accord with our own.

This is the best reply to certain objections which have been made to us. Objections have not been lacking; some have been just; but others have been childish. In an Italian review it was declared that our tests were too easy. The experiments of Decroly and Mlle. Degand seem to have lent support to this criticism. Whipple, in spite of the friendliness of his analysis, has associated himself with these unreservedly. Truly, without wishing to defend to excess a method which is only being tried, I repel these objections; Miss Johnston's results are there to prove that they are not well founded.

I again requested Miss Johnston to indicate the tests that are easiest for each age. Here is an extract from her communication which shows not only the tests that are easiest but those which are the most difficult.

41 children of 7 years

	Failures
Lack in pictures	24
Naming 4 pieces of money	19
Repeating 5 figures	18
Number of fingers	10
Counting 13 sous	7
Description of pictures	5
Copying a diamond	4
Copying a written model	2

22 children of 8 years

	Failures
Counting backwards	17
Reading with 2 memories	16
Dictation	3
Naming of colors	2
Comparing two objects from memory	2
Counting 3 single and 3 double sous	1

30 children of 9 years

	Failures
Definitions superior to use	23
Arranging weights	21
Giving change from 20 sous	16
Reading with 6 memories	14
Date	10
Days of the week	2

38 children of 10 years

	Failures
Difficult questions	26
3 words in 2 sentences	21
The 9 pieces of money	19
Easy questions	6
The months of the year	0

24 children of 12 years

	Failures
Abstract definitions	21
Putting words in order	13
3 words in 1 sentence	12
Criticism of sentences	7
More than 60 words	5

If one compares these results with those we have indicated in our Table II, it will be found that except for tests where our little Parisians are decidedly in advance of their neighbors (lack in pictures, counting backwards, abstract definitions) the other results are almost analogous.

Finally, I recently asked my devoted collaborator, M. Morlé, director of a school in Paris, to take the measure of the level in two primary schools presenting extreme social differences. It seemed to me advisable to entrust the two parts of the experiment to the same experimenter. M. Morlé had already taken the measure of the level of the children in his school (rue-Sambre-et-Meuse) which is one of the poorest in Paris; with these indications and with the authorization of the inspector, M. Belot, he made the supplementary investigations in the school, rue Marseilles, where the children belong to a population in easy circumstances. M. Morlé took all the necessary precautions not to let himself be influenced; he even voluntarily ignored the school standing of the pupils examined. His findings are very significant. In comparing from the point of view of level 30 children from the school of the poorer class with 30 children of the class in easy circumstances, the age being the same in both, he found the distribution indicated by the following table:

Comparison, from the Point of View of Intellectual Level, of a Primary School Attended by the Poorer Class, with a Primary School Attended by Those in Easy Circumstances.

	SUPERIOR INTELLECTUAL LEVEL		LEVEL EQUAL TO THE AVERAGE	INFERIOR INTELLECTUAL LEVEL	
	2 years	1 year		1 year	2 years
Poor Primary School.............	1	4	13	11	1
Primary School Easy Circumstances.................	6	10	10	3	1

Thus, on one hand, there are 16 students in the better class school in advance, while in the poorer school there are only 5; and on the other hand there are 4 children in the better class school who are backward, while there are 12 backward children in the poor school.

If from these figures we try to estimate in years the mean divergence which separates these two groups of children, we find that it is about three-fourths of a year. The total of the poor children is below the average by one-fourth of a year and the children of the better class are above it by a half year. Certainly this advance of one-half year is not equal to that which Mlle. Degand found under conditions much more favorable; it points, however, in the same direction and is consequently a valuable confirmation. Let us add, in passing, that the school standing of the children in the poor school was less advanced than that of those in the better school as the following table indicates:

Comparison from the Point of View of Scholastic Level in a Poor Primary School, and in a Primary School of the Better Class

	SUPERIOR SCHOLASTIC LEVEL		AVERAGE SCHOLASTIC LEVEL	INFERIOR SCHOLASTIC LEVEL	
	2 years	1 year		1 year	2 years
Poor School.....................	0	3	18	7	0
Better Class School.	2	12	12	3	0

The difference shows itself also in the same direction; the average scholastic level in the poor school is very little removed from the normal average; while that of the better class school is slightly in advance, about a half year. That need not surprise us since we have already seen that the scholastic level and the intellectual level go hand in hand.

A word in conclusion. A singularly interesting idea arises from these investigations which I have already noted in my previous articles but perhaps without sufficient insistence. For the first time I now see its full meaning. This idea may present itself first as a criticism of past methods. For a long while the psychologists have tried to establish correlations of experiments; they study among adults and more often among children some aptitudes which seem to them different and afterwards they wish to know what bearing they have upon one another. Legitimate investigation certainly and timely; but more often they can lead to no real result, so that the calculations of correlations has become one of the most delicate questions of psychology.

We now understand why. It is because the aptitudes studied have not been the object of a sufficiently profound investigation. One has contented himself with an experiment or two. Thus, to take a simple example upon which we can reason, one has studied by short and rapid tests suggestibility by lines then by weights; afterwards one tries to find if a child, suggestible to one form of test is also suggestible to the others; and naturally one never finds appreciable correlation. An American investigation published this year arrives at this conclusion. But what we should do first and above all else during this period of groping in which we now are, is not to make a comparison of tests, an analytical investigation of their correlations, but just the contrary, that is to say, a comprehensive study of their significance, a calculation of their results. Just as it is perilous to investigate whether one form of suggestibility is correlated with another, so on the other hand is it advantageous to try to group all the tests of suggestibility, to make of them a mass, and to make a classification of pupils from this point of view, to afterwards see if the most suggestible pupils are the youngest, more docile in the class, or have such and such mental qualities more pronounced than less suggestible pupils. This is what we have tried for the measure of intelligence; we have grouped all the tests supposing that they all more or less tend in the same direction and we have thus arrived at a classification of pupils from the point of view of the intelligence.

What is the reason for proceeding thus? Obviously it rests upon the principle that a particular test isolated from the rest is of little value, that it is open to errors of every sort, especially if it is rapid and is applied to school children; that which gives a demonstrative force is a group of tests, a collection which preserves the average physiognomy. This may seem to be a truth so trivial as to be scarcely worth the trouble of expressing it. On the contrary it is a profound truth, and good sense is so far from being sufficient to divine this so called triviality, that up to the present it has been constantly disregarded. One test signifies nothing, let us emphatically repeat, but five or six tests signify something. And that is so true that one might almost say, "It matters very little what the tests are so long as they are numerous."

In support of this, I shall cite what Mlle. Giroud[7] recently proved in applying to pupils a method of measuring the intelligence devised by our colleague M. Ferrari. This method is composed, very much like that of Blin, of a long series of questions which one puts to the subjects; the questions are often badly formed and Mlle. Giroud has made a detailed criticism which shows that out of some forty of them scarcely more than 8 or 10 can be retained; furthermore, I hasten to add that this criticism can in no way touch the author of this list of questions because they were not organized for the study of children but for the study of patients. But in spite of the immense majority of the questions being poorly made for children, the total result is far from being bad; one succeeds in proving that the total number of questions to which good replies are given grows quite regularly with the age, which is the touch stone of the test. It is necessary that the principle of the methods which we employ be excellent in order that they can lead to such useful conclusions even when they are badly applied. It is then chiefly to the principle of the multiplicity of tests that the attention of the psychologists must be drawn. Without doubt great benefit will be derived from these methods in the future for the study of aptitudes of character and even for the psychological condition, in a word for the realization of a measure of individual psychology.

ALFRED BINET.

[7] Mlle. Giroud. *Study for a New Process for Measuring the Intellectual Level.* Soc. libre pour l'étude psychologique de l'enfant, No. 69, Mars, 1911.

INDEX

BIBLIOGRAPHY ON BINET-SIMON TESTS

BUFFALO COMMITTEE. Informal Conference on the Binet-Simon Scale. *Jour. Ed. Psych.*, February, 1914, Vol. IV, No. 2.

DOLL, E. A. Note on the Intelligence Quotient. *Tr. Sch. Bull.*, Vol. 13, No. 2.

GODDARD, H. H. Four Hundred Feeble-Minded Children Classified by the Binet Method. *Ped. Sem.*, September, 1910, Vol. 17, No. 3.

GODDARD, H. H. Two Thousand Normal Children Measured by the Binet-Simon Measuring Scale of Intelligence. *Ped. Sem.*, June, 1911, Vol. 18, No. 2.

HUEY, E. B. Backward and Feeble-Minded Children. *Ed. Psy. Mon.*, Baltimore, 1912.

KITE, E. S. The Binet-Simon Measuring Scale for Intelligence. *Bull. No. 1*, Committee on Provision for the Feeble-Minded, Philadelphia, 1916.

KOHS, S. C. The Binet-Simon Measuring Scale for Intelligence. An Annotated Bibliography. *Jour. Ed. Psych.*, April, May, June, 1914, Vol. V, Nos. 4, 5, 6, (254 titles).

KUHLMAN, F. Results of Grading Thirteen Hundred Feeble-Minded Children with the Binet-Simon Tests. *Jour. Ed. Psych.*, May, 1913, Vol. IV, No. 5.

ROGERS, A. L. AND McINTYRE, J. L. The Measurement of Intelligence in Children by the Binet-Simon scale. *Brit. Jour. Psych.*, October, 1914, Vol. VII, No. 3.

SCHWEGLER, R. A. A Teacher's Manual for the Use of the Binet-Simon Scale of Intelligence. Univ. of Kansas School of Education, 1914. (Selected Bibliography of 56 titles.)

STERN, W. Psychological Methods of Testing Intelligence. *Ed. Psych. Mon.*, 13, Baltimore, 1914. (Bibliography appended.)

STERN, W. Der Intelligenzquotient als Mass der kindlichen Intelligenz, insbesondre der unternormalen. *Zt. f. Angew. Psych.*, January, 1916, Vol. XI, No. 1.

TERMAN, L. M. The Stanford Revision and Extension of the Binet-Simon Scale. Buckel Foundation, 1915.

TERMAN, L. M. Suggestions for Revising, Extending and Supplementing the Binet Intelligence Tests. Psychological Principles Underlying the Binet Scale. *Jour. Psycho. Asthenics*, Vol. XVIII, Nos. 1 and 2.

TOWN, C. H. (Translator), BINET, A., AND SIMON, TH.—A Method of Measuring the Development of the Intelligence in Young Children. 1913, Lincoln, Ill.

WHIPPLE, G. M. Manual of Mental and Physical Tests. Baltimore, 1910.